THE GREEN AND THE BLUE

THE GREEN AND THE BLUE

Naive Ideas to Improve Politics in the Digital Age

LUCIANO FLORIDI
Yale University

WILEY Blackwell

Contents

Preface

This is a moderately optimistic book about improving politics, understood as the transformation of the possible into the preferable. It is *optimistic* because it looks at the wealth of opportunities to combine *green* environmental policies with *blue* digital solutions to reform capitalism, strengthen democracy, and pursue a sustainable and equitable human project for the twenty-first century. However, it is only *moderately* optimistic because it also highlights how politics is currently unable to take full advantage of such opportunities. Finally, it is a book about improving politics, because it regards good politics as the only means by which we can prevent moderate optimism from degrading into a frustrated and bitter regret about what humanity could have done but has failed to achieve.

Liberal democracies require good political strategies to enhance and promote their potential to help humanity and save the planet. Many countries are emerging from a protracted social, political, and cultural crisis, which has affected various aspects of life. The changes in *social factors* precipitated by these crises are evident in the fracture of the social pact, above all concerning intergenerational issues; the reduction and impoverishment of the middle class; poor social mobility; and inequality of opportunities. The *political* aspects are dominated by the collapse of trust in institutions, disputed forms of sovereignty, populism, nationalism, the personalisation of politics, and a vast wave of misinformation. The *cultural* aspects encompass issues ranging from national identity to immigration, and the role a superpower or any country may play in a globalised world (and in the European Union, for Member States). The social, political, and cultural panorama is not encouraging. It could be much improved. In this delicate phase of recovery, it is not essential to be original at all costs or to look for fanciful political solutions. Governments should not merely imitate each other in finding new universal answers. They should instead recognise and maximise their specific strengths while mitigating their weaknesses and identifying potential obstacles to recovery. In light of this strategy, I hope the ideas presented in this book may contribute to improving politics.

In the following chapters, I advocate a politics and economics of care in opposition to one of consumption. In contrast to the consumerist model, the framework presented here focuses on the quality of relations and processes, and hence of experiences, and much less on things and their properties, to ensure a sustainable environment and develop an equitable information society for all. Given this broad and inclusive goal, the book is not written for experts. Instead, it is a text intended for anyone interested in understanding the present and how to improve it by designing good policies for our future. For this reason, I have avoided overloading the reader with bibliographical references and explanatory notes. I have also explained relevant technical terminology whenever I thought it was worthwhile to do so. But above all, I have not discussed the "debates" circulating among experts. Instead, I have tried to address some philosophical questions directly, without recourse to the questions that philosophers ask themselves. So, this is a book on philosophical problems, not philosophers' problems.

As I have argued elsewhere (Floridi 2019), I conceive philosophy as *conceptual design*. At its best, philosophy identifies and clarifies fundamental problems—those with the most substantial consequences, which can have a positive domino effect if resolved satisfactorily—and articulates, as far as possible, the best solutions that are factually correct, reasonably persuasive, and up to date. I have aimed to present these solutions in a logically coherent manner. They are designed to remain open to reasoned, informed, and tolerant discussion because the problems with which philosophy deals are inherently open.[1] Throughout this book, I apply this concept of philosophy to understand our information society and formulate what I hope is a plausible proposal for its future improvement. Scholarly or rhetorical trappings weigh philosophy down unnecessarily, concealing its rational and functional structure.[2] They are too often distracting, digressive, and unhelpful. I have sought to avoid them.

The book is divided into twenty-eight chapters and a Postscript. Inevitably, but also to facilitate reading, I organised them through a linear narrative, with the first chapter as an introduction and the last as a conclusion. However, the truth is that Chapter 28 acts as the centre of the book, as if it were a planet

---

[1] For a debate on a short essay containing some of the ideas presented in this book see (Buchheim et al. 2021).

[2] The indirect reference to the Bauhaus is deliberate, see (Forgács 1995).

around which all the other chapters orbit like moons at different distances. These preceding chapters introduce some ideas that help elucidate Chapter 28 and can be read independently. Anyone in a hurry could head directly to Chapter 28 and read it before the others. I have structured Chapter 28 into 100 theses to make it easier to critique them more granularly, with the hope that each reader will find at least some of the theses convincing. In closing, I have added a Postscript in which I briefly comment on the crisis precipitated by the COVID-19 pandemic, but only insofar as it relates to the ideas presented in this book.

Yale, 4 September 2023

Acknowledgement

"The composition of this book has been for the author a long struggle of escape, and so must the reading of it for most readers if the author's assault on them is to be successful – a struggle of escape from habitual modes of thought and expression. The ideas which are here expressed so laboriously are extremely simple and should be obvious. The difficulty lies, not in the new ideas, but in escaping from the old ones, which ramify, for those brought up as most of us have been, into every corner of our minds".

John Maynard Keynes,
The General Theory of Employment,
Interest, and Money, 1936.

Chapter 1
The Importance of Naive Ideas

In this book, I offer some ideas[1] that I hope may help understand and improve politics in today's information society. My ambition is philosophical, namely, to try to understand and improve the world. That is all. I realise it may seem a lot, indeed overambitious. But I hope that, instead, it may be interpreted as a contribution to a far greater, collective effort. Of course, this brings us to the usual paradox: how significant is a vote or, in this case, a conceptual contribution? Well, I contend, as much as a grain of sand on the beach: one counts for nothing, two still for nothing, but millions can make a huge difference, if only because, without them, there would be no beach. This is the *relational value* of aggregation.

While the ideas in this book are philosophical, they are not meant to be so abstract to the point of being inapplicable. I hope that the ideas I share will help clarify some practical discussions and may generate some positive political changes. I have tried to find the appropriate balance between politics as a theory of governance and politics as a policy practice.

---

[1] From here onwards, I am talking only about ideas that guide politics rather than about good ideas in general (e.g., scientific ones).

The Green and The Blue: Naive Ideas to Improve Politics in the Digital Age, First Edition. Luciano Floridi.

Thus, the ideas proposed may be defined as *translational*, a term I borrow from medicine, which uses the concept of *translational* research because even the most fundamental findings of a Nobel Prize winner and the most applied practice of a family doctor are not disconnected, but are instead linked by a continuity determined by a shared interest in understanding and improving human health. Insofar as the ideas in this book can be translational, they seek to articulate a primary, or rather foundational, reflection, which can inform clear, strategic guidelines to implement specific political, legislative, economic, organisational, and technical actions in the future. I do not claim this as an original idea. Good philosophy has sought to be translational at least since the time of Socrates. All that was missing was the label.

Offering ideas to improve politics is inherently a political action. This is even more the case today. While politics has always been a *relational activity* that includes its own negation, such a status is increasingly apparent and understood more widely in our society. Let me clarify.

The idea of politics as a *relational activity* serves as a central theme of this book. Now, it is a characteristic of some relational phenomena to internalise their negation. A few examples can illustrate this point. If you think about it for a moment, any lack of interaction is still a form of interaction. Likewise, a lack of communication is itself a mode of communication, because silence also speaks volumes about who is silent and about what. Similarly, a lack of information is a form of information because it has a communicative value: unanswered questions may fail to satisfy our need for an answer but are still informative in confirming our need to know something. Politics belongs to these kinds of relational phenomena. Not participating in politics—i.e., abstentionism—is still a political act, at least insofar as it involves delegating to others one's political power, often in the form of a protest at, or rejection of, political alternatives that have been offered. It follows that it is an illusion to think that one may live in a society without being political. If the idea of a social contract makes any sense (a real conditional, see Chapter 10), we must acknowledge that it is a contract imposed on every individual at all times, no matter whether the individual wishes to subscribe to it. Nobody can escape it. Only solitude can be genuinely apolitical (not solipsism, which is just *believing* to be alone, as opposed to really being alone). If a desert island is home to just two people, like Robinson Crusoe and Friday, politics is already inevitable. Every friendship is political, and every family is political. Aristotle, then, was partly right in saying that we are all political animals,[2] but in the sense that trying not to be political means being political nevertheless. He was wrong, however, to think that we are political actors *voluntarily*, *continuously*, and *rightly* (not in the sense of "justly", but in the sense of "in the right way"). All three of Aristotle's conditions are somewhat problematic, and today none of them is satisfied, for the reasons I shall now outline.

First, in all existing democracies, we are political actors *involuntarily*, i.e., against our explicit will, not just unconsciously. This can lead to frustration and conflict, as it is impossible to escape politics even when we would like to reject it, for example, because it has disappointed us, and we do not like it. Civil society is only one side of the coin; the other side is political society. Neither exists without the other: their separation is inescapably abstract. Therefore, no one can mark out a private space in civil society without also marking out some public space in the political society, and vice versa. The illusion that such a separation is possible does not directly generate monsters, like the sleep of reason,[3] but it does allow monsters to grow into beasts, such as political apathy (*qualunquismo*[4]) and populism.

Second, in a *mature information society* (see Chapter 8), we are never "always-on politically".[5] Instead, we are increasingly often political actors *discontinuously* (intermittently), *on-demand* and *just-in-time*,[6] usually when social attention is called upon to express its opinion, judgement, or preferences. For this reason, the communication mechanisms of politics are analogous to the communication mechanisms of *marketing*, especially in countries where comparative advertising is allowed (e.g., "this product is better than that one"). This is simply an observation, not a criticism, and I will return to it in Chapter 17. Here, I would like to emphasise that political communication and marketing pursue the same end: to attract or renew, and thus maintain, peo-

---

[2] See Aristotle, *Politics* (Aristotle 1996).

[3] The indirect reference to Goya's etching is deliberate.

[4] On the "Common Man's Front" (Italian: Fronte dell'Uomo Qualunque, FUQ), also translated as "Front of the Ordinary Man", see https://en.wikipedia.org/wiki/Common_Man%27s_Front.

[5] The indirect refence to (Cellan-Jones 2021) is deliberate. A system is always on if it is continuously powered, tuned on, and working.

[6] The indirect reference to the manufacturing, just-in-time approach is deliberate; see (Cheng and Podolsky 1996).

ple's *attention*, be they customers or citizens, on a topic, be it a new product or a new social or political issue. If this happens often, the result is a constant renewal of the stimulus, which requires ever more intense doses of attention-grabbing communication to take effect. For this reason, marketing carefully considers timing: no one launches a new product randomly, if they can control the timing of innovation. At least a year or two must be allowed to pass, so that the habit of the new product takes hold, and its memory is less vivid. Just look at how often a new iPhone is launched:[7] after a while, the old model is discontinued, at which point it becomes replaceable by the new model. This has the added advantage that the risk of obsolescence is transferred from the "old" product to its outdated user. The iPhone does not age—by default, one refers to the latest model, which is always "new"—instead, it is the users who age because they still rely on an older model. The iPhone is always "new" because the latest model is always new, and the pressure is on the customers to "renew" themselves by buying it. Apple enjoys a self-reinforcing leadership position because it has the power to dictate when innovation cycles take place. As long as this cycle is unbroken, the company's hegemonic position remains difficult to challenge. Those under pressure from the competition cannot afford to control the timing of innovation, whether commercial or socio-political. This is why antitrust laws rightly prevent (or at least they should) the synchronisation of innovation in the hands of one or only a few players, and instead promote competition between many. The same analysis holds in politics. Dictatorial politics is like a market monopoly controlling any policy's innovation. However, if politics becomes a constant pursuit of populist, attention-grabbing consensus, in an unregulated political market where only *laissez-faire* options dominate, and competition rules allow a handful of actors to dictate the "market", then politics renounces any control over its renovation agenda. Another move must counterbalance every move, politicians engage in fight or flight, and no one leads. There is no becoming accustomed to the political solutions that have been implemented, only familiarisation with how they are communicated. Not all current politics shares this asynchronism. Nevertheless, the fact remains that while we depend on the political call to action, we are also beginning to show signs of addiction to this call. Unless politics shouts, we do not pay attention. The result is that for us to listen, communication must be of ever-increasing inten-

---

[7] https://en.wikipedia.org/wiki/Template:Timeline_of_iPhone_models.

sity, simplification (right down to the repetition of a few, elementary slogans, like "Brexit means Brexit" or "make America great again"), and novelty (it does not matter so much what is communicated, but whether that message is "new" or presented in a "new" way), while all the time normalising emergency messages (the "crying wolf" effect). The UK's withdrawal from the European Union (EU) after the June 2016 referendum (Brexit) is a striking example. The populist marketing of two problems—chiefly, immigration and the bureaucracy of the EU—led to the UK's withdrawal from the EU being sold by the Vote Leave campaign as a panacea. The campaign was successful for many reasons, one of which was that it constantly served to renew an advertising message disconnected from the real needs or reasonable aspirations of the consumer-citizens.

To distance oneself from all this, I hope that the following pages may be read without alarmism and serve to re-evaluate a rhetoric of content (semantics) over one of form (syntax). It is preferable for timing not to be tactical (i.e., merely reactive to the novelties of the political market), but to maintain its strategic quality, that is, focused on the design and *implementation* of the right *human project*.

Finally, let us consider Aristotle's third condition. Aristotle was partly justified in calling us political animals. Still, we invariably face a problem when we are called upon to be political actors, insofar as we run the risk of being so in the wrong way, namely when political power is abused. Power for its own sake promotes selfish interests and unjustly privileges some people over others.

For all these reasons, it follows that, while politics can never be absent in any society, it can easily be damaged. The bad politics of populism, nationalism, sovereigntism, intolerance, violence, extremism, passive and indifferent abstentionism, and sometimes the mere protest vote, *also* manifest a frustration about the impossibility of non-politics. But the more such bad politics becomes established, the more it remains a political move, and the more it escalates, eventually occupying all the space of the political dialogue with negative variants, in a confrontational spiral that ultimately leads to polarisation. It undermines society's confidence in its political capacity to solve problems that require cooperation, solidarity, tolerance, and multipartisanship. Today, there is no shortage of good, well-thought-out solutions to problems because more educated and intelligent people are around than ever before. The difficulty is finding the right approach to remove the obstacles impeding the implementation of these good solutions. Goodwill is not in short supply but has withdrawn from politics, where it is no longer represented. This withdrawal is self-defeating and reinforces the vicious circle of bad politics. By trying not to engage in politics, goodwill only leaves room for bad politics, which negatively influences how goodwill is exercised. The optimism of the heart is eventually joined by the frustration of reason[8] at seeing so many opportunities wasted, so many crucial solutions delayed, and so many pressing problems exacerbated to the point of becoming unsolvable.

Considering the points just made, the political ideas expressed in this book are intended to be constructive and impartial, as opposed to destructive and partisan. This is not for anti-party reasons—as I have argued above, it is well known that anti-party and anti-political sentiments today form part of the most widespread party rhetoric and sometimes the most cunning politics. I offer my ideas to anyone (political forces included) who may find them helpful as a means by which to improve politics. In other words, the ideas presented here are *open source* and unconstrained. They are adaptable by anyone who wishes to use them, however they see fit, and to the extent that they may consider them useful. All that remains now is to explain the sense in which the ideas presented in the rest of the book are "naive".

The ideas are naive not in the sense that they are *empty* of "the cunning of reason",[9] or unaware of the shrewd calculation of expediency or opportunistic cynicism in the abuse of power. Instead, they have been intentionally *emptied* of all this, *a posteriori*, with disenchantment, but without disappointment. Another analogy may help to explain the point. Let us consider the difference between a brand new Moka pot, one that is empty because it has never been used to make any coffee, and a used Moka pot that has made coffee but has been cleaned and emptied. It is generally accepted that coffee tastes better in the used, emptied Moka pot; in other words, the patina of use (the patina of reflection) improves itself. This is why historical memory is of enormous value: it is a reminder of the persisting presence of meaning, which requires a mental life to be appreciated, and not as a mere record of facts, for which, say, a Wikipedia entry is sufficient. I have emptied the ideas—rendered them naive, so to speak—to welcome back-in the tenets of good politics, namely social altruism and solidarity; the intergenerational pact; sustainable care

---

[8] The indirect reference to Gramsci's "Pessimism of the Intellect, Optimism of the Will" is deliberate, see A. Gramsci, "Discorso agli anarchici", in *L'Ordine Nuovo*, i (43), 1920.
[9] The indirect reference to Hegel is deliberate (Hegel 2019).

for the world; a sense of a shared home; civic and ecological responsibility; political vocation as a service to institutions, to the state, and to an equitable *res publica* (but we will see that, today, it is better to speak of *ratio publica*); human rights and constitutional values; a cosmopolitan and environmentalist vision of the *human project*, understood as the individual and social life that we would like to enjoy together; and, finally, the very possibility of talking about good and bad politics. All these *moral* relations exist within a nexus of values, as we shall see later.

Today, it takes courage to use the above expressions because political naivety is too often seen either as the ignorance of incompetent beginners or as the cunning of cynical politicians. So, many people either deride it or suspect it is mere rhetoric, a feigned attitude behind which other meanings, ambitions, messages, or manoeuvres hide. This coded language can be deciphered according to the refined art of the most advanced "secondguessology", a term that could be used to translate the common Italian word "dietrology", namely the "study" of what lies behind (the word is based on the root "dietro" (behind), a message). People who wish to engage in this kind of second-guessing can stop reading the book. It is not written for them, because the book intends to say only what it shows and does not intend to show anything beyond what it says,[10] an aspiration of simplicity that should characterise the most thoughtful and mature politics. Or, as Paul of Tarsus writes in the *Letter to Titus*: "To the pure, all things are pure [*Omnia munda mundis*]; but to those who are defiled and unbelieving, nothing is pure, but both their mind and their conscience are defiled" (1:15). The defiled should not take offence, but their punishment is already their very attitude: they will never understand.

My decision to adopt this "naive" approach was the outcome of discussions and dialogue with experienced individuals (see the acknowledgements at the end of the book) who have studied the works of Plato, Aristotle, Machiavelli, Hobbes, Locke, Rousseau, Kant, Mill, de Tocqueville, Marx, Weber, Keynes, Hayek, von Mises, Arendt, Galbraith, Rawls, Berlin, and many others. Yet, ultimately, they have preferred to follow the far-sighted strategy propounded in Matthew 18:3, although in a secular manner: "unless you are converted and become as little children, you will by no means enter the kingdom of heaven".[11]

---

[10] The indirect reference to Wittgenstein is deliberate (Wittgenstein 2001).
[11] New King James Version.

Like Ithaca, naivety is the point from which one starts, but also the point to which one must return after the enriching journey of reflection. Hence, rather than a lack of judgment, it is sometimes the highest degree of sophistication to which one can aspire. And if this "forward" return to naivety (as opposed to a backward, unsophisticated regression) cannot, perhaps, save the soul, it may at least help politics. Therefore, maybe a less ambitious and more appropriate title for this book would have been: "ideas that *would like* to be 'naive'".

Chapter 2
The Digital Revolution

Digital technologies, sciences, practices, products, services, and experiences—in short, what we can conceptualise as *the digital*—are profoundly transforming the world in which we live and how we conceive of it, that is, both the *realities* we inhabit and the *ideas* we have about these realities. We are at a stage where this is obvious and uncontroversial. The real questions about the digital changing the world and our sense of it are *why?, how?*, and *so what*? The answers to these questions are far from trivial and certainly open to debate. To explain those answers that I find most convincing and to introduce what I mean by the "digital revolution", I shall start *in medias res*, by addressing exactly *how* the digital exerts its influence. I hope this will make it easier to move back to understand the *why*, and then move forwards, to address the *so what*.

The answer to the *how* aspect is simple: the digital has caused a revolution by *cutting and pasting* many fundamental elements of the world and the ways we think about them. In a moment, I shall provide four concrete examples of this process. In more abstract terms, the digital-first detaches or decouples (*cutting*) aspects of the world, attaches or couples (*pasting*) them with others, and sometimes re-attaches or re-couples (*pasting back*) those parts it cut. This remodels our corresponding ideas about such aspects, which we have inherited

The Green and The Blue: Naive Ideas to Improve Politics in the Digital Age, First Edition. Luciano Floridi.

from modernity, especially that of the nineteenth and twentieth centuries (I shall return to the different concepts and timeframes of modernity in Chapter 23). Before the advent of digital technology, we never thought—at least as a culture—that some features of reality that we perceived as fundamentally separate could be united so indissolubly; or, conversely, that what we perceived as intrinsically connected could be separated so straightforwardly. In metaphorical terms, it is as if the digital splits and fuses the modern "atoms" of our experience and culture, creating something powerful and unprecedented. To use a second, Wittgensteinian, metaphor, I would add that the digital revolution resembles altering the river's bedrock, which I describe in Chapter 3 as our deep philosophy, or *Ur-philosophy*. Now, let us move to four everyday examples to illustrate this idea.

Our first example deals with one of the most significant cases of *pasting* together formerly separated aspects of the world, namely personal identity, and personal data. Today, these two aspects are conceptually fused because we speak of *personal identity* in terms of *personal information*. This fusion is a story with deep roots. Censuses have been used for millennia (Alterman 1969); remember the one that led Mary and Joseph to Bethlehem. More recently, the invention of photography in the nineteenth century fundamentally affected privacy; the classic article by Brandeis and Warren (Brandeis and Warren 1890) initiated the debate on the very value of privacy. From the First World War onwards, European governments made it compulsory for citizens to travel with a passport, for reasons of migration and security, thereby extending state control over the movement of its citizens (Torpey 2018). Yet, it is only now, with the digital and its unlimited capacity to record, monitor, share, and process vast amounts of data about Alice,[1] that it has become possible to connect fully *who* Alice is with her *individual self*, *public profile*, and *personal information*. All these strands constitute a single conceptual unit, to the extent that personal data protection is discussed in EU legislation in terms of human dignity and the personal identity of *data subjects*. Alice is her personal information and vice versa. It is also owing to this pasting of

---

[1] The use of "Alice" as a synonym for "agent" is not merely an Oxford-related reference (*Alice in Wonderland*). Readers acquainted with the literature on quantum information will recognise "Alice", "Bob", and "Carol" as the more memorable and concrete placeholder names for otherwise abstract agents or particles; see http://en.wikipedia.org/wiki/Alice_and_Bob.

personal identity with personal data that privacy has become such a pressing, widespread issue.

The second example concerns a case of *cutting*, which causes a disconnection or separation, between *location* (where Alice is physically) and *presence* (where Alice is interacting). In an increasingly digital world, it is now taken for granted that one can physically be in one place, for instance, at home, and be present interactively in another place, such as at the office when working together remotely with a colleague, in another location, on a shared document. Yet all previous generations who have lived and experienced an exclusively analogue world have always conceived and experienced *localisation* and *presence* as two inseparable facets of the same human condition: being situated in space and time, here and now. Up to only recently, an action performed at a distance and telepresence belonged exclusively to fantastical or science-fiction worlds. In the *Iliad*, even the Greek gods themselves must be physically located under the walls of Troy to maintain a local interactive presence and thus exercise an influence over human events. Telepresence was not possible even for them. Today, this disconnection between location and presence simply reflects an unremarkable experience in any information society. We are the first generation for whom "where are you?" is not just a rhetorical or metaphysical question. Of course, this disconnect has not severed all analogue connections. For instance, geolocation works only if Alice's telepresence can be monitored, which is possible to ascertain only if Alice is in a physically connected environment. However, *localisation* and *presence* can now be completely separated, with the result that localisation is becoming of slightly less value than presence: where you are counts less than where you can interact. If all Alice needs and cares about is to be digitally present in a particular corner of the *infosphere* (a simultaneously digital and analogue space and an idea to which I return in Chapter 4), it no longer matters where in the analogue world she is located, be it at home, on a train, or in a café. This is why bank branches and bookshops, for instance, are "modern" places, first created when *location* and *presence* were still conceived as part of an inseparable block. Today, they are looking for a new role where *presence* counts above all. So, when a bookshop opens a café, it is not only trying to diversify and increase its profits but also to reconnect presence and location back together. This is why banks, bookstores, libraries, and retail shops are all *presence* places searching for a *location* repurposing.

The third example involves another powerful *cut* operated by the digital, namely between *law* and *territoriality*. For centuries (roughly since the Peace of Westphalia in 1648 onwards), political geography has provided jurisprudence with an easy answer to determining the scope of law enforcement: legal authority operates within national boundaries. The modern pasting together of law and territoriality can be summarised as "my place my rules, your place your rules", or, in terms of religious tolerance, "whose region, his religion" (*cuius regio, eius religio*). While it seems an obvious principle to us today, reaching such a straightforward approach took centuries and immense suffering. Such an approach still functions perfectly in terms of the territoriality of the law, so long as one operates only within a physical space. The problem of territoriality, however, arises from the infosphere, which exceeds physical space and emerges from a lack of alignment between the normative space of law, the physical space of geography, and the logical space of the digital. This new variable "geometry" of the infosphere is one that we are still learning to manage. For instance, the problems encompassed by the disconnect ("cut") between law and territoriality became evident during the debate on the so-called "right to be forgotten" (more on this in Chapter 7).[2] Search engines like Google operate within an online logical space of nodes, links, protocols, resources, services, web addresses, interfaces, etc. This means that any information is just a click away. Therefore, when the European Court of Justice, in 2014, decided that Google, under specific circumstances, must remove links to someone's personal information from the results that appear on its search engine, it is crucial to remember that this removal would take place only on the European versions of the search engine and not, for instance, the American version.[3] Although this significantly reduces the efficacy of the decision, the disconnect between law and territoriality must be taken seriously. France, however, complained at the time, and tried to impose a global removal of the links, an anachronistic attempt that failed. The General Data Protection Regulation (GDPR) achieves France's intention better, as it ingeniously overcomes the post-Westphalian decoupling ("cut") by instead exploiting the connection between personal identity and data that I illustrated in the first example, to justify the fact that *wherever* the data of a European citizen are processed, European law applies. The GDPR ties the data to the source (Alice is a data subject), and not the law to the territory

---

[2] I was a member of the advisory group organised by Google.

[3] Things are slightly more complicated, but there is no need to go into details here, for a comprehensive analysis, see (Floridi 2015).

(as would be the case in an anachronistic Westphalian system). This is a bit like the logic of the passport, which does not give the right to expatriate (e.g., sometimes a visa is also needed) but to return home, thereby tying the holder to their nationality. Finally, it should be noted that spaces misaligned by the digital not only cause problems but can also provide solutions. The non-territoriality of the digital offers an excellent mechanism for the free circulation of information. In China, for instance, the government must make a constant and sustained effort to control and censor online information that is contrary to the government's politics and ideology.

Finally, let me offer one last example to emphasise that some digital "cut and paste" phenomena can be more accurately interpreted as "re-pasting" or "pasting back together". In his 1980 book *The Third Wave*, Alvin Toffler coined the term "prosumer" to refer to the fusion of the roles of producer and consumer (Toffler 1980). Toffler attributed this tendency to a highly saturated market and the mass production of standardised products, which favoured a process of mass customisation and, thus, the increasing involvement of consumers as producers of their customised products. The idea was anticipated by Marshall McLuhan and Barrington Nevitt in the 1970s, in their attribution of the phenomenon to electricity-based technologies (McLuhan and Nevitt 1972). Almost twenty years after Toffler, at the end of the 1990s, and entirely unaware of the precedents just mentioned, I introduced the word "produmer" to refer to the production/consumption of digital products by the same group of users (Floridi 1999). Today, examples of this mode of consumption are represented by Facebook, Instagram, YouTube, or TikTok, all platforms on which "produmers" consume their digital output. In all such cases, we are not witnessing a "new", unprecedented "pasting" of two previously separated phenomena onto each other. Instead, to be precise, it is a re-pasting or re-coupling of two features that have been linked together for a long time. For 90% of human history, humans have survived by hunting and gathering (Lee and Daly 1999). During this time, producers and consumers (in this case, primarily of food) normally overlapped. In other words, the "produmers" who hunted wild animals and gathered fruit were the norm, not the exception. Only with the development of agricultural societies, and the first forms of urbanisation some 10,000 years ago, do we witness the gradual separation and specialisation of producers and consumers. This articulation into distinct roles gradually grew to the point at which it became culturally codified. In light of this "re-pasting", it is not surprising that online human behaviour patterns, and the way we forage for information, have been studied in comparison with the way we searched for food in the forest for tens of millennia (Pirolli 2007). The practices of a few millennia are now ending, and digitally reinvigorated *produmers* are returning to a type of behaviour deeply rooted in the human psyche.

Having understood the answer to *how* the digital is profoundly changing our world and how we think about it, it is now easier to apply it to interpret other cases of "cutting and pasting". For instance, consider the difference between *virtual reality* (*cut* from ordinary reality) and *augmented reality* (*pasted* to everyday *reality*), or, in the context of the *sharing economy*, the disconnection ("cut") between the *authorised use* of something (contract law) and its *legal ownership* (property law). Because of this *cut*, people do not actually buy digital books on Amazon, as one cannot re-sell them; the situation is more akin to renting them permanently. The digital revolution has nullified the distinction between *authenticity* and *reproduction*: because two files are exact clones of each other, it makes no sense to ask which one is the original in the way it does for an analogue object such as the *Mona Lisa*, for instance. Today, however, blockchain technology can re-paste authenticity to a given artefact, even one that happens to be digital, thereby reintroducing the possibility of certification that was previously applied only to the analogue realm. A key example in this regard is digital works of art. Non-fungible tokens (NFT) stored on blockchains have become a popular way to certify digital assets, such as photos, videos, or audios, as unique and not interchangeable. In particular, NFTs can provide a buyer with a proof of ownership for a digital work of art. In 2021, there was an NFT buying frenzy, and on 11 March, the American digital artist Beeple sold his work *Everydays: The First 5000 Days* through the auction house Christie's for $69.3 million, breaking all previous records for NFTs. Memory (i.e., a file) reverts to being authentic or inauthentic, as in the case of a smart contract. Another disconnection ("cut") engendered by the digital is seen in how Uber and Airbnb have decoupled a function—third-party car transport and rooms rental, respectively—from the professions of taxi driver and hotelier. The process of "uberisation" refers to the innovative decoupling enabled by digital technology. There are myriad other examples. The reader does not have to look far to find additional instances of this cut-and-paste dialectic, which abounds in the digital era. The time has come to move from the *how* to the *why*.

Why does the digital have the power to cut and paste both reality and how we think about it? Why have other innovative technologies not had such an impact? The answer lies in the combination of two factors.

On the one hand, the digital is a *third-order technology*. The terminology is easily explained. Consider a technology (your choice) as something that is between a user, Alice, and something with which she is interacting. The digital is not simply a technology that mediates between Alice and nature, like an axe she can use to cut down a tree. That would be a first-order technology, that is, an instance of a technology interacting with something that is not a technology, but rather part of the natural world. Nor is the digital just a technology between Alice and another technology, like a hammer she uses to hit a nail. That is a second-order technology, a kind of technology that interacts with another technology, no longer with the natural world. Instead, the digital is a technology that operates between one technology and another, like a computer system that controls a robot building a car. To use an everyday example: Roomba, a robot vacuum cleaner, is a first-order technology because it deals with dust on the floor, something it finds in the natural world. The app Alice uses to control Roomba is second order: it is between her and another technology. The smartphone's operating system that automatically upgrades the app that controls Roomba is a third-order technology: it interacts with another technology to interact with a third. So, if Alice does the updating herself, she works like a third-order technology: she could and perhaps should be replaced. Because of the autonomous processing power of digital technology, there is no need for Alice to be involved in the process at all, or, at most, she needs to be involved only to the extent that she monitors and controls it. So, rather than being *in the loop*, she is *on the loop*, or perhaps only *after the loop*. Simply put: an axe or a hammer need Alice to perform the tasks for which they are designed, but digital technology can bypass her altogether. Thus, digital technology creates a distance and an unprecedented space for "artificial autonomy", between humanity and reality, that is wider than any other first- or second-order technology. This distance makes it easy for the digital to cut and paste aspects of the world, including how we conceive of it, because it multiplies the opportunities (affordances) and reduces the constraints to perform various tasks.

On the other hand, we have seen that the digital not only enhances or augments the reality we engage with but also transforms it by creating new environments in which we live, and by giving us new abilities to coordinate interactions with people or things. We do not live on television, but we do live on the Web or in the infosphere. Not only does the digital enable the *design* of new constructs, structures, and systems (e.g., a society, a machine, some artefacts, some services, some experiences, etc.), it radically transforms both their intrinsic nature and the way we conceive of them. If the digital allows one easily to cut and paste facts and ideas, it also equips one to design and re-design them with fewer constraints and more affordances. For this reason, our age is the *age of design*—a point to which I shall return at the end of this chapter.

The previous considerations suggest that the digital owes its power of cutting and pasting reality, and our ideas about it, to its being a third-order, design-oriented technology. This unique quality is why we rightly speak of a digital *revolution*, and why no other technology has ever had a similar effect on humanity, its life, and its environments.

If we consider all this plausible, even if only approximately, then it can help us make sense of two current phenomena that may initially seem unrelated, but that both owe their new influence in society to the digital. These are two cases in which the ability to cut and paste features of modernity is frequently misinterpreted, namely artificial intelligence (AI) and direct democracy. The latter theme is more closely aligned with the overarching topic of this book, and Chapter 20 is entirely devoted to it; here, let me briefly dwell on AI.[4]

Let us recall the basic premise: the digital marks a revolution because it cuts, pastes, and hence can more easily design or re-design reality and how we think about it. If this is true, does AI represent an outcome of a similar cut or a paste? Today, many people seem to believe that AI is about a *paste*: coupling artificial agency and intelligent behaviour into new artefacts, a kind of marriage between engineering and biology. This is a misunderstanding. The opposite is true: AI is about decoupling (*cutting*) successful agency (the ability to solve a problem or complete a task in view of a goal) from any need to be intelligent. It is a divorce between two formerly united traits. It is only when this decoupling can be achieved that AI works and has value. Let me explain.

The best definition of AI remains that propounded by the scientists and mathematicians McCarthy, Minsky, Rochester, and Shannon in their classic *A Proposal for the Dartmouth Summer Research Project on Artificial Intelligence*, the document, and ensuing event, that founded AI as a new field of research in 1955. In that seminal text, they wrote:

> For the current purpose, the problem of artificial intelligence is considered to be that of making a machine behave in ways that would be called intelligent if a human being behaved in the same way.
>
> *(McCarthy et al. 2006)*

---

[4] I have discussed this point in detail in (Floridi forthcoming).

It is what philosophers call a counterfactual statement: if Alice behaved in the same successful[5] way as the AI, we would call her behaviour intelligent. That does not mean, however, that AI is intelligent. This is an error that betrays superstition. Imagine a river that, over time, by flowing and shaping its best possible course, reaches the sea by removing obstacles and optimising distances on its way. If this "optimising" were Alice's behaviour, we would consider it intelligent, but it does not follow that we consider the river intelligent.

The above definition is reminiscent of the Turing test (Turing 1950). The test involves an assessment of the ability to perform a task successfully. A judge asks the same questions to two participants for five minutes. One of these participants is a computer, and the other is a human being, our usual Alice. The judge does not know who is who and needs to spot the difference by interpreting their answers alone. Imagine that this happens through emails. If the answers are such that the judge cannot distinguish between the computer and Alice, then the machine can be said to have behaved *as if* it *were* as intelligent as Alice. Using a household example, a dishwasher does not clean the dishes the same way as Bob does, but at the end of the process, its washed dishes are indistinguishable from Bob's, and may even be cleaner. So, by looking at the clean dishes, an observer may be unable to tell whether it was Bob or the dishwasher that did the washing up. The same concept applies to AI. These examples remind us that we are talking about engineering, for which the result is essential, and not cognitive science, for which it is not so much the result that is important, but whether the agent or its behaviour displays even a slight degree of intelligence. AI is not about reproducing human intelligence or producing superior intelligence, but rather about being able to do without it, obtaining the same or even better results, without relying on it. It is not a marriage, but a successful divorce (or *cut*) between agency and intelligence. Thus, to paraphrase Carl von Clausewitz, one may conclude that AI is the continuation of human intelligence by other means. This is why autonomous vehicles are not driven by robots sitting behind the wheel, as in *Star Wars*, but instead are vehicles that re-design mobility and the conditions that make it possible and safe. Today, successful AI *decouples* (*cuts*) the ability to perform tasks and solve problems successfully from the need to be intel-

---

[5] A qualifier like "successful" must be added to capture "in ways that", otherwise any failing behaviour would count.

ligent to do so. It is a revolution, but not the kind envisaged by believers in true AI, the sci-fi kind. Thanks to this decoupling, AI can take over increasingly larger shares of tasks to be performed and problems to be solved, whenever these can be effectively dealt with without recourse to understanding, awareness, sensitivity, embodiment, concerns, intuitions, meaning, experience, taste, passions, even wisdom, and all those other factors that contribute to what we understand by human intelligence. In short, it is precisely when we stop trying to reproduce human intelligence that we can succeed in solving an increasing number of problems with AI. If we had waited for even a spark of true AI, my smartphone would never have beaten me at chess (something it now does regularly). John McCarthy knew this very well: that is why he never stopped complaining about the way the game of chess had been used in AI (McCarthy 1997). He was partly right: it is not by creating systems that play chess (or any other board game) and consistently win that we will succeed in reproducing human intelligence. However, he was fundamentally wrong in thinking that this was not the course that AI should take. He did not like it because he believed in true AI, the kind you see in *Star Trek*. It is precisely the engineering direction, however, and not the cognitivist direction (which has failed completely) that society has taken. It works, even if the resultant AI is as intelligent as a Moka pot. Disconnecting (digital "cutting") intelligence from the ability to perform tasks successfully is the outcome of the extraordinary capacity of human ingenuity.

I can imagine the almost convinced reader still pondering various questions. How can a divorce between agency and intelligence be successful in the first place, in terms of efficacy? Isn't intelligence fundamental for any behaviour to be successful? I already offered the example of the river to illustrate how this is not necessarily always the case. But more needs to be said in terms of a positive explanation to answer the previous question that can double task as a reasonable objection. The success of AI is mainly attributable to the fact that we are building an AI-friendly environment in which smart technologies thrive. Recalling the cut-paste-design process, there is a "pasting" that enables AI to be successful with zero inherent intelligence, achieved by pasting the digital and analogue environments together into a single infosphere. We are adapting the world to AI, not vice versa. We have seen how the digital is changing the very nature of our environments (and what we understand them to be) even as the infosphere is progressively becoming the world where we spend most of our lives. While we have not successfully developed true AI that can interact with the world as well as, or better than, us, we were actually modifying the world to suit the engineered artefacts that we call AI. The world is becoming an infosphere that is increasingly well-adapted to AI-bounded capacities. To understand this, consider the development of the car industry.

Since the beginning of the digital revolution and the advent of AI, the car industry has been at the forefront, first with industrial robotics and now with AI-based driverless cars. Now take a third-order technology, as we saw above, such as a robot that paints a vehicle component in a factory. The three-dimensional space that defines the boundaries within which such a robot can work successfully is defined as the robot's *envelope*. The car industry has been working with enveloped robots for decades. Some of our domestic technologies, such as dishwashers or washing machines, accomplish their tasks because their environments are structured (*enveloped*) around the elementary capacities of the "robots" that make them function. The same applies to Amazon's robotic shelves in "enveloped" warehouses. It is the environment that is designed to be robot-friendly and not the other way around. Thus, we do not build droids like C-3PO from *Star Wars* to wash dishes in the sink precisely as we would. Instead, we envelop micro-environments around simple robots that splash soap and water around, to suit and maximise their limited capacities to deliver the desired output.

Enveloping used to be either a stand-alone phenomenon (you buy the robot with the required envelope, like a dishwasher or a washing machine) or implemented within the walls of factories carefully tailored around their artificial inhabitants. Now, enveloping the environment into an AI-friendly infosphere has started to permeate all aspects of our lived experience. This "marriage" between AI and our environment happens daily, whether in the house, the office, or the street. When we speak of smart cities, we mean not only urban places that rely on different forms of technology to collect, process, and use data, but also social habitats that are being transformed into places where digital technologies of all kinds can operate successfully. We have been enveloping the world around digital technologies for decades, both invisibly and without full awareness of doing so. The future of AI lies in the continued expansion of enveloping, e.g., in terms of 5G and the Internet of Things. As we spend more and more time in the infosphere, all new information is increasingly born digital. Returning to the car industry example, driverless cars will become a commodity when we can envelop the environment around them. So, expect them to be successful in environments like airports, but not in the countryside.

In the 1940s and 1950s, the computer was a room; Alice used to walk inside it to work with and within it. To program it required using a screwdriver. Human-computer interaction was mainly a physical relation. In the 1970s, Alice's daughter walked out of the computer to stand in front of it. Human-computer interaction became less a *somatic* and more a *semantic* relation, facilitated by Disk Operating System (DOS), lines of text, Graphic User Inter-face (GUI), and icons. Today, Alice's granddaughter has returned to walking inside the computer, which now takes the form of a whole infosphere that surrounds her, often imperceptibly. We are building the ultimate envelope in which human-computer interactions have returned to their somatic origins through touch screens, voice commands, listening devices, gesture-sensitive applications, proxy data for location, virtual or augmented reality, and so forth. As usual, entertainment, health, and military applications are driving such innovation. But other industries are not lagging far behind. If drones, driverless vehicles, robotic lawnmowers, bots, and algorithms of all kinds can move "around" and interact with our environments with increasing ease, this is not because true AI (the Hollywood kind) has finally arrived. It is because we have rendered the environment increasingly suitable for our engineered artefacts and their extraordinary but limited capacities. In such an AI-friendly infosphere, the default assumption is that any agent performing a task may be artificial. This is why we are regularly asked online to prove that *we* are *not* robots by clicking on a so-called CAPTCHA (the Completely Automated Public Turing test to tell Computers and Humans Apart). The agent is tested on its ability to decipher a slightly altered string of letters, symbols, or images, pos-sibly mixed with other graphical elements, to prove it is a human and not a robot, for instance, when registering for a new online account. It is a trivial test for humans but an apparently impossible task for AI. This demonstrates how little progress has been made in the cognitive area of the production of non-biological intelligence, and how much the environment we inhabit is, in fact, increasingly populated by artificial agents.

Every day brings more computational power, more data, more devices (the Internet of Things), more sensors, more tags, more satellites, more actuators, more digital services, and more humans connected and living "onlife" (see Chapter 7), in other words, more enveloping. More jobs are becoming digital, as are all kinds of activities, such as playing, educating, training, dating, meet-ing up, fighting, caring, gossiping, or advertising. We do all this and more in an enveloped infosphere where our role is more of an analogue guest than a digital host. No wonder our AI systems are performing increasingly well.

We have altered the world enough for it to be their environment. As we shall see in the rest of this book, this profound ontological transformation implies significant political and ethical challenges.

Assuming that the previous answers to *how* and *why* the digital revolution is happening are sufficiently correct, the third question, it will be recalled, concerns the consequences and significance: *so what*? What difference does it make understanding the revolutionary power of the digital in terms of its cut-and-paste dynamics? While I have already hinted at the answer, an analogy may help to introduce it more intuitively.

If you have only one piece of paper and absolutely nothing else, not even another piece of paper to put next to it, the only thing you can do with it is to enjoy it, perhaps by playing with it. However, suppose you cut the paper into two, and can glue the two pieces differently. In that case, you are already presented with several possibilities that result from combining and recombining the pieces. Two pieces of paper thus provide more opportunities (*affordances*) and fewer *constraints* than one piece of paper. The more you can cut and paste, the greater the affordances and the fewer the constraints. We saw that cutting and pasting a single piece of paper—a proxy for reality and our understanding of it—is precisely what the digital does. Taking advantage of affordances and constraints to solve a problem in this way becomes a matter of *design*.

Design is, among many other things, the production of an artefact that maximises opportunities (the affordances) within some given constraints, to solve a problem or conduct a task successfully, in view of a particular goal. Alfonso Bialetti's Moka pot does precisely that: it makes good coffee by safely and inexpensively solving the problem of steam production and brewing. This understanding of design helps to explain why design is so important and prevalent today. By cutting and pasting reality and how we think about it, the digital increases the opportunities for what can be done and decreases the constraints on what previously could not be done, or what would be too costly, complicated, or challenging to do. We have seen, for instance, that digital technologies allow us to interact with others at a distance (presence) while remaining physically distant (location). In a purely analogue world, Alice must go to the bank to deposit or withdraw money. Online, however, everything is easier: her physical location in the house is disconnected from her interactive presence in the infosphere. With fewer constraints and more opportunities in a dematerialised (in the sense of "de-analogued") world, design becomes the kind of innovation that makes a real difference in transforming opportunities into a coherent reality. For example, a bank offers an app to scan cheques and deposit them into Alice's current account without her having to go to a branch. Therefore, the answer to the third question— *so what?*—should be clear: digital technology significantly reduces reality's constraints and dramatically increases its affordances, turning design into the kind of *innovation* that defines our age. To understand and improve the present, our priority must be to work on design as today's primary force for progress and innovation.

While innovation has a thousand forms, it can also be categorised into three distinctive types: *invention*, *discovery*, and *design*. Someone *invents* the wheel, *discovers* a new metal, or *designs* the Moka pot. Inventions, discoveries, and design are always connected, like a three-legged stool. For instance, without the design of the caravel, introduced around 1430 by the Portuguese, there would be no Columbus' *Pinta* and hence no discovery of America. Innovation, however, resembles a stool with one leg longer than the others. One of the three kinds of innovation tends to dominate, depending on the circumstances. There are periods when one type of innovation is more influential and drives the others. European history from the fifteenth to eighteenth centuries (the post-Renaissance and early modern period) is often described as the *Age of Discovery* or the *Age of Exploration*. The subsequent phase (sometimes known as the late modern period) was still a period of European geographical discovery. However, progress in that period owes much more to innovation in the sense of *technological inventions*, hence its common designation of the mechanical and industrial age. We live in the age of design, which drives innovation and adds value to products, services, processes, ecosystems, discoveries, and inventions. The archetypal example is the iPhone: "Designed by Apple in California. Assembled in China". Of course, all historical ages have also been eras of design, at least because discoveries and inventions require ingenious ways of connecting and shaping old and new realities. However, it is only today that one may speak of an *age of design*, where the digital offers immense and expanding freedom to organise, reorganise, and create the realities around us in a multitude of ways, by cutting, pasting, and designing them, and thus solving a range of old and unfamiliar problems.

Through the process of design, we shape an increasingly malleable reality. Design is what creates new tasks, new jobs, new trades, new processes, new techniques, new services, and new institutions. Successful entrepreneurs are first of all great designers. Entire categories of creativity or work appear, disappear, or are revolutionised. While the opportunities for those who can exploit digital design are astounding, the costs for those excluded can be severe. More-over, these events are happening extremely quickly, which is a real cause for concern. There is a genuine risk that the digital metamorphoses from being part of the solution to being part of the problem. While this is a real dilemma that should be considered, we can avoid or at least minimise risks by rethinking the world of ecology, education, and political collaboration, as I shall argue in the remainder of this book. Every design requires a project. In our case, the pressing question regarding design is that of the *human project* for our digital age. We live in the age of design. The most important "object" of such design is us and how we live together. So, we need to ask ourselves: what society do we want to design, in the twenty-first century? What human project is worth pur-suing today so that future generations will be grateful for our efforts? These are political questions. We do not seem to have articulated this project yet, but we must define it as soon as possible, given the global challenges we face. We must not let chance or unchecked dynamics shape the world without us having any plan of our own. We must make a critical effort to decide in which direction we wish to steer the digital revolution, to ensure that the information societies we are designing are open, tolerant, equitable, and not merely sustainable but supportive of both the natural and social environments, as well as future human development. The hope is that the following chapters may contribute to the design of this much-needed human project.

Let me summarise the chapter. Once we realise that the digital cuts, pastes, and consequently (re)designs what we inherit from the past (facts, things, what happens in the world, in short: *ontology*) and how we understand this inheritance (ideas, concepts, our cultural frames of reference, in short: *epistemology*), it becomes evident that the digital revolution is a *re-ontologisation* and *re-episte-mologisation of* modernity that requires a new *design* of the *human project* as a *political* effort. These are strong assertions, which may be slightly off-putting to some readers. However, I hope they can be understood simply as a more concise way of communicating the previous analysis. It is of the utmost importance that the digital revolution, with its power to re-ontologise the world and us in it and re-epistemologise our knowledge of it and our self-understanding, must be eth-ical and political to enable a deeper understanding of the present to design the future better. To ensure this, we need to understand how the digital has trans-formed our ways of understanding reality. This is the topic of the next chapter.

Chapter 3

The Transition from Things to Relations

Our everyday way of thinking (especially in business, economic, legal, social, and political contexts) is still dominated by a deep and implicit philosophy inherited from Aristotelian and Newtonian thought. This way of thinking is now obsolete in our information society, as experts have remarked to me more than once. However, it is still pervasive in our culture and communication, as I have often replied (one only needs to read texts and reports from the Austrian or Chicago School of Economics or the Washington Consensus researchers, with their emphasis on individual agents). I will explain why in a moment. For now, we can call this "philosophy behind philosophy"— the everyday cultural paradigm or conceptual perspective that we do not question or even consciously perceive—our *Ur-philosophy*.

The Aristotelian and Newtonian *Ur-philosophy* was fit for purpose in the past. As a testament to this, our way of thinking is still unconsciously shaped by it. Let us examine it briefly, to understand why it would be a mistake to continue applying it, and to adapt it to obtain the correct answers to the new questions posed by today's information societies.

The Green and The Blue: Naive Ideas to Improve Politics in the Digital Age, First Edition. Luciano Floridi.
© 2024 John Wiley & Sons Ltd. Published 2024 by John Wiley & Sons Ltd.

To use an analogy, an Aristotelian *Ur-philosophy* conceives of society as if it were a set of Lego bricks. Many units connect to other units, from the bottom to the top, creating complex structures interacting with one another. The Lego bricks or *atomistic* (i.e., indivisible) entities represent the physical (e.g., Alice and Bob) or legal persons (e.g., the companies employing Alice and Bob). Their combinations give rise to various formations: a couple, a family, a generation, a social class, an ethnic group, an industry, an administration, a district, a municipality, and so on. The *properties* (what qualifies the bricks for what they *are*, e.g., a "manager" or a "limited company") and the *behaviours* (what qualifies the bricks for what *they do*, e.g., "responsible for quality control" or "produces semiconductors") of the brick-persons are combined in a relatively complex way. Moreover, according to this *Ur-philosophy*, the combination of brick-persons gives rise to properties and behaviours that may be *inherited* (e.g., brick persons that behave honestly create a society-building that is itself honest) or *emergent* (e.g., brick persons that are privileged by birth create an unequal society-building). In more technical terms, our Aristotelian *Ur-philosophy*—and the related sociological and political ways of implicit thinking informed by it—uncritically assumes an ontology formalised by "naive set theory".[1] This conceptualises a whole (in our case, society) as a collection of complex and diversely structured simple objects, called elements or members of the set. It also interprets all other non-atomic "social objects" (e.g., family, generation, social class, party, trade union) as sets of natural or legal persons.

This Aristotelian *Ur-philosophy* of *things* is complemented by a Newtonian *Ur-philosophy* of *space* (that is, the house, the shop, the office, the square, the neighbourhood, the city, the region, the territory, the nation, the country, the borders, the land, the sea, the sky, the Moon, Mars, etc.) and of *time* (e.g. days, months, and years, history, tradition, recurrences, deadlines, festivities, weekdays and working days, weekends, Bank holidays, coffee breaks, vacations). Space and time are understood as two rigid and absolute reference containers insofar as they are not relative to anything else. They are conceived as dynamic only to the extent that they tend towards an ideal, definitive stability. The fascist concept of a territorial "living space" and the Nazi concept of *Lebensraum*, or the idea that a nation has a destiny to fulfil in this space, are ideological variants of this Newtonian *Ur-philosophy* of physical space as a geographical territory, and of physical time as a calendar.

---

[1] Axiomatic theory, on the other hand, analyses sets based on the relation of satisfaction of certain axioms.

To summarise: let us imagine space as a large box, in which elements (such as people) interact along the arrow of time, linearly and irreversibly. Our Aristotelian-Newtonian *Ur-philosophy* conceives reality as made up of *things*, *space* as a box, and *time* as a moving arrow. It emphasises the concept of *action* as the crucial point (the "ontological variable", in philosophical terminology) on which to exert pressure, constructively, to modify or improve the behaviour or properties (that is, the nature) of the elements themselves, focusing primarily on their structural combinations, and thus of the society they constitute. Put more simply, according to this view, the way to change society is to modify (shape, punish, reward, nudge, etc.) the *actions of* the natural or legal persons who constitute it. Therefore, actions are the system's pressure points, which can be managed, guided, directed, or modified to achieve the desired changes. This philosophy leads to a vision of law as a system to regulate the *actions* of brick-persons (and their compounds) in time and space.

Metaphors of society as a body, organ, or coordinated system have been based on this *Ur-philosophy* since the time of Agrippa's *Apologue*. They can be found in Hobbes' *Leviathan* or Kant's *Perpetual Peace*. Furthermore, from Weber[2] onwards, the emphasis on the centrality of action shows how the design of social architecture remains focused on shaping and directing *behaviour*, prioritising actions and their effects as the only initial entry points to any policy.

The main achievement of the Aristotelian-Newtonian paradigm is the idea of building and regulating the *social mechanism*: atomic entities, on account of their properties and behaviours, are combined in a structure that has its properties and behaviours, like an analogue clock, or a construction built from Meccano. The construction of the desired mechanism (in our case, the society) in terms of properties or behaviours, starts with identifying the necessary and sufficient components required to build it. If the mechanism (society) does not work, or works in an undesirable way, then the relevant parts are repaired, modified, or added, until they function as desired. The concept of "performance" and the quantitative analysis of it represent the contemporary translation or update of this mechanistic approach.

The Aristotelian-Newtonian paradigm had its merits. But it has become so ingrained in our ways of thinking that even Actor-Network Theory (ANT),

---

[2] See M. Weber, *Sociology of Power. The Structure of Power and Bureaucratic Power.*

insofar as I understand it, treats actors (or actants) as existing logically before the network to which they belong:

> A central assumption associated with actor-network theory is that "society, organisations, agents, and machines are all effects generated in patterned networks of diverse (not simply human) materials" (Law 1992, p. 380). Hence, actor-network approaches understand human actors to be *embedded* [my italics] within relational networks of human and nonhuman actors, and seek congruent methods of analysis (Latour 1984, 1987; Law 1994). Sayes suggests that "the term 'nonhuman' is intended to signal dissatisfaction with the philosophical tradition in which an object is automatically placed opposite a subject, and the two are treated as radically different" (Sayes 2014, p. 136).[3]

ANT seems to focus on, and understand, *agency* and *actions* relationally, rather than as *agents* (*actors*, *actants*) themselves. This is a step in the right direction, but it still relies heavily on the Aristotelian-Newtonian paradigm based on the primacy of things.

Today, such a paradigm no longer meets the needs of a *mature* information society (see Chapter 8). Since the twentieth century, the more formal and quantitative sciences, namely, mathematics, physics, and logic, when faced with increasingly difficult conceptual challenges, have abandoned the old Aristotelian-Newtonian *Ur-philosophy*; or, when it has been necessary to adopt it, have done so critically, with an awareness of its limits. Their "new" (but, in fact, now a century old) *Ur-philosophy* can be defined as *relational*. A fundamental obstacle is that the combination of our mammalian brain, our sensory apparatus, our Indo-European languages, and our Western culture, by their very nature, seek to objectify or "thingify" (i.e., hypostatise or reify) the world, organising it as if it were a Lego set: first there are the things (*nouns*); second, there are the *properties* of things (*adjectives*); and finally, the *behaviours* of things (*verbs*). For instance, "Alice writes with the blue pen on the white paper" is thing + behaviour + thing + property, and so on, for the rest of our experiential world. This is how we are used to think, and it is a conceptual framework difficult to abandon. A relational and non-thing-based *Ur-philosophy* does not reject the concept of "thing", of course, but it does not consider it primary, instead replacing it, in order of ontological importance, with the

---

[3] *Lost in delegation? (Dis)organizing for sustainability*. Available from: https://www.researchgate.net/publication/322307885_Lost_in_delegation_Disorganizing_for_sustainability [accessed Jan 26, 2022].

concept of *relation*. It looks at the world as a *network*, in which nodes are the outcome of relations, not as a *mechanism*, in which components come first and then are related. With an analogy, the threads (relations, links, and functions) pre-exist the nodes (things), which are as real as the threads, but are born from the crossing of the threads, and logically form after them. Mathematically, it can be modelled by edge-centric graph theory, in which edges are primary, vertices are defined in terms of edges, and there are no isolated vertices, that is, vertices with no incident edges (in the same sense in which there are no roundabout without roads).

To overcome the obstacles that Aristotelian-Newtonian intuition and common sense pose to adopting a relational *Ur-philosophy*, science uses sophisticated mathematical tools in different fields. For example, the theory of relativity requires vector spaces, in which tensors are used to describe space-time in a four-dimensional curved variety. Category theory replaces the theory of sets to offer a general theory of *functors*. It also disengages the foundations of mathematics from the hypothesis of prime elements as things, which is frequently explained according to the old metaphor of apples (elements) in the basket (set). These two examples are important, but they are also somewhat disheartening. Not only do they not work perfectly well. Admittedly, they are very complicated, and if the intention is to change our way of thinking in our politics—similarly to how we have been forced to think differently in physics or mathematics—it is almost certain that this experiment is likely to end in resounding failure.

How can we abandon such an intuitive *Ur-philosophy*, given that the Aristotelian-Newtonian mode of thinking is so ingrained in our everyday mental habits, culture, and ways of perceiving and thinking about the world? This question is especially pressing when we consider that, while we should all be able to engage in dialogue with one another, not everyone possesses the necessary conceptual vocabulary, especially when human reflection engages with its intellectual, cultural, and factual parameters and products (such as society, ecology, jurisprudence, or politics) which, by their very nature, compel us to linger in "thing-based" thinking. We not only interpret and think of society but also physically construct it in material parts, as we do with a Lego set. To do otherwise may seem an almost impossible conceptual transformation, much harder than accepting that the earth is round, or not at the centre of the universe, or that each of us is composed mainly of water. This is because the phenomena being discussed (in our case, society, and politics) impose a paradigm shift in a much less decisive manner (i.e., in terms of complex and recalcitrant problems to be solved), and with much weaker standards (i.e., in terms of evaluating proposed and varied solutions) as they do in physics and mathematics. In other words, the change does not impose itself on our collective way of thinking. Moreover, it is difficult to overcome our reluctance to abandon a worldview in terms of things and their properties. Our mammalian brains find the Aristotelian-Newtonian ontology too intuitive and appealing to relinquish it easily.

An illustrative example of this inability to think outside an Aristotelian-Newtonian paradigm is offered by Margaret Thatcher (she read Chemistry at Oxford, specialising in crystallography). The inadequacy of the ingrained "Lego" model is evident in this famous Thatcher quotation:

> There is no such thing [as a society]! There are individual men and women and [end p. 29] there are families and no government can do anything except through people and people look to themselves first. It is our duty to look after ourselves and then also to help look after our neighbour and life is a reciprocal business and people have got the entitlements too much in mind without the obligations, because there is no such thing as an entitlement unless someone has first met an obligation [...].[4]

Note the admission (couched in political rhetoric) that the family is one of the basic elements of society. In fact, this admission is contradictory: the family is not an atom, but rather a social molecule. Besides, where does a family end? Do we include only parents and offspring, or grandparents, uncles, and aunts, as well? What about cousins? And on what basis do we admit the extended family and not, for instance, a group of related families? And why not admit the whole human family? In the passage quoted, individualist rhetoric has paid the price of allowing incoherence to become demagogically palatable. In fact, political nominalism accepts only individuals, not families. This is clear if one looks at the statement issued by No. 10 (this is the equivalent of saying "by the White House", as a way of referring to the British Prime Minister or the government), at the request of the *Sunday Times* and published on 10 July 1988:

---

[4] Keay, *Woman's Own*, 31 October 1987, pp. 8–10. Thatcher Archive (THCR 5/2/262): COI transcript, available here: https://www.margaretthatcher.org/document/106689.

All too often, the ills of this country are passed off as those of society. Similarly, when action is required, society is called upon to act. But society as such does not exist except as a concept. Society is made up of people. It is people who have duties and beliefs and resolve. It is people who get things done. She prefers to think in terms of the acts of individuals and families as the real sinews of society rather than of society as an abstract concept. Her approach to society reflects her fundamental belief in personal responsibility and choice. To leave things to 'society' is to run away from the real decisions, practical responsibility and effective action.[5]

Here, the reference to "family" comes almost as an afterthought and, again, a somewhat inconsistent one, given that a "family" is also just made up of people, and is no less a concept than "society" itself. Quoting once more from Thatcher, the same Aristotelian-Newtonian *Ur-philosophy* is evident in the following simplistic conception of politics and economics[6]: "who understands the problems of running a home will be nearer to understanding the problems of running a country".[7]

Aristotle would have been delighted. Today, however, it is becoming increasingly difficult to understand (and, *a fortiori*, to manage successfully) phenomena through a simple framework of home-grown governance and Aristotelian-Newtonian insights, as in the following examples:

- stock buybacks, i.e., the repurchasing of stock shares by the company that first issued them;
- negative interest rates, namely, a tax on owning money, in the words of the economist Silvio Gesell, supported by a monetary policy;
- the recent popularity of negative-yielding bonds, such as those issued by Germany, whereby the investor receives less money at the bond's maturity than the original purchase price for the bond;

---

[5] Thatcher Archive (THCR 5/2/262): COI transcript, available here: https://www.margaretthatcher.org/document/106689.
[6] Indeed, the etymology of economics, namely "regulation of the home (*oikos*)", is equally unsatisfactory.
[7] "Any woman who understands the problems of running a home will be nearer to understanding the problems of running a country", BBC (1979), quoted in J. Blundell, *Margaret Thatcher: A Portrait of the Iron Lady*, Algora Publishing, New York 2008, p. 193: https://en.wikiquote.org/wiki/MargaretThatcher.

- the advocacy for exercising austerity when it is possible but not necessary (i.e., in times of economic growth), and not when it *seems* necessary but is not really feasible (i.e., in times of crisis) because it only ends up doubling the damage (think of the Greek crisis);
- the economic value of a minimum degree of inflation or level of unemployment;
- the populist and self-defeating phenomenon of democratic degradation, seen in Brexit and Trump's presidency.

These examples illustrate why society cannot be viewed as a Lego set and managed like a house. Keynes was right, and Thatcher was wrong: neither politics nor economics is akin to housekeeping. It is as if scientists at CERN (the European Organisation for Nuclear Research) were to use Newtonian physics to understand the behaviour of subatomic particles: the point is not that Newtonian physics does not work or have any value, but rather that it is insufficient and no longer works in this case, and that this case is now the most important one.

To meet the new challenges posed by mature information societies, where there is generally greater affluence and more free time than was available in the past or is available in other developing societies, our way of thinking about politics must take a step forward and reimagine and update the intuitions of common sense espoused by the Aristotelian-Newtonian paradigm. A new way of thinking is required to address adequately the characteristics of mature information societies, in which basic goods are cheap, information and other services are free or paid in-kind (by sharing personal data), network economies often lead to *de facto* monopolies, and the degree of complexity and interconnectedness is now profound. The concept that can and should replace the Aristotelian-Newtonian paradigm of *social things* is that of *relation*.

In 1920, a great German philosopher, Ernst Cassirer, published a brilliant essay, *Substance and Function* (Cassirer 2003), in which he analysed the transition in mathematics and physics from the centrality of the concept of *substance* (things) to the centrality of the concept of *function*, and hence the end of the Aristotelian-Newtonian paradigm as I have described it here. Cassirer was right, and the next step we need to take is to understand how to move from functions to relations. A *function f* is just a special type of *relation* that associates each element of a set to only one element of a set. For example, squaring natural numbers (1, 2, 3, …) is a function, and can be written like this: $f(x) = x.^2$ In the example, for every natural number, you get one and only one natural number, $1^2 = 1$, $2^2 = 4$, $3^2 = 9$, etc. A *relation R* is more general than a function because it is any predicate that qualifies one or more elements of a set and can associate each individual element to many other elements, not just one. It is easier to see how this works in the case of $2^2 = 4$: squaring *relates* 2 and 4. One can then use the same concept of relation to say that Alice is taller than Bob. This relation connects two elements, so it is *binary* and can be written thus: "Alice is taller than Bob" = *is-taller-than* (Alice, Bob). Note, however, that *is-taller-than* also connects Bob to many other people, so "is taller than Bob" could give us Carol as well, not just Alice, as in *is-taller-than* (x, Bob). If you have three elements, then the relation is described as ternary, as in Alice *is sitting between* Bob and Carol or: *is-seating-between* (Alice, Bob, Carol). You can see that the "arity" (bin-*ary*, tern-*ary*, etc.) determines the number of elements qualified by the relation.

At this point, mathematicians make a move that may seem counterintuitive, but it is helpful to unify our language and conceptual framework under a single concept. They tell us that *any predicate* (or qualification or property) of any element—human, natural, artificial—is a relation, even if it has an "arity" of only one, as in "Alice is tall", which is written *is-tall*(Alice). Speaking simply of *relations* allows us to indicate simultaneously "is old" and "is older than" as relations with different *arity*. The penultimate step to arrive at a new way of thinking is to understand Alice as the whole set of relations that, in the end, uniquely qualify her and only her. Alice becomes a signifier for all the relations to which she is connected. Using different vocabularies, one may also say that Alice is a bundle of relations (to use a more Humean perspective), or that Alice is an encapsulation of multiple properties and processes (to adapt the terminology of object-oriented programming).

The final step is to understand change as a transition from a set of relations to another set of relations, as when Alice becomes taller than Bob: a transition from *is-taller-than* (Bob, Alice) to *is-taller-than* (Alice, Bob).

Let us return to the analysis of the fundamental transition from a thing-based to a relation-based *Ur-philosophy*. There are reasons to be optimistic about the feasibility of this conceptual paradigm shift. The conceptual vocabulary of relations is sufficiently rich, semantically, to express everything we require and to translate the old political vocabulary of things, their properties, and actions. In more precise terms: relational thinking is sufficiently expressive to define all the necessary ontology to put it into

We can explore the possibility that it is not things but *relations* (which constitute all things) that can play a foundational role in our way of thinking politically by considering the "digitalisation" of money. Consider Bitcoin, other cryptocurrencies, or even Facebook's project *Diem* (formerly known as Libra). According to the Diem Association, its aim is "to enable a simple, global financial infrastructure and currency that facilitates billions of people". 1.7 billion adults worldwide do not have access to banking services. Of these, one billion have a mobile phone, and half have access to the Internet. In theory, Diem, or something similar, could help these people by making financial transactions as simple and cheap as sending a text message with an app. This all sounds very promising, but it must come under scrutiny. There is a difference between *money* and *currency*. This difference is usually drawn by saying that money is intangible, whereas currency is its tangible counterpart, but this explanation may not be sufficient. A better way of thinking about the difference is that money depends on the "receiver", relationally: it is whatever the market accepts for financial transactions. A currency, however, also depends on the "sender": it is the circulating, tangible coins and banknotes issued by a state or a union of states, such as the dollar or the euro. So, money is defined by its function, that is, by its relations with the market. In this sense, Bitcoin, other cryptocurrencies, and Diem are not a currency (a state does not issue them), but rather a type of money (the market accepts them). The Deutsche Mark, the French Franc, and the Italian Lira were currencies and are no longer money; salt (from which the word "salary" comes) and sheep (the etymology of "pecuniary" derives from the Latin word *pecus*) were at one point a form of money, but never currency, bearing a resemblance to Bitcoin but not to the dollar.

In the modern era, we have thought that the state-sender and the market-receiver were perfectly coordinated, like two sides of the same coin (pun intended). Hence, that money and currency were essentially synonymous. That is why we sometimes speak indiscriminately of cash. However, it is sufficient to recall periods of hyperinflation, from the Weimar Republic to present-day Venezuela, to remember that a currency can "devalue" and function no longer as money but merely as useless paper instead. In reality, it is its function that makes the object. It is worth considering some examples. If something serves as a unit of measurement (e.g. to answer the question "what is the price?") or a

(Continued)

medium of exchange (e.g. to answer the question "what can I buy with it?") or a repository of value (e.g. to answer the question "how much do I have in the bank?"), then its function is money, no matter whether that something is shells, golden coins, dollars, euros, or cryptocurrencies. For decades, international currencies have performed these three functions solely on trust (fiat money), that is, based on a social relation, because they can no longer be converted into gold, that is, into things. English banknotes still carry the words "I promise to pay the bearer, on demand, the sum of...". However, since 1971, all you can convert a ten-pound note into is two five-pound notes or an assortment of coins. The dollar and the euro promise nothing (take a moment to check). Today, in our increasingly cashless societies, the three functions of the paper-and-metal currency are performed by the digital currency, which is often an even more convenient and efficient form of currency. In addition to functions, trust too is now being transferred, from the state-currency to the market-money. This is where Bitcoin or Diem come in. Both are money based on blockchain (a digital ledger), but Bitcoin is decentralised, with its value created by computation and the market without being pegged to any currency, and therefore swings up and down like a yo-yo. By contrast, Diem looks like a kind of stablecoin: it is centralised, and its value does not depend on the blockchain; its stability will continue to be ensured by parity with real assets that are not particularly volatile (i.e., bank deposits and short-term government bonds), denominated in the currency of reliable central banks.

At least initially, Diem will be managed by the Switzerland-based Diem Association, which incorporates several organisations. The debate surrounding Diem has already identified many potential problems: technological reliability, security, privacy, regulatory uncertainty, economic and financial policy risks linked to the "Diem-isation" of weaker currencies and the rigidity of parity, and its possible use by criminal or terrorist groups. For this reason, the US administration quickly asked Facebook to stop the development of Libra (Diem's previous name), pending clarification. I do not know whether Diem, or something like Diem, will ever be a reality. Regardless, it serves to illustrate three main points in this chapter.

First, the digital world is trying to override (not replace) the analogue world, in this case, represented by the modern state and its currency. The US dollar still bears the anachronistic motto "IN GOD WE TRUST", but God is dead, and modern trust is placed in the secular state.

Now that even the state is in poor health, the question is whether contemporary trust will shift again, this time from the state-currency to the market-money, or whether the state will recover and re-invent itself as worthy of trust. The way cryptocurrencies have crashed, and the related scandals that surrounded them in 2022 may be a case of "peak market-money", or a powerful lesson in how difficult and much more regulated the transition will have to be. In any case, the unmistakable impression is that the physical nature of physical currency (the Aristotelian-Newtonian paradigm) will become increasingly obsolete.

Second, managing the world's digital money is a matter of pure power as well. Countries such as China are developing their digital currencies. Sometimes, talking about power with economists is like talking about sex with biologists: they forget that it is often an end in itself. I will return to these points in Chapter 18 when discussing the new "grey power".

Third, it is clear that we can no longer interpret the world in the same way as we did when, for example, we exchanged gold coins (Aristotelian-Newtonian Ur-philosophie). We need to embrace a relational worldview and understand how we can design robust and resilient relations of trust, for instance, via a well-functioning digital currency. Cryptocurrencies will flourish not despite but because of international regulations.

practice.[8] This semantic capacity gives rise to something much more important than a mere translation exercise. It has the enormous advantage of shifting and broadening our focus towards the *analysis and design of relations*, rather than on the implementation of specific *actions* (recall the Actor-Network Theory approach above) as the main pressure point upon which to operate to try to enact societal changes for the better in a lasting, non-ephemeral way. In simple terms: ecology, law, sociology, economics, and, above all, in the case of this book, political philosophy, can all be rein-

---

[8] We saw that entities are reducible to the totality of their properties, and all properties are reducible to n-posed relations (unary, such as "x is of age", binary, such as "x works for y", and so on), so entities are reducible to the totality of their relations. The behaviour of entities and changes in their properties are reducible to state transitions, and state transitions are reducible to transitions from one set of relations to another.

terpreted as *sciences of relations*—those that constitute and connect *relata*, not only people, but all things, natural and constructed, and therefore their environments and ecosystems—even before they are interpreted as *sciences of the actions or behaviours of* the physical and legal persons understood as things, or indeed any other non-human actors also capable of actions, following here the Actor-Network Theory approach. Thus, Hegel and Marx were right to emphasise not *the persons* themselves but the dialectical relations between people as a crucial focus for political thinking.

Our question concerns how to move from an approach based on things and their properties to a relational approach, to attain an adequate understanding, and design our information society better. Such a shift requires thinking of politics as the governance and management of the *ratio publica* ("ratio" in the sense of relation, not reason) first, and only then of the *res publica*. I return to this fundamental point in the final chapter. Here, it is essential to underline that the implicit operational model and world view changes: it is no longer grounded in the Aristotelian-Newtonian *mechanism*, which is comparatively rigid and restrictive, but in the relational *network*, which is much more flexible and inclusive. We have seen that, in any network, the nodes (including, but not limited to, all persons) do not pre-exist their relations, only to be connected by relations (or actions), as is the case with the components of a mechanism and the analogy of the Lego bricks. Instead, the relations create the nodes in a co-dependent and symbiotic way. Thus, to improve the properties or behaviours of the entity-nodes, the nature, quality, and number of relations constituting them must be addressed first. By prioritising relations at the centre of the socio-political debate, the new model can encompass all entities (*relata*) more easily: not only people, but also institutions, artefacts, and nature. In a network, there is no external, independent node, isolated from the others, something that is instead imagined to be perfectly possible—and idealised—in a mechanism.

A thing-based philosophy easily discretises societal elements into sets. For instance, the set of all Italian citizens, the set of all British citizens, and the set of all citizens with dual Italian and British nationality. On the contrary, social relations tend to be intertwined and continuous, with varying degrees of intensity, from the weak to the strong. By way of example, imagine Italian citizens who have relations with British citizens, where such relations can be many, few, intense, meaningful, superficial, etc. Consequently, in *relational* as opposed to *thing-based* politics, the primary evaluation parameter is no longer how much the "performance" of things can be quantified (in terms of actions or behaviour), but instead the degree of *robustness* and *resilience* of the relations that compose things and bind them together. For instance, today, we observe, in various contexts, that financial, political, and health-related crises have been tackled in part thanks to the efforts of families. If one looks more deeply, one can see that it is the social *network* that makes possible and less traumatic the transition from a post-industrial world (the linear production of things and quality of things) to a world with a green and blue digital economy (the circular production of services-functions and quality of experiences). This phenomenon does not contradict globalisation; on the contrary, a relational view of society (according to a network-oriented philosophy) explains the current tendency of politics to become global and cosmopolitan.

The paradigm shift, which has been necessary (and ongoing) for some time, implies abandoning both an Aristotelian ontology of the primacy of things and a Newtonian ontology of space and time as rigid containers, within which things are positioned, interact, and change properties. Let us consider how this is achieved.

First, a network is a logical space, not a physical one, in which distances are not measured with Euclidean metrics. Consider an elementary example. In chess, the distance between a Pawn and the Queen is symmetrical in the Euclidean sense (e.g., 10 centimetres from the Pawn to the Queen and thus from the Queen to the Pawn) but is asymmetrical in the logical sense (e.g., it is one move from the Queen to the Pawn, but three moves from the Pawn to the Queen). Similarly, the diagonal is necessarily longer than the column from a Euclidean point of view, but on the chessboard, it has the same length in terms of the number of squares. The King then, for instance, takes the same number of moves in crossing either. In our case, the space of politics (which is relational and thus qualifies as a logical space) no longer overlaps indistinguishably with the geographical territorial space (thing-based, and therefore physical space) of national sovereignty (see also the old Westphalian identification between political and legal space). Instead, it occupies the spatiality of social relations—including those of force. The old concept of "spheres of influence" already partly anticipates this idea. By way of example, when in geopolitics one speaks of "indo-pacific region", one is seeking to relate, conceptually, economies that would be merely juxtaposed in terms of physical geography. Using a homier example, Italy's Mediterranean identity is, above all, cultural, i.e., relational, and not merely geographical. For this reason, one day, the European Union could reform both Article 7 of the Treaty on European Union

(TEU), to allow for the possibility of expelling European Member States that do not respect the agreements and shared values, and the Copenhagen criteria (see Article 49 of the TEU), which prevent a *geographically non-European* state from joining the Union. An expanded EU would also require the courage to abandon the primacy of the twentieth-century geographical space on which the European Union was founded (Aristotelian-Newtonian ontology) and adopt a relational notion of space instead. Doing so would make it possible and easier both to exclude European countries that repeatedly flout the values of the European Union, because geography is no longer a sufficient reason to join, and to include new countries that are outside of the continent, but that share the values of the European Union, because geography is no longer a prerequisite for membership status. Today, the European project should be based on a union of values and human rights, that is, on relations, not physical borders. For example, it would be very reasonable to think of Canada as a possible future member of the European Union from this perspective, as has already been considered in the past.[9] If this relational approach seems counterintuitive, it should be noted that it has already been adopted with Cyprus, a state that, in terms of Newtonian space, belongs geographically to Asia, but which rightly and justifiably joined the European Union in 2004 because its spatiality was considered not in accordance with a thing-based, geographical ontology, but rather historical-cultural relations.

Similarly, the time of politics does not correspond to the time of physics but to the *temporality* of human history and social relations, a concept to which I shall return, with regard to the notions of *hyperhistory* and *onlife experience* (see Chapters 6 and 7). Something becomes possible only after something else has happened, in terms of the logic of chronological relations (before, during, and after), rather than following fixed dates and times that align with the logic of the calendar year. For example, a concrete discussion on the feasibility of *Eurobonds* becomes possible only after the German government approves them. In addition, intergenerational relations are no longer understood as relations between the person-bricks of an Aristotelian-Newtonian ontology, but rather as relational links between person-nodes that the political vocabulary itself describes as "the *social fabric*".

To understand this crucial concept, it is useful to refer to another version of the same Thatcher quotation we saw above, concerning the sole existence

---

[9] https://mowatcentre.ca/canada-should-join-the-eu-sort-of.

of individuals (and families) and the non-existence of society. A transcript of the interview published on the Margaret Thatcher Foundation website differs in some details but not in substance:

> There is no such thing as society [end p. 30]. There is living tapestry of men and women and people and the beauty of that tapestry and the quality of our lives will depend upon how much each of us is prepared to take responsibility for ourselves and each of us prepared to turn round and help by our own efforts those who are unfortunate.[10]

Note this time the absence of the family. Tapestry is a fabric in which the weft dominates: the warp is not visible when the work is finished. Warp and weft are sets of threads. Each thread is individual, and the figures in the tapestry and the warp are the detailed results of the interweaving of the threads. So, Thatcher was right in her conclusion: her use of the concept of "woven" as a tapestry is correct, if you look at the internal coherence of her metaphor. A fabric, however, does not have to be *woven* like a tapestry: it can also be knitted, like a blanket, in which case it is a fabric made of knots created by the intersection of a single thread. The knots do not pre-exist but co-exist because of the common thread. The structure makes them possible. So, Thatcher was mistaken in her choice of the premise, because the social fabric is much more like a crocheted blanket than a woven tapestry. We have used this textile metaphor since at least Plato (see *Republic*, pp. 308–311). It is better to speak of the *common social fabric*, of which everyone is a part, and which should therefore be for the protection and benefit of all, as Aristophanes suggests in *Lysistrata* (pp. 565–586):

> [...] mixing all [...] understand what separate threads of wool are for us: from all of these we need to take, gather them into one and make a large ball of wool and with this then weave a cloak for the people.

Good metaphors tend to recur throughout the history of ideas.

Finally, the personal fabric is the *inter-temporality* of an individual life, that is, the fact that human existence, both individual and social, is itself like a crocheted thread, the knots of which must be interrelated and follow a coherent design. For example, if Alice invests in her studies and receives a good education, she should be able to find a place in the job market. There must be

---

[10] Thatcher Archive (THCR 5/2/262): COI transcript, available here: https://www.margaretthatcher.org/document/106689.

inter-temporal links that give meaning to paths, trajectories, expectations, individual and social human projects, and so forth. Politics must be able to support the inter-temporality of people's lives and the intrinsic relationality and connection of the phases of human existence, addressing not only their interests but also their hopes.

The social fabric is the systemic interdependence and manifold connections between the individual fabrics just mentioned. In many countries at present, the social fabric can also be interpreted in terms of the information society; indeed, in some cases, one can already begin to talk of a *mature information society*, where life is now spent *onlife*, within a simultaneously digital and analogue space that can be called the *infosphere*. These are concepts I shall use throughout the remainder of the book. It is now time to address them in detail, starting with the infosphere (in the next chapter) and its polluted state (in the form of *fake news*, discussed at length in Chapter 5).

Chapter 4
The Infosphere

On 29 October 1969, Charley Kline, a research student at the University of California Los Angeles, sent the first message to Stanford on the Advanced Research Projects Agency Network (ARPANET), a network that connected four universities in the USA. This was the birth of the Internet. The experiment was also a partial failure: the connection dropped almost immediately, and only the first two letters of the word "login" appeared. The irony is that "lo" could almost be taken as a greeting, as if the network wanted to announce itself. The achievement, however, did not make the news, as two other events monopolised public attention that year. On 20 July, Neil Armstrong landed on the Moon, and between 15 and 18 August, 400,000 people gathered at Woodstock in an unprecedented musical experience: two extraordinary and unparalleled events. And yet, half a century later, it is easy to see that the event with most impact was that first message. Today, the Internet touches the lives of approximately 5 billion users out of 8 billion people.

For twenty years, the Internet was used to control computers remotely and exchange data. In 1986, after Great Britain, Norway, France, and Italy joined the network, the Internet was the preserve of the military and academia. The Internet is still the network that structures the environment where we spend most of our time, thanks to the Web, born in 1989. Yet, in surveys, people sometimes respond that they do not use the Internet but contradictorily note that they shop on Amazon (launched in 1994), watch movies on Netflix (launched in 1997), send tweets (Twitter was launched in 2006), and post pic-

The Green and The Blue: Naive Ideas to Improve Politics in the Digital Age, First Edition.
Luciano Floridi.

tures on Instagram (launched in 2010). They think the Web is something else. In reality, the Internet is a bit like the pastry in a tart: you may not see it, but it supports, circumscribes, and organises the jam that is the Web. Without the Internet, all those experiences and what I have termed *onlife* (i.e., living simultaneously online and offline, as in the case of a smartwatch that geo-localises us and monitors our biological functions), which we now take for granted, would simply be impossible. It was on Facebook (launched in 2004) that I saw the photo of Nick and Bobbi Ercoline, the couple who appear on the cover of the famous 1969 Woodstock soundtrack album, and on YouTube (launched in 2005) that I saw the 50th anniversary of Armstrong's landing.

To understand the transformation of the Internet into a simultaneously analogue and digital environment (i.e., the *infosphere*) imagine drops of water on glass. When the drops are sufficiently close, they merge. The more drops we add, the greater the volume of water, until we reach a point when we start talking about an environment: a river, a lake, a sea, or an ocean. In fifty years, the Internet has grown from four drops—the ARPANET universities in 1969—to 50 billion various systems in 2020, with zettabytes of data. Today, the Internet connects tablets, phones, watches, cars and bicycles, intercoms and household appliances, satellites and robots of all kinds, fire alarms, road traffic, waste collection and entire cities (*smart cities)*, and more. It is what is termed the *Internet of Things*. The Internet is the ever-expanding ocean in which we are immersed, without even realising that we are wet. That is why our society may be described as the "mangrove society": mangroves grow in brackish water, where the river mixes with the sea. In such an environment, there is no point asking whether it is freshwater or saltwater; it would be to miss the point. Today, the question "are you online?" belongs to an obsolete past that no longer has any bearing on the present. Thanks to the Internet, we increasingly live *onlife* in the *infosphere*.

The opportunities and risks of the Internet can be understood only if one grasps the fact that, for decades, the Internet has not just been a communication system but, above all, the backbone of our reality and a habitat that we are building, to which we are adapting, and on which we are increasingly dependent. Let us start by considering who the actual natives of the Internet are, referred to as *digital natives*. Rather than considering generational taxonomies that pile up and overlap—scientists and futurologists compete to separate generations into ever finer slices of time—I prefer to distinguish between those who knew and experienced the world as entirely and only analogue, before the Internet (just think of the telephone token), and those for whom the world has always included the Internet. I belong to the first group, and my students belong to the second. For them, iTunes, and Wikipedia (born in 2001) have always been part of their world, while cassette tapes have never been (the distribution of music on cassettes ended in 2002). Yet even this distinction is unsatisfactory. In a couple of generations, humanity will belong to a post-Internet world, in the same sense we belong to a post-electricity world. Therefore, the most crucial distinction is a different one: the real digital natives, who are truly autochthonous and live on the Internet naturally, are artificial agents, embedded in the digital to interact with the digital. They are the actual fish; we are merely scuba diving. This will not change in the future, because even the post-Internet generations will continue to be partly analogue. They will be used to surfing (to use another aquatic metaphor), but they will not develop gills. Artificial agents or, more generally, AI systems can learn and act autonomously *for* us, *instead* of us, and *better* than us, because they produce, exchange, and consume bytes, splashing around in the digital ocean of the infosphere in ways that we will never be able to emulate. Just think of large language models. Or to take an example that has already been used: future cars will also operate thanks to the infosphere, not because we will have androids driving like us, but because we will have turned cars into digital systems that are entirely embedded in the digital environment, more like nodes in a network.

In an infosphere where billions of people and new artificial agents live and interact, the rules of conduct become paramount. We made a mistake with the Internet. In the 1990s, a decision had to be made whether to regulate the Internet or let it grow first. Historically, society has generally preferred not to shackle free competition during growth phases, from newspapers to electricity, from the telephone to television. The Internet was interpreted as merely another *utility*, thus the decision was taken to postpone the implementation of regulations. Then the Web came along, and the eco-systemic nature of the Internet as an environmental component of our reality via the infosphere became clear even to non-philosophers. But it was too late, because the Internet, now synonymous with the Web, had been commercialised. Today, governments are finally beginning to regulate a space that should have been planned as social and public from the outset. Another analogy may help to illustrate the difference between the Internet and other revolutionising utilities. If the Internet is like the telephone, competition between providers is expected, and freedom of expression and privacy are fundamental factors. As in the case of the phone, one can choose the provider one wants, say what one wishes on the phone, and expect the conversation to be private (neither recorded nor censored), unless overriding legal reasons require otherwise. However, if the Internet is like the only public park in town, freedom of expression is limited by the rules of good coexistence. I cannot do or say whatever I want, how and when I want; there is less privacy, because it is a public space; and choice is practically non-existent (there is only one park). The Internet was always going to be part of our new infosphere, and it is, therefore, more like the park. Still, instead of managing it collectively, we have entrusted it to a few multinationals, which behave like states. They do not do a terrible job, but their management is certainly not what we expected in the 1990s. Today, Internet policies shape a global social habitat, but they are determined by the private sector. There is only one park, and while it is public, it is run by private companies that often operate as if privacy protection were an obstacle (they treat the Internet as if it were a public environment) and freedom of speech a non-negotiable right (they treat the Internet as if it were a matter of individual communication and expression, as opposed to a public environment). The contradiction is explicit, and the resulting mess is for all to see and experience. The current "solution" has been to give even more power to these companies responsible for the problem, from managing the right to freedom of speech (Google, founded in 1998) to the removal of fake news (Facebook, Twitter).

In any discussion of the past, a key lesson is to acknowledge how difficult it is to predict the future; who knows what vagaries we are ignoring or failing to anticipate today? As Shakespeare writes in *Macbeth*, only the witches can "look into the seeds of time, / and say which grain will grow and which will not". We, humans, must be content with actively trying to build the future we want. In 1994, I was invited to speak at the UNESCO plenary assembly on the future of the Internet, in celebration of organisation's 50th anniversary. Re-reading that report, I realise that, while the Internet still has an enormously positive social potential, many of the main actors capable of developing it for the good of humanity and the planet belong to the private sector. It is clear and urgent that society harnesses their capacities for the public benefit. The Internet can potentially be a significant positive force to solve the most critical challenges of our time: climate change and ecosystem collapse, social injustice, human intolerance and conflict, public health (just think of the COVID-19 pandemic). It requires an enormous effort to confront these challenges. However, it is possible, through effective forms of coordination, collaboration, and cooperation, which the Internet could realistically achieve. The Internet will become the safe, open, public space we imagined when it was created, and thus support the infosphere we want, only if the public and private sectors commit to working together, to turn the park into a garden for all and not just a jungle to be exploited by the fittest. Such a task can be done, but we need the most appropriate policies and business strategies. Therefore, as I shall argue in the following chapters, the real challenge for the future of the Internet, the infosphere, the digital world, and our information society, is not further digital innovation but rather ensuring a focus on the *governance of the digital*. By this, I mean that it is not so much designing new technologies but designing better ways to use and manage them that will be increasingly crucial. Let us hope we do not forget the importance of regulation and slip up again. Unfortunately, things are currently moving in a worrying direction, not least because we are polluting the infosphere with *fake news* and misinformation, the topics of the next chapter.

Chapter 5
Fake News

In the beginning, the digital was blue. The electric blue of technologies operating at the speed of light. Blue represented its potential, akin to the "the sky is the limit" maxim. Yet the blueness soon faded. The digital began to turn yellow, in some corners growing old, like an old Polaroid. It has degraded to the yellow of paedophiles who lure children online, and of radicalised fundamentalists on web forums. It is the colour of cowards (*yellow-bellied*) who hide behind an anonymous screen to commit all kinds of vandalism. This is the colour of "post-truth", which denies evidence, rejects reasoning, and is addicted to eye-catching headlines and clickbait. In short, this yellow is the colour of the mounting pollution contaminating the infosphere.

The yellowing of the infosphere is not a new phenomenon. In the ferocious newspaper battles of 1890s in New York, the emerging sensationalist style of journalism in Joseph Pulitzer's *New York World* and William Randolph Hearst's *New York Journal* was dubbed "yellow journalism" by those concerned with maintaining standards and accuracy to defend and generate informed public debate. The current yellowing of the digital is not the result of an intrinsic fault in the digital, but rather a consequence of a long-established type of pollution that caught it unprotected. Indeed, the more people live onlife, the greater the background noise, and the more disagreements mount. The truth is that, in its relatively short existence, the digital aged poorly, because we lowered our guard against the deterioration and pollution of the infosphere. We mistake online abuse for freedom of expression, profiling for personalisation,

The Green and The Blue: Naive Ideas to Improve Politics in the Digital Age, First Edition. Luciano Floridi.

spying for security, apathy for tolerance, and populism for democracy. We have let the infosphere develop haphazardly, without guidance, regulation, or straightforward socio-political projects. It grows on the yellow fuel of the market, happy that it is giving us exactly what we want. And what we want is making us addicted and sick.

Humans have always been prejudiced against different views, and intolerant of them. Francis Bacon's philosophical masterwork *Novum Organum*, published in 1620 (Bacon 2000), analyses four kinds of idols or false notions that "are now in possession of the human understanding, and have taken deep root therein [...]". One of these types of false idol, the "idols of the cave", refers to our conceptual biases and susceptibility to external influences:

> Everyone [...] has a cave or den of his own, which refracts and discolours the light of nature, owing either to his own proper and peculiar nature; or to his education and conversation with others; or to the reading of books, and the authority of those whom he esteems and admires; or to the differences of impressions, accordingly as they take place in a mind preoccupied and predisposed or in a mind indifferent and settled; or the like.

Likewise, the human appetite for shallow gossip, pleasant lies, and reassuring falsehoods has always been enormous. The difference is that today, for the first time in human history, the infosphere feeds that appetite a constant supply of semantic junk—transforming Plato's and Bacon's caves into cavernous echo chambers, which are referred to as "bubbles". In this sense, we have always been "post-truth" because "post-truth" is the default position. A "truth-friendly" society requires constant and renewed efforts.

The result of such overconsumption of semantic junk is evident. It leads to digital-ethical problems representing a defining challenge of the twenty-first century. They include breaches of privacy, security and safety, ownership and intellectual property rights, trust, and fundamental human rights, as well as the possibility of inducing exploitation, discrimination, inequality, manipulation, propaganda, populism, hate speech, racism, and violence. No one precisely knows the exact human costs of these multiple and combined problems. But they must be immense. The political responsibility of media websites for distorting discussions around Brexit in the UK, or the misinformation disseminated by the "alt-right", a loose affiliation of people with far-right views, during the election campaign waged by Donald Trump, are but two dramatic examples with long-term consequences.

Thus far, the strategy has been to confront the ethical impact of digital technologies after the harm has been inflicted, only when some "yellowing" has already occurred. For instance, Facebook and Twitter started to combat online disinformation only after the Cambridge Analytica disaster caused public outrage, and Trump won the US presidential elections. This is no longer sufficient to deal with the scale of the problem at hand. The old, Silicon Valley mantra of "fail often, fail fast" has always been a poor strategy when it comes to the ethical and cultural impacts of these businesses. It is equivalent to being content with "too little, too late". It has very high long-term costs of global impact that cause harm that could be prevented or mitigated, and it incurs a waste of resources, missed opportunities, lack of participation, misguided caution, and lower resilience. A lack of proactive ethics foresight thwarts decision-making, undermines management practices, and damages strategies for digital innovation. It is also bad for business. In short, addressing damage after it has taken place in this way is too expensive. Moreover, owing to globalisation and the almost instantaneous dissemination of digital innovations, some of the costs of digital pollution are hard to reverse, especially when confidence and trust are undermined.

Today, we can and must do better. We must clean and remove all those yellow stains that disfigure the infosphere and ensure that we coherently steer the extraordinary potential force of the digital for individual, social, and environmental well-being in a better direction. We have a fundamental need for an ethical infosphere to save the planet and ourselves, from ourselves. Restoring the infosphere and making it flourish again requires enormous effort. We must rebuild trust through concerted credibility, transparency, responsibility, and accountability. Our information society must be built on the resilient foundations of solidarity and benefit-sharing. Such an endeavour will require significant resources and a great deal of patience, cooperation, and determination. But it can be done. We need an open and independent forum to bring stakeholders together to participate in dialogue and decision-making and implement these solutions to common problems caused by the information revolution and the pollution of the infosphere. It is time to design a new and better model of the infosphere that incorporates good policy to shape and guide, and not merely pursue, the future of a fulfilling mature information society. This is especially important in our increasingly digital age, when we live more and more *onlife*, as we shall see in the two chapters.

Chapter 6
Digital Time

In 1972, the first commercial digital wristwatch was released, the Hamilton Pulsar P1. James Bond wore the P2 model in *Live and Let Die*, the following year. Since then, thanks to digital innovation, we have been quantifying our everyday time far too precisely. I belong to the generation that has experienced the shift from being told that "it is almost 11 o'clock" to being told that "it is 10:57". Admittedly, things have recently improved. Today, digital watches often hide behind analogue interfaces, and the clock hands of a modern smartwatch may restore some healthy approximation at the user interface point. And yet, the automatic system of a delivery service still warns me that the package I am expecting will be delivered between 10:57 a.m. and 11:57 a.m. Computers do not joke and do not round up. Of course, the couriers simply arrive when they can.

How has the digital revolution over this half-century changed our relation with time? Time is a classic topic of philosophy. There is the time of physics, with which Einstein was concerned. There is the time of metaphysics, which occupied Heidegger. And there is the time of daily experience, that of Alice the courier, of me, waiting for her, and of which Ecclesiastes ("Kohelet" or "Qoheleth" in Hebrew) speaks in the Bible, when we are reminded that "there is a time for everything, and a season for every activity under the heavens" (Ecclesiastes 3:1, more on this in the next chapter). Digital technologies are profoundly transforming this experiential, everyday time. Yet, the story started a long time ago.

The Green and The Blue: Naive Ideas to Improve Politics in the Digital Age, First Edition. Luciano Floridi.
© 2024 John Wiley & Sons Ltd. Published 2024 by John Wiley & Sons Ltd.

For millennia, we have used space to quantify and structure time, moving from an approximate notion to a universe of increasingly accurate measurements (Koyré 1957). The shadow of the obelisks and sundials, the flow of water or sand in the hourglasses, or the oscillation of the pendulum are all systems that use space to measure the duration of time (*how long*: for example, the train arrives at its destination an hour after departure), and to establish when things happen (*when*: for example, the train leaves at 10:30), and finally to compare or synchronise events (*while*: for example, I will meet you at the railway station while you are there). The continuity of time was soon organised through the continuity of space, which in turn was quantified using the sexagesimal system (ratio 1/60 between units of measurement and its submultiple)—think of the hour, minutes, and seconds (Holford-Strevens 2005). Today we are so used to treating time as space, and this kind of spatialised time as a numerical quantity, that we often fail to distinguish between the experience and the measurement of time, marvelling that the same time spent on the train lasted a moment for Alice but an eternity for Bob. So far, nothing new; one may just read Bergson.[1] Things only recently began to get complicated with the arrival of digital technologies.

For over half a century, the digital has been transforming (re-ontologizing) the relation between space and time by modifying a third variable: the speed of the processes of *communication* (both in the sense of *interacting* and in the sense of *transferring*) and *manipulation*.

In modern times, the trend was already underway. It preceded the digital with the evolution of faster transport, which rendered distances ever shorter and thus made it increasingly natural to think of space in terms of travel times. When it became possible to travel around the world in 80 days,[2] it became increasingly intuitive to reverse the relation and use time to measure space. Today it is the ETA (Estimated Time of Arrival) that counts, not how many kilometres away Alice lives from the city centre, for instance. Or think of the "15-minute city" concept, which defines urban space based on the time required to reach essential services on foot or by bicycle (Moreno et al. 2021). In all these conceptualisations, the digital still belongs to the same modern trend, amplifying it in ways that are not necessarily surprising.

---

[1] Originally *Essai sur les données immédiates de la conscience*, Bergson's doctoral thesis, first published in 1889 (Bergson 2014).
[2] Originally *Le tour du monde en quatre-vingts jours*, by Jules Verne, first published in 1872 (Verne 1995).

However, an absolute novelty introduced by our digital culture is *latency*, one of today's most interesting and influential concepts to understand the humble time of everyday experience. Latency is different from bandwidth, even though both refer to speed. Bandwidth indicates the speed of a connection, and it measures how many data can be transferred between two points of a network in a specified time. In everyday experience, it relates to the time it takes to download a file from the Internet, for instance, or stream a movie. Latency is also a matter of speed, but it refers to the time (sometimes called delay or lag) between a cause (usually a user's action) and its effect (usually the response to a user's action). So, rather than how many data one can transfer over a specified time, it refers to the speed of interaction. For example, there may be a long latency between clicking on a web page and that web page responding accordingly, depending on many variables, including the connection speed, but overall, it remains a matter of latency. Likewise, the latency between pressing a key on the keyboard and seeing the letter appear on the screen is usually less than 40 milliseconds (ms) on a good keyboard.

Latency combines the concepts of *communication* (the time for a signal to arrive at its destination and return to its starting point) and *interaction* (the return of the signal indicating the resulting effect produced by the signal itself) with that of *causality* from a distance. Alice does something here to change something elsewhere intentionally. High latency means a slow interaction time; low latency is the opposite.

In a way that is only superficially paradoxical, we are organisms that are well-adapted to a given range of latency. Above very high and below very low latency, we no longer perceive any change or interaction. If a web page takes minutes or even longer to load when interacting with it, one may think it is simply "frozen". That is why Operating Systems have various ways of indicating that an app is still busy. Apple officially calls it the "spinning wait cursor"; Microsoft prefers the "Windows wait cursor". In a Wittgensteinian move, one may be tempted to conjecture on the family resemblance between "cursor" and "curse". All this is relatively intuitive. Increase the latency, and the world slowly grinds to a halt: for all you know, the touchscreen you interact with may be made of marble.

What happens when the latency of a signal becomes increasingly low is less intuitive. Imagine Alice bouncing a tennis ball against a wall. Its "latency", so to speak (how long it takes to come back), is sufficiently high so that Alice can easily catch the ball when it returns. Now let us imagine that the ball makes the round trip increasingly quickly, that is, with ever-decreasing latency. There will be a moment when it will be difficult for Alice to catch the ball because it returns to her in ever shorter times. However, at some point, if the speed increases still further, it will become very easy to "catch it" because she will not be able to make the ball leave her hand, as it were, or, to be more precise, it will become impossible for Alice to register visually the ball leaving her hand, given that the ball will return to her in a few milliseconds. She may just feel the ball vibrating in her hand. This is what happens when we play online: it seems that "we are there" (telepresence) because our sensory apparatus perceives interactions below 100 ms of latency as immediate, in the etymological sense of *not mediated* by anything else. Therefore, serious video gamers choose their keyboards, as well as their displays, very carefully.[3] It is called "real-time", that is, unmediated time (sometimes only at the appearance level). The concept merits further explanation.

"Real-time" is a technical expression coined in the 1940s to discuss the design of "electronic digital computers", as they were called. Allegedly, the first recorded usage was in 1946 by John Eckert, who, along with John Mauchly, designed the first general-purpose electronic digital computer (ENIAC) and later the first commercial computer in the United States (UNIVAC). After that, "real-time computing" became a technical expression for any computation constrained by a time limit, meaning it must provide an outcome within a "deadline". However, the more general concept of "real-time" now refers to something (an event, a process, etc.) that is simulated, represented, communicated, interacted with, or shown, *at the same time* or *at the same rate* as it happens. The distinction is essential. Real-time news about an event, for instance, is news that arrives "live" concurrently with the unfolding of the event being reported; there is no delay. Likewise, so-called "nowcasting" is a kind of short-term forecasting that monitors something (often meteorological or economic conditions or events) in real-time. However, a real-time movie is not a CCTV camera monitoring a bank, but a film that records an event, such

---

[3] Video-gamers are interested in "frame rates" or "frames per second" (fps) because better graphics cards and better monitors, with higher fps, provide a competitive advantage. Standard monitors are usually 60hz (capable of displaying 60fps), but 120-hz, 144-hz, and 240-hz monitors are also available, with 120-hz displays available also for some mobile phones. Many thanks to Prathm Juneja for this note. See also https://www.wepc.com/gaming-monitor/compare/60hz-120hz-144hz-240hz.

as a five-minute walk, in one-take precisely as it occurs (not when and not live) without any edits or jumps, and that lasts the same amount of time as the event itself. Let us concentrate on this latter, more narrative meaning.

If the latency of a digitised interaction is sufficiently low, a surgeon can operate on a patient from thousands of miles away by controlling a robot in the operating room in real-time, as if they were there, interacting *at the same time* and *at the same rate* at which events unfold. 5G, which has a latency of 10–30 ms (the latency of 4G is about 50 ms), is responsible for this transformation. Low latency and high-speed translate not only into telepresence— whereby the place at which one is *located* physically is no longer a constraint to be able to interact as if one were *present* elsewhere—but also into faster travel times of increasingly heavier tennis balls, to continue with the previous analogy. The limit of how many bits can be transferred becomes less and less important at high speeds and very low latency. It is this combination that makes, for instance, autonomous vehicles possible.

In the infosphere, latency determines real-time experiences, and it is a significant metric for determining the space in which we live. Too high a latency means living in the suburbs, distant or even detached from the rest of the infosphere. Very low latency (where everything is immediate, i.e., in real-time and interactable) means living at the centre of the infosphere (telepresence). Bad latency means feeling sick while being immersed in a virtual reality environment. Zero latency everywhere could be a definition of omnipresence.

Consider next the speed at which something can be *manipulated*. Computer scientists do not speak precisely in this way, but, philosophically, this speed can also be interpreted as a matter of latency—in this case relating to the time it takes to transform data into information (latency between input and output in a simulation is also called transport delay). When Turing decrypted the secret messages of the German army, one of the main problems he had to deal with was time. It is useless to decrypt a message if, by the time it is cracked, the event to which it refers has already occurred, in precisely the same sense in which it is useless to take 72 hours to predict the weather for the next day. The solution was Colossus (Copeland 2006), the computer that Turing helped design, capable of processing up to 100,000 instructions per second (IPS). Finally, and crucially, it enabled messages to be read *before* the events they referred to had happened. Today, an ordinary PC with a Ryzen-type processor, manufactured by AMD, completes 2,356,230 million instructions per second (MIPS). It "render[s] time irrelevant", as AMD's advertisement puts it.[4] It is only with this low "latency" between inputs and outputs that AI can work, often better than us, for example, when reaction times must be immediate (in the sense of being unmediated, i.e., in real-time, as we have seen above). An example would be algorithmic trading in capital markets. The availability of quantum computing will mark another leap in the history of latency, making possible calculations, simulations, and interactions that would otherwise be utterly unfeasible in reasonable spans of time. As early as 2019, Google's quantum computer was 158 million times faster than the fastest of the classic supercomputers.[5] The future belongs to those who can simulate it. This is not the place to elaborate on this remark, but suffice it to say that quantum computing will mark the return of the crucial role of space (think quantum superposition and entanglement) in changing how we determine time.

Digital technologies are technologies of "unreal-time", that is, of time that is *mediated* by the technology itself. However, this digital unreal-time may be experienced as "real-time" because the mediation can reach such a low latency that what is mediated may be experienced by people as immediate. So, it is unreal-time *de facto*, which is not unreal but real *de experientia*. Following Amazon's example of "Artificial, Artificial Intelligence"[6]—that is, AI that is not really AI because real people are involved—digital time may be described as "unreal, unreal-time". This essentially means time that is mediated to be perceived as immediate and hence real. It is this kind of time that enables us to be present and interact at a distance (telepresence, the metaverse), do more things simultaneously (i.e., multitasking), transform more and more data into the information we want, simulate what is possible, and predict what may happen. This is why the experience of time is changing for anyone living onlife. We saw that digital technologies create and shape our environments, the infosphere, where we spend increasingly more of our time. Precisely because the infosphere is not entirely "natural" but also artificial and designed and managed by human beings for other human beings, we need to reflect a great deal more on its nature and dynamics, to guarantee

---

[4] https://subscriptions.amd.com/newsletters/commercialchannelnews/archives/2019_11_en.html.

[5] https://www.forbes.com/sites/chuckbrooks/2021/03/21/the-emerging-paths-of-quantum-computing/?sh=150799356613.

[6] https://www.economist.com/technology-quarterly/2006/06/10/artificial-artificial-intelligence.

the equitability and sustainability of its design. We must ensure that we manage as well as we can "the new speed of politics and the new politics of speed", as Josh Cowls put it,[7] and to understand how we want to protect the time we have (think of the job market), how we want to enhance it (think of public and individual health), how we want to use it (think of entertainment), and how we want to distribute it (think of time management). We also need to know more about digital technologies and regulate better those in power who control the "unreal, unreal-time" of our lives. We must proceed quickly, because *tempus fugit* and there is no time to waste. But we must proceed with caution, because we must deal with such fundamental issues correctly. *Festina lente* ("make haste slowly"), as the Romans used to say.

---

[7] https://medium.com/josh-cowls/flattening-the-curve-forwards-the-new-speed-of-politics-and-the-new-politics-of-speed-3f19c1fad8ee.

Chapter 7
The Onlife Experience

The digital world is changing our conception of ourselves. We are amid a fourth revolution, no less fundamental and radical than those initiated by Copernicus, Darwin, and Freud (Floridi 2014). Following the Copernican revolution, heliocentric cosmology stripped away the illusion that Earth and humanity were privileged at the centre of the universe. The Darwinian revolution highlighted how every living species on Earth is related and has evolved from common ancestors through natural selection, thus calling into question the centrality and exclusivity of humanity in the biological realm. Freud gave us a framework to recognise and analyse that the mind is made up of the unconscious and not solely the conscious. Upon closer inspection, we (or our conscious selves) are no longer at the centre of our mental sphere. It was Freud himself who lined up these three decentralising revolutions. Today, computer science and digital technologies are the agents of a fourth revolution, which radically changes how we conceptualise who we are, further undermining the lingering preconception of our "exceptional centrality". We are realising that we are no longer at the centre of the infosphere. We are not independent entities but interconnected and related agents, or nodes. We produce and consume information and share a global environment substantially made up of information (the infosphere, as discussed in the previous

The Green and The Blue: Naive Ideas to Improve Politics in the Digital Age, First Edition. Luciano Floridi.

chapters) with other biological and artificial agents, i.e., other nodes. The digital has detached us from the centrality in the infosphere. If we wanted to credit one person for this, the champion of this fourth revolution would undoubtedly be Alan Turing.

We are integrated into the online world when, in the infosphere, the boundaries between online and offline life are blurred, we are constantly connected to one another as well as to continuous streams of data, and surrounded by smart systems that interact with us. The *onlife* experience is the counterpart of the fourth revolution, as it enmeshes the analogue with the digital. While the digital has untethered us from information-centricity, it has tethered us to an identity formed by the information that constitutes us and, in this way, to everything else onlife, as a system of connected nodes in the same network. This is a crucial instance of the digital *cut-and-paste* process discussed previously. This fourth revolution invites us to conceive Being dynamically and relationally (in philosophy, it could be called *relational monism*). It does not annul the existence and identity of individual nodes. Rather, it does not conceive of them as pre-existing or being entirely independent of the co-presence of the other nodes, i.e., the network. We are like roundabouts, the existence of which is determined by the roads that constitute them and does not precede them.

The onlife experience is increasingly underpinning our daily activities and interactions with the world. It structures how we communicate, interact, learn, work, shop, look after our health, have fun, and cultivate relationships. It shapes how we interact with the legal, financial, and political world and even affects how we wage war and maintain or promote peace. The digital has become an "environmental force" in every context of life, creating and transforming our realities. We have seen that, in philosophical terms, the digital is re-ontologising modernity and re-epistemologising our worldview. We perceive the world differently, reading it in terms of the types of information it imparts, from DNA to the fundamental laws of physics, from likes on social media to streaming experiences of videos and music.

By living onlife, we have finally begun to abandon the hegemony of the obsolete but deeply rooted Aristotelian-Newtonian *Ur-philosophy*. The onlife experience also makes us understand history differently, such that our era is even "more historical than before", that is, "hyperhistorical". Let me elaborate.

We saw in the previous chapter that the digital increasingly determines how we understand everyday time; what happens from day to day (i.e., *historical events*); how we remember, record, and recount what happens (i.e., the *narration of* events), and what it means to live historically (i.e., the *concept of* history itself). The way the digital interweaves our different ways of relating to time together is crucial, but simultaneously confusing. Let us take a step back to get our bearings. I shall begin with a fundamental distinction.

We saw in the previous chapter that there are various types of time, one of which is that of physics. This is quantifiable with precision, and reversible, like filling a glass with water and then emptying it (the equations of physics can be read both from left to right and from right to left), as opposed to the irreversible scenario of making an omelette with eggs. We have already seen that the time of physics does not flow in space, like a river or an arrow. Instead, it is baked with space, as a fourth dimension, in a continuum that curves in the presence of mass or energy, like when you put a weight on a bed, and it sinks, so that an ant, walking in a straight line, takes longer to cross it than if it were flat. Then, there is the time of daily experience, or *temporality*, as discussed in the previous chapter. This is the time described in Ecclesiastes 3:

> For everything there is a season. There is its time for everything under heaven: a time to be born and a time to die, a time to plant and a time to uproot that which is planted, a time to kill and a time to heal, a time to destroy and a time to build; a time to plan and a time to laugh, a time to mourn and a time to dance, a time to cast away stones and a time to pick them up, a time to embrace and a time to refrain from embracing; a time to seek and a time to lose, a time to keep and a time to throw away, a time to tear and a time to sew, a time to keep silent and a time to speak; a time to love and a time to hate, a time for war and a time for peace.

The time of *temporality* is perceived as flowing qualitatively, irreversibly, and separately from space. Our clocks measure temporality as if it were the time of physics. However, this is just an artefact to create a sense of synchronicity, something we have practised since bells structured the time of medieval towns and villages. History as a discipline studies this temporality, not the fourth-dimensional time of physics. It articulates temporality in *events*: the election of a new mayor, a short holiday, a successful celebration, an exhausting race, or time wasted in traffic. *Events* constitute our *history* as the assemblage of past lives, composed of the interlaced layers of an individual, family, social, and global history. Nobody can determine a priori *the size of events*, because this is a matter that requires reasonable and informed agreement. When did the event described as a "road traffic accident" begin and end? And how many sub-events did it include?

Digital technology increasingly influences our *temporality*, by which I mean our everyday experience, transforming how we learn, communicate, work, and interact; it shapes how we socialise and entertain ourselves and care. The very possibility of *multitasking*, or even being in several places at *once* (telepresence), transforms the nature of temporality and our former understanding of it. Increasingly, most of the everyday, temporal events that we experience are digital, at least partly. Take, for instance, selfies, the very essence of the temporal experience of temporal experience. The new mayor campaigned online, the short holiday was also spent on Facebook, the music for the party was downloaded from a website, the run burnt precisely 856 calories, and we listened to an audiobook while stuck in traffic. This is the onlife experience, comprising events in which the digital is an inevitable and sometimes fundamental ingredient, mixed with the analogue.

We narrate our temporality in a sequential, chronological, and meaningful order. This is history understood not as a discipline, but as a *narration* of events. It is not mere chronology (a life spent) but "temporalogy" (a life lived), to coin a neologism. We remember and forget, explain and reinterpret, create meaning, and narrate by repeating stories, celebrations, and traditions, as in the case of the feast of Sant'Agnello, held every year, on the last Sunday of August, in the small Italian village of Guarcino. Our experience of this temporalogy is a *consequence* that is not always objective. "Ferragosto" is no longer the feast of Augustus (*Feriae Augusti*), or a fascist holiday, but now marks the religious feast of the Assumption of Mary on the 15th day of August. When it is said that the victors write history, this is the kind of narrative "temporalogy" to which I am referring. Here too, digital technology plays a crucial role as a victor, if only because testimony, our historical memory, is increasingly entrusted to digital media: photographs, texts, videos, and audio recordings. This does not come without risk because the digital is fragile. A technology becomes obsolete, and today I can play Frisbee with floppy disks and CDs. A virus or a trivial formatting error erases the hard disk, and with that, we wave goodbye to family photos and part of our historical archive. A power surge fries the computer, and years of correspondence with my wife disappear. CDs can be demagnetised or become unreadable, and have an expiry date, as opposed to analogue vinyl. Everything can be rewritten in a constant present (think of a website) with a *reversibility* of historical narration that the glass of water I mentioned earlier would envy, impossible for the omelette. In just a few years, we have gone from a thousand-year-old culture of recording—what to save "for future reference"—to a culture of incessant rewriting and erasing—what to remove or edit "for future oblivion". This transformation is something we have yet to comprehend fully. All the while, digital data accumulates in nature, like dust in a house—think of the music or photos on your smartphone. The debate on the right to be forgotten, and on controlling the sedimentation of our past, would be inconceivable without the digitisation of our history and the onlife experience.

We thus arrive at the *concept* of history, not as a discipline, or a series of events or narrative, but as a *transcribed record*. In this sense, prehistory ends, and history begins when a society discovers a way of recording the present for future use, by inventing writing. Thus, *prehistory* started its decline in this corner of the world (Eurasia) about 6000 years ago (at least according to some scholars: the debate is ongoing), with the appearance of writing in Mesopotamia (writing was invented in several other places in different times). It is one of the most important inventions in the evolution of human society. In the fifth century BC, about halfway between us and cuneiform writing, Plato was still animatedly discussing the invention of writing, preferring remembering to written memory, a bit like a great philosopher lamenting the invention of the computer 2500 years from now.

With writing, and thus with the beginning of history as a form of archived documentation, information technologies drove individual and social development. Writing makes it possible to give permanent names to things and places, fix the census of a region, draw up a contract, indicate taxes or the laws and constitution of a country, leave a will, or write down how to calculate the area of a field. Without writing, there would be no religious texts like the Bible and the Qur'ān, the basis of the Abrahamic religions: Judaism, Christianity, and Islam.

Over time, the connection between human development and recorded (primarily written but also graphically represented) documentation has become increasingly vital. It is no coincidence that the great empires were also excellent managers of their time's information and communication technologies (ICTs). The second significant moment in developing the concept of history as a transcribed record came with the invention of the printing press around 1440. It rivalled in importance the invention of writing, combining the availability of the written record with the accessibility and mass dissemination of information.

Today, humanity lives historically everywhere, except for a few Amazonian tribes, which live prehistorically because they rely solely on oral culture and have no written records. However, digital technology is bringing about an equally radical third transformation in the infosphere by automatically processing information rapidly and seamlessly. Recording, disseminating, and now manipulating: advanced societies live, thrive, and depend on these digital activities. In the past, it was already difficult to imagine a world without writing or printing and other ICTs. Today, it is impossible to conceive of a world without digital technologies, given the extent to which they inform financial markets, transport, and a large spectrum of office work, for example. What was for millennia a *connection* between human development and ICTs has become a *dependency*. This reliance on the digital means that societies can be victims of *cyberattacks*. ICTs have gone from being an engine of development to becoming a driver of innovation and a necessary support for our lives. As such, history has become even "more historical" than history itself: we have moved from *history to hyperhistory*.

The transition from history to hyperhistory is unfolding incomparably faster than the transition from prehistory to history. This epochal transformation is having an immense impact. Amid these changes, there is an enormous need to see clearly, ask the right questions, and find the best answers to the new challenges, including political ones, posed by hyperhistory. The past can help, but only partly because history never truly repeats itself, and the difference in what is happening this time is significant. Every historical revolution has been accompanied and partly guided by a conceptual revolution. In other words, every era has its unique philosophy, guiding and giving it meaning. Today, the more we live hyperhistorically, in symbiosis with the digital, the more the philosophy we need to understand our world must deal directly with the infosphere. Therefore, the philosophy of our time and for our time must be a philosophy of information. Giving it an articulated form will not be easy, but it is possible, and above all necessary, if we want to create a better future.

I briefly mentioned that a clear indicator that we live in a hyperhistorical society is its susceptibility to cyberattacks. To put it more dramatically: in hyperhistorical societies, those who live by the digit can die by the digit. Therefore, cyberattacks are a good test of whether and to what extent one lives onlife in a hyperhistorical society. It is a new form of dependency and fragility. To understand this, let us begin with a somewhat personal example.

On 27 May 2017, the computer system used by British Airways went down due to a technical failure. The result was that 75,000 passengers between Heathrow and Gatwick were left stranded, including me. It took three days for the computer system to return to normal. The inconvenience and damage to passengers were considerable. The costs were enormous. The loss of reputation was severe, especially in such a competitive and low-margin airline context.

The day after I was stranded, a similar but unrelated problem occurred: the damage caused by the WannaCry cyberattack. The malware targeted Microsoft Windows systems, encrypting the files of infected computers, and then demanding a ransom to decrypt them. This time, I was spared. However, it was estimated that WannaCry infected more than 230,000 computers in 150 countries. Eventually, more than 300,000 computers were affected, making WannaCry one of the most infectious computer viruses of all time. Among the organisations in trouble were Deutsche Bahn, FedEx, Telefónica, Renault, and the Russian Ministry of the Interior. The English National Health System (NHS) was forced to cancel appointments and send patients home, and for a few days, it was back to analogue pen and paper. Fortunately, there were no casualties.

These two almost simultaneous disasters are two not-so-exceptional examples of how fragile the digital world is, how wide-ranging and risky our hyper-dependence on the digital is, and how systemic the problems caused by ICT failures really are.

Fragility can be a positive, even valuable quality, if, for example, we are talking about the delicacy of a crystal vase. It becomes a problem, however, when it denotes a system's unreliability or lack of resilience. So, it is natural to be concerned when the system in question is the digital one on which our information society is increasingly "hyperhistorically" dependent. We live in ever more complex environments that function only thanks to digital technology. Suffice it to say that by 2025, 70% of the world's population will be urbanised. The question is whether something can be done to make these digital systems less fragile and more reliable. Resignation, like crossed fingers, is not a workable strategy. On the contrary, much can be done to strengthen the digital, or at least to ensure that damage is limited when it occurs. Action is urgently needed, not only from individuals, but also from institutions and companies, because the cost of doing nothing has become unsustainable and dangerous.

Let us examine a classic solution: if the system collapses, the backup system takes over. This is what is known as resilience through redundancy. We add a leg to the sofa or make sure there is at least a spare wheel, like on my old Vespa. The trouble with British Airways was that it had cut costs so radically that, when the spare wheel was needed, it was not there (like, most unfortunately, with my new Vespa). In the case of digital technology, there is a constant need for a complete and up-to-date backup of your computer. If the computer is blocked by malware, it is painful, but you can format it and reinstall a clean copy. If only it were that simple for the analogue world, too.

Another solution is reflexivity. In digital systems, everything is made up of binary zeroes and ones: the operating system, the programs managed by the operating system, and the data manipulated by the programs. We are accustomed to this by now. It seems trivial, but it is extraordinary when you think about it. It is as if a car's chassis, engine, and petrol were made of the same interchangeable substance. Or as if bottles and glasses were both made of ice. Thanks to such reflexivity, the digital can work with itself, on itself, and for itself. WannaCry infected many computers because many had not been updated to block it. Users forgot that reflexivity makes digital technology both fragile and resilient: malware is made up of zeros and ones, but zeroes and ones also enable a computer to defend itself and repair itself, for instance, with an antivirus. In the future, we will increasingly call upon the positive reflexivity of the digital, without which we will not be able to protect our car software, for instance. Watch out, because the next malware could be called WannaDrive, and it might leave us stranded.

The reference to cars reminds me that there is always the old solution of insurance. According to an article in the *Financial Times*, the cyber insurance market jumped after the WannaCry cyberattack. Predictably, as with the response to cleaning up the pollution (fake news) of the infosphere, we run for cover only after the trouble has started. In 2022, the cyber insurance industry had a premium value of about $3 to $4 billion per year. According to Allianz, it is expected to reach $20 billion by 2025, making it one of the fastest-growing segments in the world insurance industry. Insurtech should refer not only to what the digital can do for the insuring sector but also to what insurance can do to make the infosphere safer.

Finally, the usefulness and value of fragility should not be underestimated. Fragility is woven into the systems we build, with fuses, valves, and even glass designed to be broken in an emergency; it is found among all kinds of life-saving devices. If something goes wrong, the system degrades in a calculated and limited way, indicating where and how to intervene. The same should apply to the digital. This is what happened with WannaCry, albeit only accidentally. The reason is unclear, but before infecting a computer, the malware checked whether an obscure website had been registered. The malware encrypted the files when the answer was no—that is, the website did not exist. A British researcher then registered the targeted site. The result was surprising: the malware stopped functioning upon finding the site. In other words, the creation of the website acted as an emergency stopgap.

We were lucky with WannaCry. There were no human casualties, but it was an obvious warning sign. The time has come for all of us to take responsibility, but digital organisations must surely take a lead here. The National Security Agency, for instance, was aware of the vulnerability of Windows that WannaCry exploited. They should have warned the world, rather than keeping it secret so that they could exploit it as a cyber weapon in the future. They raised the alarm too late after the information had been stolen from them. Then there are companies like Microsoft that increasingly have to take responsibility as the first line of defence. Abandoning old operating systems when they can no longer be upgraded to the latest version is not an acceptable solution, because they remain in use, and it is well known that a chain is only as strong as its weakest link. Finally, there are us, the users. We must be more responsible because, just like in medicine, it takes only a small part of the population being unvaccinated to put the entirety of society at risk. The digital can heal the digital, but as in all systemic contagions, the cure works only if everyone cooperates. No matter how strong the other legs of the sofa are, if one of them is fragile, we will always end up hurting ourselves, and it will be our fault for not taking care of ourselves.

Digital technology has changed how we understand ourselves, our world, and our everyday lived experience, or temporality. In the immediate future, will the digital lead us towards expanding our abilities and opening new possibilities, or will we find ourselves imprisoned within its boundaries? The answer demands an ecological and ethical approach that coordinates natural reality and the human-made (digital) universe. We need to devise an *e-nvironmentalism* that successfully confronts the new challenges generated by digital technologies. How we will construct, shape, and regulate the new infosphere and living onlife from an ecological perspective is one of the crucial challenges of the digital revolution. The good news is that overcoming this challenge is entirely within our grasp, as we will see at the end of this book. But first, we need to explore some more basic ideas. The next idea that requires discussion is that of a *mature information society*, which I have frequently mentioned. In such a society, our everyday experiences are increasingly *onlife*, within the *infosphere*, and *hyperhistorical*.

Chapter 8

A Mature Information Society

The expression "information society" is by now so familiar that sometimes we forget that there are multiple information societies, often different from one another. Therefore, it is more appropriate to refer to them in the plural and ensure that we do not over-generalise or ignore any meaningful distinctions. There is always a level of abstraction at which something can correctly be associated with something else: the Moon is like an umbrella, which is like a pizza, if the point of comparison is that they are all more or less round objects. The point is not to take pleasure in one's acrobatic equations (x is like y, which is like z), but rather to be critical in identifying the correct level of abstraction, whereby the adopted equation is the most effective one by which to achieve a given objective. In other words, it is crucial to ask how useful it is ("what for?") to see an umbrella, the Moon, and a pizza as round objects.

All of this should clarify why, when considering the multitude of very different information societies, it is essential both to distinguish and to associate

The Green and The Blue: Naive Ideas to Improve Politics in the Digital Age, First Edition. Luciano Floridi.

them in terms of meaningful criteria, and more specifically, why it is crucial to understand what it means for an information society to be more or less mature than others. As I will explain next, I refer to maturity as a question of *expectations* rather than technological or economic development.

The Organisation for Economic Co-operation and Development (OECD) collects many useful statistics to assess the developmental stage of an information society. The data mainly concern technological progress as far as the OECD is concerned. They measure development in four main areas: broadband and telecommunications, the Internet economy, consumer policy, and digital status. Taken together, it is reasonable to believe that these four pillars offer a framework to assess what it means for an information society to be mature. However, while the OECD approach to defining the development of an information society is widespread, it is far from satisfactory. Take the worldwide percentage of fibre broadband connections. The information in the OECD's December 2021[1] update showed Korea, Japan, Spain, and Sweden at the top, which is not surprising. However, it also placed Colombia above Canada and the USA, Turkey above the Netherlands, while Germany and the UK languished near the bottom of the list, after Italy. Yet both Germany and the UK can easily be considered mature information societies. What becomes apparent is that the percentage of fibre connections is not a critical factor in assessing a country's information maturity. A similar criticism can be made of all the other statistical data provided by the OECD. The problem with many technological and economic measurement approaches is that they capture only some of the conditions that facilitate the development of an information society. Think of connectivity, Internet usage, the number of computers per household, governmental open data projects, *e-health* services, digital skills, the use of social media, the *per capita* investment in digital technologies, the presence of policies against the digital divide, etc. These conditions are *jointly* necessary, representing valuable and meaningful opportunities and possibilities. They must be coordinated to make a difference, but—perhaps partly because they are not strictly necessary separately—they are also insufficient to explain how and why one information society can be more mature than another. Something fundamental is missing, and that something is the *population's expectations*. The following analogy may help to explain why.

---

[1] Source: OECD, Broadband Portal, http://www.oecd.org/digital/broadband/broadband-statistics.

Suppose you are in a hotel in Rome. You rightly expect the water in the bathroom to be drinkable, because Italy is a mature society in terms of water management. In fact, you do not think for a moment about the possibility that it might be dangerous. The idea does not cross your mind that the hotel should provide you with information about the potability of the water, let alone for you to ask. Italy is a "mature water society", not only because of its water system and related quality controls, but above all because, given these conditions, the population considers and expects drinking water to be something essential, a given, ordinary, a topic about which there is no need for questions to be asked. It is part of life, what everyone expects in a hotel in Rome, implicitly, without thinking or a shadow of a doubt. At the same time, we all know that water potability is anything but a trivial matter. According to the World Health Organisation and UNICEF (Joint Monitoring Programme), in 2015, around 700 million people (10% of the world's population) did not have access to safe drinking water. In 2019, another report published by the same sources indicated that approximately 2.2 billion people worldwide lacked safely managed drinkable water services, 4.2 billion people did not have access to safely managed sanitation services, and 3 billion had no basic handwashing facilities.[2] The expectations that water is unquestionably safe to drink thus change if you go on an adventurous holiday. It becomes normal to ask whether tap water is safe to drink, even if you wish only to brush your teeth. Of course, expectations also change depending on the context. They provide a suitable metric by which to calibrate the maturity of a society with regard to a specific social characteristic. The formula is simple: if the presence of a social characteristic f is no longer informative, but its absence is informative, then that society is mature in terms of f. According to this interpretation, mature information societies already exist in some parts of the world. In such societies, people live onlife, in the infosphere, hyperhistorically. They take it for granted that they can order any product online, pay for it digitally, exchange any kind of content on the Web, find any sort of information, take advantage of services, mass media and digital entertainment, rely on smartphones and apps, and so on. They can do all of this, at any time, in any place, continuously, quickly, and reliably, without having to ask or wonder whether it is possible. We realise that we belong to a mature information society only when we go somewhere else where our expectations are not fulfilled. For years now, I have

---

[2] Source: https://www.unicef.org/reports/state-worlds-drinking-water.

not asked a hotel where I am staying *whether* they have an Internet connection, but *how* I can connect to it.

When information societies are analysed in terms of their members' implicit and unreflective expectations, such as those about potable water, we move from quantitative assessments to qualitative ones. This enables us to examine some practical consequences. For our chief purpose, which is to understand those ideas that can help improve politics, three are more important than the rest. Here I shall expound them in no particular order of importance.

First, consider *education*. Let us reject the myth that "nowadays young people all know how to use [add your favourite digital technology here]". Young people differ from older people because of what they take for granted: their implicit and unreflective expectations, not because they are born with unique, innate abilities. Lamarck was wrong, and Darwin was right in that successive generations do not evolve genetically. Hence, their abilities are not automatically or intrinsically better than any other member of the society in question. Children have no innate knowledge of how to use a touch screen, but they are surprised if a television screen does not respond to their touch, because that is what they expect as normal, on account of the games they play on touch-screen tablets. Another analogy using cars can help with the comparison to a mature society. Precisely because it is not a question of knowledge, ability, use, or ownership, but rather one of implicit assumptions and expectations, Alice or Bob can live in a car-mature society—in which everyday life consists of vehicles, car parks, roads, motorways, traffic lights, zebra crossings, petrol stations, traffic, speed limits, fines, and so on—even if they do not own or know how to drive a car, or have no idea how an engine works, or how they might repair a car. They may take the availability of public transport for granted, for instance, and not have a driving licence. "The young generation" still has to learn to use new technologies, like any other generation, but more importantly, it is *irrelevant* whether they do, insofar as assessing the expectations of a generation matters to understand whether they live in a mature information society. This is one of the reasons why education is crucial: it makes us aware of our implicit expectations and how they may or may not be reasonable, socially justified, and determined by historical factors.

Second, let us consider *innovation*. We have seen how expectations determine what is considered ordinary and extraordinary, normal, and abnormal in a society. In short, expectations determine what is informative: to be told that the water in your hotel in Rome is not drinkable—for instance, because of some works in progress—would be very informative, in the same way that it would be informative (unexpected) to be told that you have access to a high-speed Internet connection on a beautiful but remote island. Therefore, from a cultural point of view (but not a technological one, as we discussed earlier), digital innovation is more difficult to achieve in a mature information society than in an immature one. In a society where people take cars and TV for granted, car and TV maturity has been achieved, no matter how much these technologies keep changing, as their presence is expected. Similarly, once people get used to living *onlife*, the proliferation of digital products, services, opportunities, or facilities will no longer make that society any more mature.

Finally, we can move on to *knowledge*. Expectations can be dazzling compared with alternative realities. As in the analogy of potable water in Rome, it is essential to know what one can legitimately expect from a given society (i.e., potable water or a good Internet connection) while keeping in mind that these are privileges, and that the situation is probably far from what billions of people can enjoy in many other parts of the world. To return to a previous example, if one expects, as is common in many countries, one's bank to provide an app that scans cheques to be deposited automatically online without the need to go to a branch and fill in a form, then it seems legitimate to file a complaint when this does not happen, as opposed to appreciating the service by thinking that many people cannot even access an ATM. The more a society treats a specific right as obvious and taken for granted, the more surprising its absence becomes. Thus, the ethical and legal debate on privacy began only once privacy was deeply challenged by photography's development and widespread use (Brandeis and Warren published their seminal article "The Right to Privacy" in the *Harvard Law Review* 15 December 1890).

Information societies are maturing worldwide, and more will continue to appear. Consequently, similar expectations to the ones I have discussed here will become increasingly prevalent. To paraphrase Tolstoy in *Anna Karenina*, all mature information societies are similar in terms of their expectations, while each immature information society is different in its own way. Therefore, the next stage of development in information societies, whether ten or one hundred years from now, will not be a further maturing of their members' expectations regarding their digital opportunities or technologies. Instead, only another total, unprecedented, and unexpected transformation will lead to further maturity, of which the digital will no doubt implicitly be part. It is difficult to describe or imagine such a future when we are still going through the digital revolution. History tends to surpass our imagination. In 1920, just after the First World War, nobody could have imagined what the world would be like in 2020. The same consideration applies to the next hundred years. That said, alongside this unpredictability—which is composed of related events that join, converge or diverge, and amplify or cancel each other out, like so many random or causal vectors—there also exists an aspect of human history that is the fruit of shared aspirations, of coordinated efforts, of joint intention. This is what I have termed the *human project* throughout this book. Therefore, an urgent question we must ask ourselves today is the following: to the limited but not negligible extent that the vectors of history can be controlled, managed, and steered by the cooperation of good wills, what should the human project look like for a mature information society in the twenty-first century? As I have argued, a promising answer might come from applying a relational and non-thing-based approach to our socio-political ontology. This is the basis of what I argue in the next chapter, where I analyse the idea and significance of the human project.

Chapter 9
The Human Project

By "human project", I mean the kind of society we would collectively like to build and live in. More simplistically, it is the vision that political parties try to capture through election slogans, often without critical awareness. For instance, in 2017, in the UK, we had "for the many, not the few" by the British Labour Party, and "building a country that works for everyone" by the British Conservative Party. Approached analytically, the human project is the kind of human life—conceived in its individual and collective, private and public manifestations—that a society presents and promotes as preferable, at least implicitly. It is also dependent on historical events. Perhaps the closest philosophical term to describe the idea of a human project is Wittgenstein's *Lebensform*, with the significant difference that a human project is not only *descriptive*, as in the case of *Lebensform* (what human project can be found in a society), but also *normative* (what it should be and how it can be realised). In reality, it is probably impossible to give complete form to any human project. Therefore, it should be understood only as a *regulatory ideal*[1] towards which to strive, hoping that at least some of its aims will be achieved. However, despite this limitation, one can still make two crucial observations.

---

[1] The reference to Kant's *Critique of Pure Reason* is deliberate.

The Green and The Blue: Naive Ideas to Improve Politics in the Digital Age, First Edition. Luciano Floridi.

The first observation is that every society has and pursues its own human project (or sometimes projects), whether implicit or explicit. Such projects can be coherent or contradictory, such as when several projects cannot be reconciled, pragmatic, realistic, or utopian. This happens for at least two reasons. First, because individuals, either voluntarily or involuntarily, come together as a polity and form an identity based on a shared purpose. Such a collective identity can be positive and result in a higher degree of trust, coordination, collaboration, and cooperation, as in Locke or Rousseau. However, it can also be negative, resulting in a higher degree of distrust, conflict, or insecurity, as in Hobbes or Kant. Furthermore, because not participating in politics and striving to be apolitical is inevitably a political act, as I argued before, the very absence of a human project is still a project. Not having a project does not mean doing without one, but instead opting for a bad project. Therefore, a society without any human project does not exist. There are only societies whose human projects can be understood on a spectrum ranging from good to bad, which are either coherent or incoherent, explicit or implicit, inclusive or exclusive, compatible or incompatible with one other (and so forth), and thus ultimately feasible or unfeasible.

The second observation is that, although every society tends to absolutise (even if only implicitly) its own human project as *unique* (there is only one, its own), *eternal* (its own is forever valid), and *universal* (its own is valid and needed everywhere), in reality, there is only a plurality of human projects. There are as many human projects as there are polities and societies, their stages of evolution, and the historical or hyperhistorical circumstances in which they find themselves. This *pluralism* is not relativism, which would argue that each human project is as good or bad as any other. Instead, such pluralism invites us to adopt a relational way of describing the multiplicity of design opportunities to question something made feasible only by what has already been achieved, and is therefore known, and by what has not yet been achieved, but can conceivably be so. The human project described by Cicero in *De Republica* (Cicero 2000) is very different from that described by Tocqueville in *De la démocratie en Amérique* (Tocqueville 1955), and neither can easily be applied to information societies today. With an analogy, the human project is like a chair: there can be a very large yet bounded number of ways of designing and implementing it, some of which are more successful than others. However, just because one is aware of this pluralism, one should not fall into the trap of thinking that anything goes: a lamp or a bed are not chairs as a matter of fact, and some poorly designed chairs (for example, too fragile, too expensive, too ugly, too uncomfortable) are chairs nobody wishes to have or use. The same holds for the variety of human projects we encounter in the history of humanity. So, the question is: what is the right human project we can and need to design and build for the digital society in the 21st century? The answer I defend in this book is the Green and the Blue.

One factor that can explain the radical transformation, disillusionment, and uncertainty that characterise our time is an implicit perception that we lack a well-articulated and coherent human project for the information societies maturing before our eyes. In metaphorical terms, it is as if we were on an ever-faster journey that we do not control, in a direction still unknown.

We have not conceived a human project for the digital age. However, we have a *postmodern* (here and in the following chapters I use this term in a chronological and not philosophical sense, see Chapter 23) starting point, in the sense of an *incomplete meta-project*, inherited from modernity and shared by the industrial and post-industrial consumer society that now characterises many advanced economies. Both terms, "meta-project" and "incomplete", need to be clarified.

The *postmodern meta-project* refers to how an information society seeks to render the *individual* human projects of its members feasible and compatible. The implementation and fostering of education, equal opportunities, more capabilities, empowering and enabling policies belong to such metaproject, or project of projects. Politics is seen as a way of avoiding or mitigating conflicts between individual projects and at best facilitating and coordinating them, in the sense of ensuring that they do not undermine each other. Since this is also what the logic of an open market best delivers, the overall coherent picture is that of a market-oriented, individualistic, postmodern metaproject, where the driving force is well-regulated competition, in life, in education, in politics, in business, and so forth. Thus, simply put, what is pursued is not a happy society, but an individualistic society in which each person can pursue their own happiness, provided that this is not to the detriment of others; not a wealthy society but a society in which each individual can, in theory, become rich within the limits of the law; not a healthy society but a society in which each individual can live a healthy life within the limits of legality and available resources, and so on.

The postmodern meta-project is clearly part of the *liberal* tradition. The exhaustive purpose of the state is to defend and promote the rights of each citizen, in a mutually compatible way. Here the metaphor of the state as a referee, as opposed to a player, applies. In the previous chapters, we have already seen that there is a reliance on, and expectation that, a socio-political and sometimes economic mechanism will "spontaneously" emerge out of the desired social-relational properties. It is sufficient to start by implementing the individual properties that one intends to support. In the previous example, a happy society would emerge spontaneously if all its members were happy. In economic terms, this emergentism (or *trickle-down economics*) fits well with *liberalism*: the state ensures that individuals have access to the free market to produce and trade, within the limits of compatibility, property rights, and competition rules. In some cases, ethical liberalism and economic liberalism end up supporting political *libertarianism*, which promotes the maximum reduction of state functions in favour of individuals' unregulated freedom and responsibility. I shall argue that this is, at best, insufficient and, at worst, mistaken.

Let us now consider the *incompleteness* of the postmodern liberal and liberalist meta-project. Its incompleteness is linked to its focus solely on the interests and hopes of the individual, including the legal person (e.g., taxation or tax relief for companies), while neglecting relational nodes. It does not intend to provide a programmatic, collective framework for the kind of society that we would like to build *together*, one for which the efforts of the majority, and sometimes everyone, need to be more than just *coordinated* (where nobody hinders anybody), to give rise to *collaboration* (individuals assisting in different parts of the same project) and *cooperation* (all individuals taking care of the whole project). I will return to the cooperation point in the next chapter. Here, it is worth noting that, since the beginning of the twentieth century, the incompleteness of the postmodern meta-project has been overshadowed by the horrific disasters of the two world wars and the corresponding effort directed towards recovery, the Cold War, and the clash of political and religious ideologies. Whenever it has been necessary to fight *together* against something, for good or bad (e.g., the COVID-19 pandemic), or to build or rebuild *together* what was inherited from this conflict, or to adopt a *collective* ideological or religious faith, the postmodern project has been externally supported by other social or community projects, which have veiled its incompleteness. The great protest movements for various human rights— e.g., the civil rights movement, the peace movement, the feminist movement, and the environmental movement—have provided, as a sort of support, the social component lacking in the postmodern human project, which otherwise would have remained limping on the single leg of the individualistic human meta-project. At best, these external social projects have been "included" in the human project, providing it with non-individualistic components. Think of Martin Luther King's work in the USA, the fall of the Berlin Wall and the reunification of Germany, or the end of apartheid in South Africa. The same applies to political and religious ideologies. Fundamentalism is also a reaction against the incompleteness of the current human project. Today, the disconnect between social and political projects is profound, and the former can no longer conceal the incompleteness of the latter. Whatever form it takes, the social project is no longer part of the political project; on the contrary, it often wilfully distances itself from it in an anti-political way, falling into the negative dialectic described at the beginning of the book.

Civil society cannot replace politics, but it must ask politics to perform its job well. In this sense, one may positively welcome the phenomenon of Greta Thunberg, for instance. On the contrary, the disconnect between the two fuels the illusion that civil society can do without politics and successfully pursue and realise its own independent human project. Evidence of this sentiment is that the world of voluntary work and, thus, *social commitment* is growing in correlation with the disenchantment and rejection of *political commitment*. For example, according to AmeriCorps, a federal agency, "an estimated 23.2 percent of Americans or more than 60.7 million people formally volunteered with organisations between September 2020 and 2021. In total, these volunteers served an estimated 4.1 billion hours with an economic value of $122.9 billion."[2] Their work was unpaid and done for the common good. Considering what has been said, this is not a contradiction but a consequence: politics does not command a social, human project. Instead, this human need, which is not satisfied by the individual human project, is satisfied outside politics, in civil society. This generates at least three significant risks.

We have already seen the first: community activism, by detaching itself from the human project, risks leaving it limp while masking its incompleteness and incurring high operational costs, because a civil society must still rely on good politics to implement the required changes effectively. The second is the illusion that community activism can overcome or substitute the absence of a social human project, and that politics can, therefore, not only be lame but also remain so without any negative consequences. Civil society, however, cannot thrive alongside bad politics, for it will achieve less and with more difficulty. The third risk is that community activism is confused with the social,

---

[2] Sources: https://americorps.gov.

human project and tries to replace it, through movements that call themselves political but do not intend to do politics positively. Such movements
fail to heed that good politics would effectively support the evolution of
community cooperation and fulfil its needs.

All of this leads to a crucial question, one that is essential to consider if
we hope to outline a good human project for mature information societies.
If it is possible to adopt an individual meta-project alongside a social project
(this "if" is not rhetorical), is it possible to do so today without falling back
into right-wing, left-wing, or religious ideologies? In other words, is it possible
to have a *complete* human project that cuts across divisions—and therefore,
both a meta-project for individual projects and a project for society—that
is neither ideological nor transcendent? I shall argue in the affirmative, but I
acknowledge that there is little room for manoeuvre. Let us consider this in
more detail.

It is telling that centrist ideology at present is either unspoken or deeply
unpopular. The centre of politics lacks its own ideology because, at best, it
transcends it, by adopting *ethics* as its main guiding principle. As in ethics—
from Aristotle to Rawls—the aim is to attain a satisfactory equilibrium and to
reconcile interests collaboratively through compromise, rather than to strive
for imbalance and dominance through the clash of parties in a zero-sum game.
The centre does not engage in "political struggle" but looks for political
convergence; it connects, it does not disconnect; it does not squabble, it
dialogues. For this reason, the human project that we can hope to design
today will proceed also socially, and not only individually (and hence only
metaprojectually), if it follows an ethical-centric approach, not in a right- or
left-wing ideologically driven way, but in an immanent and non-transcendent
way, staying within history (human temporality, as discussed in Chapters 6
and 7) and improving it from within, not "coming out of it" in a salvific way,
rejecting it.

That is to say that good politics will no longer take left vs. right seriously,
but will concentrate on centrist alternatives that have more or less successful
strategies to approach the human project. To be coherent, the ethics to be
adopted will have to be inclusive of all those parts of the world and society
inevitably ignored by the meta-project, that is, those parts that do not play an
active role in presenting and managing their own interests and rights in the
first person. This is one of the great lessons that political commitment can
learn from the community commitment. The human project for the digital age
and for a mature information society must include the "silent world": the mar-

ginalized, the disadvantaged, the weak, the oppressed, the past generations who no longer speak but must be respected, and the future ones who do not speak yet, but must be facilitated, the environment (natural and artificial), and the semantic capital of culture and science, literature and art, experience and memory. In other words, the human project must adopt an ethics of the interests of all the "patient" nodes (those who receive the effects of political action), and of the various networks that they form, and not only of the individual "agent" nodes, whose interests are already taken care of by the metaproject component, which knows their requests because they are presented explicitly and constantly. It will have to listen to those who are not heard by the metaproject. This is not an oxymoron: let us remember that silence can be profoundly informative.

As regards the relation with religion, the human project for the digital age will have to support a secular and immanent society, while being wholly respectful of the multiple faiths that can coexist and flourish in it. The reasons in favour of a secular human project are many. Only a secular human project can be *coherent* in articulating and upholding the meta-project (remember, the project is to facilitate individual projects to the extent that they are mutually compatible) as well as *tolerant* (i.e., respectful) and supportive of the plurality and variety of individual human projects. And only a secular human project can avoid proselytism and zealotry and the attempt to impose a specific (religious or otherwise) view of the human project at the expense of those who hold other views, including religious ones, and a specific interpretation of the world in terms of "we" and "they" (*religious divide*). While ethics can unite, religion tends to divide. In a tolerant society, everyone must have the right to go to hell as they wish, as long as they travel alone, bringing nobody with them.

To summarise, the human project for a mature information society must primarily be ethical, then political, and only then economic. It must comprise two components: one of which is modern and classical, represented by the liberal metaproject in favour of individualist projects, and the second of which is communal and yet to be constructed, and can, in theory, provide social meaning to how we live together as a society. To quote the opening words of the US Constitution, it should also be a project of *we the people* and not only of disconnected individuals pursuing their compatible interests. The profound lack of valuable utopian thinking today speaks to this yet-to-be-developed second component. This absence is perpetuated partly because politics is now often seen as an outcome of economics, when instead, the ethics and semantics of a human project should guide good politics, which in turn should only then implement the right economy. Therefore, in the following chapters, I will present two additional ideas: first, that of an economy of experience, consistent with the human project of green and blue; and second, that of a good ethical infrastructure, which I will call *infraethics*, that encourages and enables the coordination and care of the social fabric, facilitating the building of the human project through good politics and an economy that supports it. But first, we must rethink another modern idea, the social contract.

Chapter 10
From the Social Contract to a Universal Trust

Various forms of contractualism, both in ethics and political philosophy, argue that moral obligation, the duty of political obedience, or the justice carried out by social institutions have their origin and foundation in the so-called "social contract". This can take the form of an actual, implicit, or hypothetical agreement among those that constitute a society, e.g., the people and the sovereign, or the members of a community. The parties agree to adhere to the terms of the contract and, in so doing, obtain some rights in exchange for a partial limitation of the freedoms that they would theoretically enjoy without restraint, in an ideal setting, one which logically, if not actually, would precede the contractual state. The rights and responsibilities of the parties to the agreement constitute the terms of the social contract, with the company, state, group, etc., being the entity created to implement the agreement. It is sometimes argued that neither rights nor freedoms are fixed and may vary owing to the interpretation of the social contract and its possible revisions for different contexts and historical circumstances.

The Green and The Blue: Naive Ideas to Improve Politics in the Digital Age, First Edition.
Luciano Floridi.
© 2024 John Wiley & Sons Ltd. Published 2024 by John Wiley & Sons Ltd.

Interpretations of social contract theory tend to be markedly, if often *unconsciously, anthropocentric*, because their purview is strictly focused on rational human agents. They tend to emphasise the compulsory nature of the agreement and are based on what I have previously termed an ontological *Ur-philosophy* that stresses the primacy of parts-things (e.g., members of a group), which come together to create a larger and more complex whole-thing based on shared advantages. These interpretations and assumptions have many problematic aspects. I am not the first to point them out, but here it is worth spelling out three of them, to further the line of reasoning developed in this book.

First, as the result of the four revolutions that successively decentralised humanity from spheres at the centre of which we previously conceived ourselves, it would be preferable to approach the formation of social relations from an "eccentric" point of view, that is, one that puts relations at the centre and humanity at the periphery, serving the world, nature, and past and future generations. Second, the social contract should ground and not presuppose its mandatory aspect. Social obligations exist because there is a social contract, not vice versa. At best, such obligations may be interpreted as a natural necessity. This necessity is usually described as the convenient and calculated transition from a state of conflict and violence to one of at least non-belligerence, and at best optimally peaceful cooperation. But the typically modern assumption that we find in Hobbes or Kant, whereby the social contract would be based on a linear transition from (a) conflict, violence, discrimination, and domination of the stronger over the weaker to (b) collaboration, peace, and respect, is controversial. This is because it seems more like an abstract construct than a historical observation. It seems more reasonable to think that war and peace, conflict and coexistence, and competition and cooperation are inseparable and always bound. Often, the need to defend oneself could be replaced by the need to help each other. There is no siege (conflict) without a fortification (collaboration). As I will explain in the next chapter, even a society of angels still needs rules to function well. Finally, the third aspect, that of a thing-based ontology, is problematic because it would be more fruitful to reason in relational terms, thus focusing on the nature and construction of relations, rather than on the nodes and the individuality of mere parts.

Regardless of how one may judge the applicability of the social contract to the information society, it is interesting, if only from a comparative point of view, to consider a possible alternative that does not presuppose anthropocentrism, the compulsory nature of the contract caused by the need to avoid violence, and an ontology of things. I shall call this alternative the *universal trust*, which is neither anthropocentric nor based on compulsoriness/ necessity, that is, on a social obligation. Instead, it is based on the primacy of relations, although it shares with the previous concept of the social contract the basic idea of an *original covenant*, which is the foundation of moral, social, and political interactions.

To introduce the idea of universal trust, let me begin with a description of a trust in the English legal system, where trusts are very common (in other countries, such trusts have only recently been conceived and used in similar ways).

A trust is a legal arrangement whereby a person (the *trustee*) holds and administers the assets (*corpus*) that belong (or belonged) to another person (i.e., the *trustor* or *donor*) for the benefit of designated persons or entities (the *beneficiaries*). Strictly speaking, no one owns the assets, since the trustor has donated them, the trustee only has legal title, and the beneficiaries only have equitable title. Together, they create a foundational trust relation to manage, protect, and improve assets. This is important, because a trust relies on the relational ontology (as opposed to an ontology of things, required by a social contract) that I advocate as preferable for our digital era. This ontology does not start with the parties coming together, but with a trusting relation, which allows the participants in their various roles to become what they are and mature over time. We can now take this further by employing this type of universal fiduciary relation as a model to envisage the foundation of future human societies. Let us begin with a concrete illustration and then examine its logical structure.

Existence begins with a gift, even if it is unwanted initially. At first, a foetus will be only a *beneficiary* of the world. Once that foetus is born and has become a complete, moral, social, and political agent, it will, as an individual, be both a *beneficiary* and a *trustee* of the world. As persons mature, they will assume responsibility for caring for the world, and become *givers* of the world for as long as they are part of the living generation. Once they die, they leave the world to other human beings and transition to the *donor-only* generation. In short, the life of a human being is a journey from being a *beneficiary* to being a *donor*, passing through the condition of also being a responsible *trustee* of the world. We begin our lives as moral agents strangers to the world; we should end it as its friends.

In terms of logical structure, the universal trust is characterised as follows:

- The *agreement*, which was already present in the social contract, is here transformed into a *primordial* covenant. It is entirely hypothetical and logically prior to the social contract. All human beings are obligated to sign it when they are born, and is constantly renewed by successive generations.

- The *assets* or *corpus* are represented by the world, which also includes every human generation, past, present, and future. It is an inherently shared good, what we often call *res publica*, but which in reality is everything *in the* world when we came *into the* world (this is networked Being).

- *Donors* consist of all past and present human generations.

- The *trustees* are the current human generation.

- The *beneficiaries* are all the current and future human generations.

A network of other *relata* or nodes makes it possible for humans to exist. A new node in a pre-existing network owes its existence both to the entire network itself, and to the individual nodes that precede it, just think of the natural languages we all speak, inherited from the past and left to the future. No node precedes the network, meaning no individual precedes the universal trust, unlike the social contract, which presupposes pre-existing individual atoms that are free to enter a contractual relation. Therefore, each person-node is bound to all that is and was, the relations that compose it—hence the trust is *universal*, or as one might say more philosophically, *ontic*—both *involuntarily* and *inevitably*, and should be so with *care*. Individuals are bound *involuntarily*, because they do not will their own conception, although in theory they can (and should be allowed to) terminate their life voluntarily; and *inevitably*, because individuals can break the bond only at the cost of ceasing to exist as agents and patients. While moral, social, and political life does not begin with an individual act of freedom, it can end with one. Metaphorically, each node cannot create itself but can untie itself. Finally, one should be bound with *care*, because participation in Being by any entity, including a human being—i.e., the fact that every entity expresses existence—offers an intrinsic right to exist and an invitation (not a duty, contrary to the social contract) to respect other entities and to care for them. Therefore, the covenant does not involve any coercion, as in the social contract, but a reciprocal relation of appreciation, gratitude, and care, which is enhanced by acknowledging this mutual dependence. Thus, the universal trust is ethically good (ethics of care) and not neutral like the social contract, which could easily be unfair, as when public resources (e.g., petrodollars) are used to support and improve the standards of living of citizens while discriminating against foreigners.

The obligations and responsibilities introduced by the universal trust vary according to circumstance. However, fundamentally the universal trust establishes the expectation that actions are carried out or avoided primarily with the world's welfare in mind; that is, the whole network of Being, in relational terminology, in the past, present, and future. In this sense, the eccentric environmentalism of the human condition is fundamental: humanity has a unique *stewardship* role in *caring* for the world. Universal trust is what is assumed by the approach advocated by the ethics of information (*information ethics*, or simply IE; Floridi 2013). According to IE, ethical discourse concerns every entity (every node in the network), that is, not only all people, present, past and future, their culture, their well-being, and their social interactions, and not only all animals, plants, and their functioning natural life cycles and environments, but everything that exists in the world, from buildings to other artefacts, from sand to rivers. For IE, nothing (no node) is too humble to deserve or even require some form of disrespect. Or to put it in positive terms, every node deserves some minimal form of overridable respect. From this perspective, IE completes the process of extending the concept of what can be considered a bearer of moral claims (no matter how minimal), which now includes every instance of Being, understood informatively as a node in the network. IE holds that every entity—each node in the network (chain) of Being, to use the relational terminology introduced earlier—possesses a minimal degree of dignity, determined by its mode of existence and essence (the assemblage of all the elementary properties/relations that constitute it), which deserves respect, at least in a minimal and overridable sense. Therefore, IE raises moral claims on every interacting agent, which should guide and regulate their ethical decisions and behaviour in relation to other nodes whenever possible.

Universal trust means that every form of reality, simply because it is what it is, enjoys a minimum, initial, overridable right to exist and develop in a way that is appropriate to its nature. To simplify: according to a universal trust position, each node should take care of the whole network as much as possible.

Societal acceptance of the universal trust requires us to adopt a perspective that is as non-anthropocentric as possible, to make a disinterested judgement of moral situations. When such an epistemic virtue is lacking, moral behaviour becomes less likely. Thus, the universal trust is respected whenever actions are impartial, universalisable, and caring towards the entire world. These actions are easier to carry out the more a society's ethical infrastructure facilitates good action and hinders bad action. This is the topic of the next chapter.

Chapter 11
Infraethics

When politicians talk about infrastructure today, a true sign of our times is that they often, and rightly so, have information and communication technologies (ICT) in mind. From business success to cyber conflicts, what makes an information society work depends increasingly on bytes rather than atoms. Whether societies can grow and prosper depends on the digital infrastructure at their disposal. At the same time, these very ICTs often constitute one of societies' weakest flanks, in terms of the possibility and harm of cyber-attacks. All of this is evident. What is less clear, and more philosophically intriguing, is that ICTs have led to both infraethics and the idea of a fundamental "equation" gaining in importance. Let us consider how, and in what sense.

ICTs have emphasised crucial phenomena such as accountability, intellectual property rights, net neutrality, privacy, transparency, and trust. The best way to understand these phenomena is probably to conceive of them in terms of a platform or infrastructure of social norms, expectations, and rules, often only socio-cultural and unwritten, which facilitate or hinder the moral or immoral behaviour of the agents involved. Thus, ICTs place our informational relations and interactions at the centre of our lives in a meaningful way. In so doing, they reveal an aspect of our lives that has always been present but was much less visible in the past: the fact that moral behaviour is also a matter of "ethical infrastructure", or what I have termed *infraethics*.

The Green and The Blue: Naive Ideas to Improve Politics in the Digital Age, First Edition.
Luciano Floridi.
© 2024 John Wiley & Sons Ltd. Published 2024 by John Wiley & Sons Ltd.

The idea of infraethics is not complicated, but it can be confused with other, similar ideas. The following "equation" may help to clarify it. In the same sense in which, in an economically mature society, a business, finance, or management system requires ever-better physical infrastructures (transports, communications, services, etc.) to succeed; likewise, in a mature information society, human interactions increasingly require good infraethics to flourish. Economic affairs are to infrastructure what ethical affairs are to infraethics. This is the simple "equation" I mentioned above: [economy: infrastructure = ethics: infraethics].

The "equation" is more than a simple analogy between infrastructure and infraethics, for the following reason. When economists and political scientists refer to a "failed state", they often mean a state that no longer performs its fundamental roles, such as exercising control over its borders, collecting taxes, enforcing laws, administering justice, providing education, and so on. Alternatively, they may be referring to the collapse of state infrastructure and the consequent failure to enable or foster an environment for the expected and desired kind of social interactions. In such a scenario, they refer to how the very foundations of society have failed. This is seen primarily in the collapse of shared ways of living together, in terms of economic, political, and social conditions, which include the rule of law, respect for civil rights, a sense of political community, the ability to have a respectful and honest dialogue between people with different mentalities or conflicting opinions, ways of reaching peaceful resolutions of disagreements, and so on. All these attitudes, expectations, rules, norms, and practices—in short, this implicit "socio-political infrastructure" that can be taken for granted—provide the vital humus for the success of any complex society. As I wrote earlier, infraethics has a fundamental role in human interactions, comparable to that we commonly attribute to good physical infrastructures with respect to a thriving economy.

I alluded earlier to the risk that infraethics could be confused with other, similar ideas. I specifically mean that the economic analogy can be misleading because infraethics should not be understood according to Marxist theory, as if it were an updated version of the old idea of "structure and superstructure". The elements in question are entirely different. On the one hand, there are moral or immoral actions, and on the other, there are the not-yet-ethical *facilitators* of such actions. A further difference is that infraethics is not meant to be understood conceptually, only in terms of a second-order or meta-ethical discourse on ethics. Instead, infraethics is a not-yet-ethical but ethically-relevant framework that can facilitate or hinder evaluations, decisions, actions and situations, which then qualify as ethical or unethical. At the same time, it would also be inaccurate to think that an infraethics is morally neutral or has *merely* a dual value, that is, ethical vs. unethical. Because while it is true that every infraethics has a dual value, it is also true that this is always oriented in turn. It is the difference between a rope that does not move because no one is pulling it and a taut rope that does not move because two people are pulling it in opposite directions. In the second case, tension is high, and equilibrium is fragile. If the value of infraethics (which is like a tightrope) were to be only neutral and not dual, this would mean that infraethics would bear no influence on either ethical or unethical behaviours. Yet, this mere logical possibility is utterly unrealistic. In the philosophy of technology, it is now commonly accepted that design, in any context, including a societal one, is never ethically neutral. Rather, it always implicitly embodies some values. However, this does not mean that an infraethics simply has a dual value or use, as if it could both facilitate and hinder moral or immoral behaviour in equal measure, depending on other external factors. In the example of the tightrope, there is rarely a perfect balance: usually, one side pulls harder than the other. A textbook example of this alleged duality is a knife, which can save a life or kill someone. The duality of its very use means that its moral evaluation depends on the actor and the circumstances. This is true, but it does not get to the very essence of the duality of infraethics. To take the analogy further, not all knives are equal. The very short, blunt knife provided in a school cafeteria to spread butter has a use, to fulfil a particular purpose, that a butcher's knife can also fulfil, but with much less ease. A bayonet has a dual-use only theoretically, because it is designed to kill a human being, not cut bread, or spread butter. Similarly, any infraethics can have a perfectly balanced dual-use only in principle. If it is a good infraethics, its twofold nature is oriented towards facilitating the occurrence of what is ethically good. At best, infraethics is the oil that lubricates ethical mechanisms to function smoothly and correctly. For this reason, it is easy to conflate infraethics with ethics because they share an evaluative nature that can help good flourish or prevent evil from growing and taking root. An example may help to clarify the distinction and stress its importance. Imagine we wish to establish a reasonable balance between security and privacy. This is difficult to achieve not least because we need to establish first with which of the following tensions we are dealing:

a. within infraethics: security and privacy are interpreted as facilitators, which are in themselves non-ethical, i.e., both understood as part of the "pipes" that convey moral values or rights, or duties;

b. within ethics: security and privacy are interpreted as moral rights or values, i.e., both would be interpreted as the "water" in the "pipes" to use the same analogy;

c. between ethics and infraethics: interpreting security as a facilitator, i.e., a "pipe", while privacy is interpreted as a value, i.e., "water".

It is impossible to resolve some debates whenever (c) is the case. Thus, the debate on the right to privacy between the EU and the USA is complicated by the fact that they sometimes adopt two divergent understandings of privacy: one ethical, as a value (or "water") in the European case, and one infraethical, as an enabler (or "pipe"), in the American case.

As I mentioned earlier, in any discussion of the need for a human project to be not only meta-projective (a project for individual projects) but also social (collective or communal), every society—be it the city of Man or the city of God, to put it in Augustinian terms—pursues its own human project (even if only unconsciously), which it facilitates by adopting its own infraethics (even only implicitly), which itself may be more or less morally successful, and more or less hostile to evil. It follows that even an ideal society of angels, in which the nodes are all impeccable moral agents, still needs infraethical rules for *coordination*—so that the angels do not hinder each other or cancel out each other's efforts—*collaboration*—so that they might assign different tasks to ensure that their efforts converge—and *cooperation*—so that they all particpate in all stages of a process, designing it, developing it, owning it together. In other words, not even a society of angels can succeed if it is exclusively libertarian. Even such a society would require a well-thought-out social project and infraethics to support its development. From this, it follows that James Madison, one of the fathers of the American Constitution, was wrong (but only in part, as I will explain in a moment) when he wrote that "if men were angels, no government would be necessary" (*The Federalist*, No. 51, 1788).

Madison was (partly) wrong because his views assumed a purely negative anthropology, which was relevant in a frontier environment and inherited from Christian interpretations of original sin. This view of humanity had been well articulated and publicised by Hobbes in his *Leviathan* and *De Cive* (*homo homini lupus*). It was neither revised nor critiqued by Locke within the atomistic view of society as a mere aggregate of individuals (see the Aristotelian-Newtonian *Ur*-philosophy that continued in Thatcher's mentality). Nor did Kant modify it. Instead, he endorsed it. Consider, for instance, his famous text *Perpetual Peace*, in which he observes that a society of devils can function as long as they are intelligent and, therefore, able to moderate their behaviour according to mutual convenience. In reality, even a society of angels would still need some form of government, and therefore infraethics, in order not to get in the way of itself (e.g., with good deeds cancelling each other out), set common goals, coordinate its good deeds, and evaluate the degree of success in pursuing them. Furthermore, infraethics needs to be able to correct, when needed, the course of collective action, because what is good can always be better. The "we", in "we, the people" of the US Constitution is not equivalent to a complete register of all citizens, a mere aggregate of "me, you, Alice, Bob" and so on. Instead, the "we" implies a moral goodness that is entirely social and cannot emerge from individual moral goodness, for at least two reasons.

The first is that goodness is also the manifestation of ambitious actions: what "we, the people" can do and hope to achieve *together* as a group or community is much more than what individual and uncoordinated efforts can ever achieve. The angels still rely on an infrastructure to avoid nullifying their individual efforts and instead coordinate them, say, if they want to organise a party or push a car together that does not want to start. It is not always true that every little effort helps: if each angel pushes the car on their own, or if multiple angels push at different angles in an uncoordinated way, it will only be a waste of time and energy. A multiagent system, in which several angels successfully push the car in the same direction, needs coordination, collaboration, and cooperation. It needs rules not merely to avoid the worst (they are, after all, angels), but to achieve the best. After all, the C, in OECD stands for "cooperation", not "competition".

The second reason is that evil is also a question of *opportunity costs*, here understood as what could have been done, but was not. It is not just deeds that can be sinful, but also omissions and silences. Without comprehensive governance, the possibility of doing many good deeds that can be done only as a group will disappear, a cost that can be very high and ultimately unethical. It is one of the paradoxes of history, which could be called the *paradox of disorganised affluence*. The more a society becomes affluent, the more its members believe that they do not need social collaboration or cooperation. To put it bluntly: everyone thinks they need only to look after their own house and garden, with coordination being only a matter of not interfering with each other's projects. Politics starts relying only on the metaproject in support of compatible, individual projects. At the same time, the more a society develops, the more the problems it faces become complex, therefore requiring ever-higher levels of collaboration and cooperation to be solved.

More and more well-cooperative participants are needed to solve them: think of social or environmental problems. The result is that the more affluent and complex human society becomes, the higher its opportunity costs become. Evidence is provided by the risky "Minsky moments"[1] that become possible when good regulations supporting social action are lacking. The only way to solve this "paradox" is to create and subscribe to a human project that is not just a meta-project protecting individual projects, but is instead also a collective or community project, making the best out of *We the People* to overcome global challenges. This is the problem of *cooperation complexity* (*C-complexity*). Before seeing why Madison was only partly wrong, let me briefly explain it.

In science, there are many kinds of complexity: state complexity, Kolmogorov complexity, computational complexity, and programming complexity are among the best known. What I have in mind is related but slightly different from these four. By C-complexity I mean to refer to the degree of cooperation required among the resources needed to solve a problem. To simplify: it takes two to tango, so the C-complexity of tango is two. If push-starting a car takes the orchestrated effort of a driver and four more people pushing it, then the C-complexity of this problem is five. Now, some problems have a maximum degree of C-complexity if and only if they are unsolvable without the cooperation of the whole relevant network of agents. Global warming is a maximum C-complexity problem: it takes all to tango. So, one can reformulate the paradox I introduced above by saying more precisely that: the more affluent a society is, the less individuals in it feel the need to cooperate, yet the more the problems facing that society are C-complex, so the more individuals should cooperate to solve them. Sufficiently good locally and individually is not good enough globally and socially. That is why affluent societies need more, and not less politics, to counterbalance individualism in favour of more cooperation. Some of the most pressing problems of our time, in many ecosystems and societies, are part of a failure in the governance of the coordination complexity of our information societies. So, they are not just management problems but, first of all, governance problems. They can be solved only by a kind of governance understood as design, management and

---

[1] "A Minsky moment is a sudden, major collapse of asset values which marks the end of the growth phase of a cycle in credit markets or business activity." https://en.wikipedia.org/wiki/Minsky_moment.

care of the cooperation strategies that facilitate the growth and well-being of societies with a high degree of C-complexity, a point to which I shall return in the following chapters.

It is time to return to Madison. I anticipated that he was only partly wrong, because his famous phrase should be read in its context, in which Madison states that "if men were angels, no government would be necessary. If angels governed men, there would be no need for *external or internal controls* on government" (Ibid, my italics). The part in italics indicates that Madison refers to the need to structure government with checks and balances, and external and internal controls. With this in mind, one can then interpret his thinking more favourably: the point would not be that, in a society of angels, a government or an infraethics is unnecessary, as the first sentence incorrectly states, but rather that a government or infraethics designed based on an angelic anthropology would not be necessary. In other words, it is possible to interpret Madison as arguing not that, if we were angels, we would not need rules for coordination, collaboration, and cooperation, but instead that special controls and constraints on the *application* of such rules would be unnecessary. The line of argument runs as follows: if all men were angels, then the rulers and the ruled would always behave according to the correct application of the rules, meaning there would never be a need for controls and constraints. By analogy, Madison could be interpreted as saying that, if all human beings were angels, we would still need a highway code to coordinate driving behaviour, but not the police to enforce it.

I maintain that the first sentence of Madison's above-quoted comment is wrong, and that the best (or at least the most common) interpretation of it is that presented earlier, namely as if all law and social regulation were solely based on the dialectic between "crime and punishment" alone. However, it would also be wrong to reject the crucial importance of infraethics from a perspective that is not only libertarian but also anarchist. Here, the two positions share the same premises but draw different conclusions. According to an anarchist view, if human beings were angels, they would not need any government; but human beings are (at least sometimes) angels, and, therefore, they (at least sometimes) do not need any government. Both libertarians and anarchists seem to assume, wrongly, that what is considered to be morally good emerges spontaneously. This is not false, but it is not true enough, so to speak, because very little moral good can be achieved individually, without a shared infraethics or a government that supports, respects, and enforces it. The multiagent system of a society needs its own organisation and *gover-*

nance at the systemic level and not just at the atomic, individual level, precisely because society does not resemble an old Aristotelian-Newtonian cuckoo clock, but a network.

Let us now return to the *oriented dual-use* of infraethics, as we saw it in the knife analogy. It is reasonable to argue that a society of Nazi fanatics (an example used here just because of the considerable group uniformity, others would also work) could display a high level of trust, respect, reliability, fairness, privacy, transparency and also freedom of expression, openness, and fair competition, without any of that making them less evil from an ethical standpoint. Clearly, we want not only the successful affordances and constraints provided by the right infraethics but also the coherent combination between them and morally good values, such as civil rights. Using the previous analogy, one needs both the infrastructure of the pipes to work—that is, not to leak and to be clean, to make sure that the water that flows through them is safe to drink,—and then potable water. A good infraethics is insufficient; one also needs good values, i.e., a good axiology.

Infraethics is far from a necessary condition for ethics, which can, after all, develop without it. However, good infraethics has the function of supporting good ethics, and, thus, good values. For this reason, designing, maintaining, and continuously updating the infraethics we need is one of the crucial challenges for a mature information society, to make morally good actions and behaviours flourish, and diminish evil ones. It is also one of the reasons why, in terms of innovation, we have repeatedly seen that our age is the age of design rather than discoveries or inventions: in this case, designing the right infraethics that can support the desired human project.

When politicians talk about infrastructure today, they often need to deal not only with atoms and bytes but also with the very structures and values of infraethics as well. Above all, by addressing and improving these last two factors, politics can best support the right human project at the right time for a mature information society. For this to be so, as Kant argues, no person should ever be exploited merely as a means but should always be treated also as an end. This is the topic of the following two chapters.

Chapter 12
Human Interfaces

Everything, including ourselves, can be described in infinite ways. In a more formal context, this can be made clear and distinct[1] through a discussion of *levels of abstraction*.[2] Social scientists prefer to speak more vaguely in terms of "lenses", but the idea is essentially the same. Levels of abstraction do not aim to describe in *absolute* terms—is John a featherless biped? Or is he what his passport says he is? Or is he a combination of 60% water and 40% something else?—but rather to pose the question of whether and how well a given description fulfils its purpose compared with other descriptions. I introduced this consideration earlier when I compared the Moon, an open

---

[1] The reference to Descartes's *Meditations* is deliberate.

[2] A level of abstraction (LoA) can be imagined as an interface that allows certain aspects of an analysed system to be observed or described, while rendering other aspects opaque or even invisible. For example, a house can be analysed at the LoA of a buyer, an architect, a town planner, a plumber, and so on. LoAs are common in computer science, where systems are described at different LoAs (computational, hardware, user-centred, etc.). Note that LoAs may be combined into more complex sets and may be, but not necessarily, hierarchical, with a higher or lower "resolution" or granularity of information.

The Green and The Blue: Naive Ideas to Improve Politics in the Digital Age, First Edition. Luciano Floridi.

umbrella, and a pizza, stating that there is a level of abstraction at which all three things can be grouped together because they are round. As I explained, the real question is whether the level of abstraction (in this case, roundness) is relevant and leads to any interesting insights.

When we think there is only one way to describe something, it is usually because we take its purpose for granted. Thus, we may describe a given artefact as a "vehicle" because we assume that the specific function or purpose is static and immutable. However, this description could quickly change if, for instance, the artefact in question is the SS-100-X presidential limousine in which Kennedy was travelling when he was assassinated. Suddenly "vehicle" does not seem to be an adequate description, although it is not wrong. This is very much the linguistic function of "just": it is no longer "just" a vehicle. John is no longer "just" a featherless biped, nor "just" the sum of the details in his passport. This is because he is, above all, John Fitzgerald Kennedy, the 35th President of the USA, who was assassinated in 1963.

Returning to our discourse, it makes sense today to describe ourselves as information organisms, or *inforgs* for short, to understand why and how we can interact, flourish, develop, or suffer and harm each other, depending on the information flows in which we navigate and participate. As Vilém Flusser eloquently writes:

> The human being can no longer be seen as an individual but rather as the opposite, as a dense scattering of parts; he is calculable. The notorious Self is seen as a knot in which different fields cross, as in the way the many physical fields cross with the ecological, psychic, and cultural. The notorious Self shows itself not as a kernel but as a shell. It holds the scattered parts together, contains them. It is a mask (Flusser 2005), p. 324.

I agree. However, contrary to Flusser, we must be careful to endorse an *epistemological* and *relational* position, instead of an *ontological* and *absolute* one. By now, it should be clear that we are not "just" inforgs. Nobody is "just" a mask. Nobody is "just" something. Instead, the idea is that a level of abstraction (i.e., a perspective, or an interface) that describes us as inforgs is now preferable to a mechanistic description, for instance, to understand our identities, roles, behaviours, and interactions. Conceiving ourselves *also* as inforgs is a useful (and arguably more appropriate) approach to interpreting our human condition today. We are relational nodes in an information society, taking care of it and ultimately seeking to improve it.

To describe ourselves *also* as informational organisms that consume, produce, cultivate, curate, process, and share information while living in an environment also made of data, artificial agents, and computational processes, requires us to adopt an ecological perspective. When such a perspective can be applied in social, economic, and political terms, I would argue that we can upgrade our level of abstraction and understand ourselves not only as *inforgs* but also as *interfaces*. While the information we glean from doing so still arises from abstraction, it allows us to focus on a crucial, *functional* aspect that would otherwise remain hidden.

Describing ourselves as interfaces allows us to gain a deeper insight into several crucial phenomena that characterise our digital age and how we might manage it better. These phenomena include the transformation of politics into *marketing* (i.e., the *marketisation of* politics), as we shall see in more detail later in the book. The rest of this chapter offers several clarifications supporting this idea and reflects on some of its implications for political theory. In the next chapter, we will see why interpreting ourselves as interfaces is at odds with the idea of human dignity.

The initial point of the argument is quite simple (see Figure 12.1), although it soon becomes more complicated. We are all increasingly becoming *human interfaces*, by which I mean spaces of interactions between *agents* (human, artificial, or hybrid) who want something from us, and our *resources*, something that we possess and that these other agents want or desire (at the very least in theory) for themselves. These interactions aim to enable the effective and efficient *operation and control* of resources and the necessary *feedback* that helps agents optimise their operation and control (decision-making) processes.

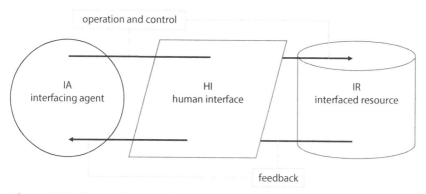

Figure 12.1 The basic model of a human interface.

While the transformation of people into human interfaces takes place in various contexts, three of these are crucial for the overarching theme of this book. First, in the world of *social media*, we serve as interfaces between them and our *personal data*. Second, in the world of *commerce*, we are interfaces between it and our *money* or *credit*. Third, we operate as interfaces between the world of *politics* and our *attention, consent,* and *vote*. I could continue, but these are the most important contexts. All three are interconnected and represent the social places (markets) where users, consumers, and citizens (on the supply side) play the role of interfaces to deal with the main demands being exercised by media, businesses (including advertising), and politics (two more examples will follow: education and welfare).

As mentioned above, describing ourselves as (also) interfaces makes it possible to clarify some crucial processes and offer a deeper insight into how such interfaces work and what could be done to change or improve them, when we do not like them or deem them unfit for purpose.

The first clarification concerns who, exactly, these interfaces are. It would be foolish to think that there is a fixed and immutable role between *them* and *us*, as if "they" were always the agents managing the interfaces, and "we" were always and only "just" the interfaces. In technical terms, "they" and "we" are indexical words, that is, their reference changes depending on the context in which they are used. In reality, "we" can also be "they", and vice versa, depending on circumstances. More specifically, as users, consumers, and citizens, we are also agents regularly using interfaces for a desired aim. By way of example, we might consider that social media act as an interface between us (the user) and their services; we (as consumers) use companies as interfaces between us and their products; and politics (or politicians or parties, the exact ontology does not matter here) serves as an interface between us (as citizens) and the society in which we would like to live. It is easy to become confused in this hall of mirrors (or, rather, hall of interfaces), but the point is simple: the roles in Figure 12.1 are fixed, but *who* plays what role, how long, and whether adequately or poorly, changes continuously, depending on the context. One final qualification needs to be made: since the human condition naturally tends to be egocentric, we generally find it easier to see ourselves as agents who use other parts of the world as interfaces to try to get what we want, rather than to identify ourselves as interfaces, that parts of the world use to get something they want from us. This natural human tendency towards egocentrism is exploited hugely by marketing strategies (more on these later), as they regularly seek to make each member of their audience feel the very centre of their attention. An entirely egocentric individual can hardly imagine being seen just as an interface used by others, to be manipulated and exploited for external gain. The current rhetoric of "disintermediation", and the plethora of *centric* design (or marketing), whether *user-centric*, *consumer-centric*, or *human-centric*, is a way of obscuring the fact that, in this new configuration, it is often us who become the intermediaries, the interfaces. For instance, L'Oréal's shift from "because I'm worth it" to "because you're worth it" is merely an update of the same marketing communication strategy intended to obscure the implicit philosophy behind it all, which is essentially saying "because you're the interface". An interface may feel important because it confuses being in the middle—between those who want something from it and what is wanted—with being at the centre.

The second clarification that emerges from seeing ourselves as interfaces concerns the equally crucial process of transforming people into interfaces, conceptually and factually. When we talk about converting some context into a market (henceforth *marketisation*), what should stand out is that what is at work is actually an *interfacisation* (the transformation into being used as interfaces) of the people involved in that context. For instance, the privatisation of a sector for projected macro-economic goals or the transformation of education into a market, with the ensuing supply and demand relations, means changing learners into customer interfaces. It also means converting companies, families, administrative organisations, and various educational institutions into interfacing agents (note that agents can be hybrid systems). This is ultimately because the drivers of marketisation are interested in manipulating learners (now the new customers) as interfaces that provide them with a quantifiable form of success that can be measured in outcomes, targets, standards, or training performance, for instance. In this newly transformed relation, success becomes the resource agents desire, and learners possess, accessible and exploitable through learners as interfaces. The more quantifiable a learner's education is, the more obtainable it becomes as a resource that can be understood and compared in terms of data, funding received, value for money, grades, credits, passed exams, labour market placements, and so forth.

Another critical example of *marketisation* and *interfacisation* today lies in promoting well-being and health care. Here *interfacisation* refers to how people are turned into interfaces between the agents providing the goods and services on one side, and the parameters determining a specific, predefined level of well-being or health on the other. For instance, think of the well-known advice to take 10,000 steps every day, which is, in reality, an entirely arbitrary target.

Note that, in this case, the roles between "they" and "we" are interchangeable (who is the interface for whom?), and agents can also be artificial. To put it dramatically, an app becomes the agent that uses Alice as an interface to achieve the target of a predetermined performance, the coveted resource. In this case, the standard meaning of user interfaces applies (i.e., visual information about an app), but it is important to note that the term can easily also refer to other interfacing agents (in this case, the user of the app). This plurality of meaning can lead to confusion. Finally, the game of cross-referencing different interfaces inevitably becomes complicated too, because an app can simultaneously be a commercial product and agent that is trying to obtain resources such as data, money, approval ratings, positive evaluations, and so on, using Alice as an interface.

Two steps are crucial in all the above cases. The first starts with moving from the marketisation of a context to the interfacisation of the people involved in this context. The second moves from the interfacisation phase to quantifying the success criteria to obtain the resource possessed by the interface in that context. People become like keypads on an ATM: if you type in the correct number sequence, you gain access to what you need or want, which is on the other side of the interface. If, in real life, Alice were to use "open sesame" as her password for a service, the joke would be on her, because fiction now increasingly meets reality. Alice becomes what she thinks she is describing, an interface, and to use her as such, all Bob needs to do is to treat her as an interface with a password.

Using humans as mere interfaces (to paraphrase the title of a famous book by Wiener, (Wiener 1954)) is not necessarily done with evil intent. The interfacisation process and using people as an interface can be done with the good of "human ATMs" in mind, for instance, to make people healthier or better educated. However, this is not entirely morally right either, as I will argue later and more extensively in the next chapter. What emerges is a third, ethical, clarification. Turning people (users, consumers, citizens, learners, patients, etc.) just into interfaces means disrespecting their intrinsic dignity and ignoring what is fundamentally ethically good for their inherent and individual nature. This contradicts the famous ethical principle, summarised by Kant in his formula of the categorical imperative, according to which one must always "act in such a way that you treat humanity, whether in your own person or in the person of another, always at the same time as an end and never simply as a means". The only difference in the present is that "treating people simply as a means" is equivalent to treating people simply as an interface. Manipulating someone, in the almost literal sense of key-padding an "interfacised" person to obtain something they possess or can provide access to, is perhaps the most common way of dehumanising a person, e.g., treating them as an enslaved person or a robot. That is why viewing ourselves as mere interfaces is, unfortunately, realistic in our information society but also causes us to shudder. This brings us to the fourth and final explanation of the processes revealed by seeing ourselves this way.

If we are increasingly becoming and treated like interfaces—regardless of the considerable and inevitable confusion this may cause, combined with the fact that it is ethically troubling and reprehensible—how exactly does the control and management of these interfaces work? This is a fundamental question *à la* Machiavelli (the Machiavelli of the *Discourses* (Machiavelli 2003)) because it is brutally realistic and pragmatic. Still, it is not *Machiavellian* (the Machiavelli of the *Prince*, (Machiavelli 2019)), or at least not yet, because the question is not posed with some cunning and cynical recommendation in mind about which ends justify which means. Neither is it a Kantian question, because it does not ask (again, at least not yet) how the situation can be improved from a moral point of view, from how things are to how they should be. The question requires an answer that provides an objective and not-yet-ethical understanding of the very situation itself. It invites us to investigate the mechanisms and logic behind the phenomenon, so we can subsequently transform them for the better. In short, asking this question privileges the epistemological and descriptive dimension over the ethical and normative one. Exploring and answering how the control and management of these interfaces works necessitates a separate discussion, which can be found in Chapter 17 on politics as marketing. Before we get to that point, it will be advantageous to address the Kantian question mentioned above: on what basis should we try to improve things from a moral perspective? The answer is: on the very foundation of what we understand by human dignity. The next chapter provides an articulation of this answer.

Chapter 13
Human Dignity

On 14 April 2016, the European Parliament approved the General Data Protection Regulation (GDPR). We encountered this EU law in Chapter 2 when discussing the disconnect (digital "cut") between territoriality and law. In the GDPR, the expression "human dignity" appears only once, in Article 88, which indicates that the regulations

> shall include suitable and specific measures to safeguard the data subject's *human dignity* [my italics], legitimate interests and fundamental rights, with particular regard to the transparency of processing, the transfer of personal data within a group of undertakings, or a group of enterprises engaged in a joint economic activity and monitoring systems at the workplace.
>
> *(Council of the European Union 2016)*

The quoted text presupposes two ontological ideas. First, the person concerned is a *natural person*, whose dignity must be safeguarded; a legal person cannot enjoy *human* dignity. Second, human dignity differs from "legitimate interests and fundamental rights". Both assumptions are correct, and the second is indicative of how the EU understands human dignity. Despite its barely perceptible presence in the GDPR, human dignity is the fundamental concept that provides the necessary framework to interpret what the GDPR— and more generally, European culture and jurisdiction—understands by *"informational privacy"*, i.e., the protection of personal data (henceforth simply privacy). The European interpretation is consistent with the concept's role in the 1948 Universal Declaration of Human Rights (Preamble and Article 1) and

The Green and The Blue: Naive Ideas to Improve Politics in the Digital Age, First Edition. Luciano Floridi.

the Charter of Fundamental Rights of the European Union. Let us consider the argument espoused by the European Data Protection Supervisor:

> [...] better respect for, and the safeguarding of, human dignity could be the counterweight to the pervasive surveillance and asymmetry of power which now confronts the individual. It should be at the heart of a new digital ethics. [...] Privacy is an integral part of human dignity, and the right to data protection was originally conceived in the 1970s and 80s as a way of compensating the potential for the erosion of privacy and dignity through large scale personal data processing.
>
> *(European Data Protection Supervisor 2015)*

I agree.[1] In the context of good politics, the protection of privacy should be *directly* based on the right to human dignity and not addressed indirectly, that is, through other rights, such as the right to property or freedom of expression. In other words, privacy should be grafted as a primary branch to the trunk of human dignity, not as a secondary branch, as if it were a separate right derived from an altogether different right.

The easiest and most effective way to graft the protection of privacy and human dignity together is to opt in favour of interpreting the protection of privacy in terms of the protection of personal identity. To clarify, this means that the possessive adjective "my" in "my data" has an entirely different value from the "my" in "my car" and is equivalent to the "my" in "my eyes". This is because personal information plays a constitutive role in who I am and can become. As we have seen in previous chapters, we now interpret individuals as their unique assemblage of information, (also) as inforgs. Protecting privacy means protecting individuals' very identity and nature as we conceptualised it today, in an information society.

The challenge is not to determine that privacy depends on human dignity (because this logical dependence appears to be solid), but that this dependence, once widely acknowledged, only serves to shift the problem further back, from explaining privacy to explaining human dignity. Unless one convincingly explains what human dignity actually is in an information society, exactly *which* interpretation of human dignity should be used to provide a foundation for privacy (as well as all other human rights) remains unclear. As Galileo said, one risks explaining *ignotum per ignotius*, that is, what is unknown (privacy) through what is even more unknown (human dignity). It is

---

[1] Disclosure: I was a member of the Ethics Advisory Group (EAG) organised by the European Data Protection Supervisor (EDPS) to formulate an ethical framework for the GDPR. This chapter is based on the work I did for the EAG.

evident that some considerable progress is required to gain the coherence necessary to protect our privacy in terms of human dignity.

To make this critical step, we must realise that what is at stake is nothing less than a *philosophical anthropology* (more on this in Chapter 21) directly addressing our times, i.e., a philosophical understanding of human nature applicable to the digital age and information society today. The stance we take on this new philosophical anthropology can lead to different notions of human dignity and, thus, different ways of defending privacy. However, any progress in taking this initial stance is still insufficient. It is necessary to admit that, no matter how much they may differ from one another, various philosophical anthropologies all share the same essential strategy and assumption: at their core, their interpretation of human dignity relies on the defence of some kind of anthropocentric human *exceptionalism*. Regardless of how they conceive of human dignity, its interpretation is ultimately the result of a shared philosophical anthropology that posits humanity as essentially different from every other species (indeed, from every other possible entity in the universe), which serves to justify humanity's status as one imbued with special consideration, dignity, and respect. Thus, the reasoning that unites the different positions on philosophical anthropology is that privacy must be protected because of human dignity, which itself must be protected because of human *exceptionalism*. This, in turn, requires a robust justification that cannot be taken for granted, especially considering the four successive revolutions that have decentralised us from the cosmological, biological, psychological, and informational spheres (see Chapter 7).

Keeping all this in mind, it now becomes understandable that—when people disagree about privacy and the meaning of human dignity—this disagreement is rooted in a philosophical anthropology that supports and barely questions human exceptionalism. This is not surprising. Four main philosophical anthropologies have contributed to the debate on human exceptionalism, at least in Western philosophy. In Greek and Roman philosophy, and especially in Aristotle and Cicero, human exceptionalism is based on human beings' unique and natural ability to exercise virtuous control over themselves (their passions, for instance) and their environment (especially animals). In Christian philosophy, and especially in Thomas Aquinas, human exceptionalism is based on the concept of divine creation that renders human beings in the image and likeness of God. In modern philosophy, especially that which followed the Enlightenment and Kant, human exceptionalism is justified because of the rational autonomy of human beings and their faculty of self-determination. Finally, in the postmodern era, human exceptionalism continues to be defended based on the capacity for the social and mutual recognition of each other's value.

The problem with these four philosophical anthropologies is that they are all weakened by their inherent anthropocentrism. Even Christianity (indeed all the three main Abrahamic religions) considers that God focuses exclusively on human affairs. However, as we have seen above, Copernicus, Darwin, Freud, and Turing consistently and repeatedly challenged this anthropocentric approach to human exceptionalism. Their research and discoveries made it clear that we are not at the centre of the cosmos, the biological web of life, the realm of reason, or the infosphere. So, if we are exceptional, we are not exceptional because of such traditional "centralities". If human exceptionalism is still defensible, it is probably so only "negatively" (*per via negativa*), from a perspective that emphasises our "eccentricity" and places our unique role in the universe at the periphery, in the marginal position of those who take care, not those who are being taken care of. From this viewpoint, "special", "unique", or "exceptional" means "anomalous" or "strange", extraneous to the ordinary course of nature, rather than "superior".

This perspective of the "eccentricity" of human beings' exceptional nature and role in the universe is far from new. It implies an ethics of care based on the decentralisation of the agent in favour of the patient (receiver) of moral actions. The gardener, the nurse, the teacher, the parent, the friend, the politician, the civil servant, the doctor, the lawyer, the team player, the colleague—when they act morally, they do so by putting the receivers of their actions at the centre of their interactions and placing themselves at others' service in a decentralised way. This is the altruistic, patient-oriented approach (as opposed to the agent-oriented approach) developed and defended in medical ethics, environmental ethics, bioethics, business ethics, and information ethics. Whenever a philosopher is caught talking about "listening" (think Heidegger) rather than "seeing" (e.g., Plato), this change of perspective from centricity to eccentricity may be assumed to have occurred. In the previous chapters, we have also seen that this ultimately produces an ethics of relations, fundamental to an ethics of care, which finally progresses from privileging the *relata* (the agent or the patient) to focusing on their relations. As an illustrative example, we are concerned with neither Romeo nor Juliet, but rather with their love.

Clearly, a decentralised approach to human exceptionalism is feasible and even preferable, and this presupposes that a defence of human dignity based on human exceptionalism is still plausible. What, then, is meant by human dignity, from an *anthropo-eccentric* point of view? Can an anthropo-eccentric interpretation of human dignity support the protection of privacy successfully *and* directly, without the mediation of separate rights?

The suggestion is that human dignity, from an anthropo-eccentric point of view that does not deny humanity's exceptionalism, resides in an absence, rather than in a presence; it is a subtraction as opposed to an addition. We are an incomplete species that desires, questions, doubts, worries over, and rejoices about the future and the possible, what could or could not be the case, what could have been and was not, what still might be. We may regret or feel nostalgia or *saudade* for the past. We are also the only species that can see both sides of the coin, has empathy even for people far away in time or space, and takes responsibility for its own life (at least partially). Other animals too, have rights, so they can be at the centre of an ethical consideration; but only we have duties, and so we must have ethical considerations for ourselves and others. We do not inexorably dwell in the here and now, like all other animals, but detach ourselves from the present through our hopes and fears, passions, memories and expectations, chatter, habits and laws, languages, traditions, religions, social structures, knowledge, stories, and so on. We are the incomplete species that cultivates semantic capital to provide ourselves with a sense of reality, which we always feel is somehow absent, although not to the extent that it drives us to insanity. Humanity is not the outcome of an overabundance of Being (almost in a Plotinian sense); it is Being's lacuna.

Such an "eccentric" vision of humanity is not entirely novel. Pico della Mirandola offers a similar perspective in his famous *Discourse on the Dignity of Man* (1486, 2003). The *Discourse* has been described as the manifesto of the Renaissance. Once stripped of its rhetorical trappings, its message is that human dignity is a perpetual work in progress, an unfinished text, or an open software, as we would say today. We are not at the top of the chain of Being, because we do not truly belong to it, and there is no place for us in that chain. We are not angels, nor are we brutes (or robots), because we can ultimately become either, neither, or both.

If we were to update the *Discourse*, we could say that we are the exception, like a *hapax legomenon*, i.e., a term that appears only once, in the book of nature, which, as Galileo said, is written in mathematical symbols. A *hapax legomenon* is an entirely natural, albeit exceptional, phenomenon. Our exceptionalism reveals itself in our unique and seemingly irreproducible way of being positively dysfunctional. We are nature's extraordinary anomaly, *the beautiful glitch*, in a universe-system that has fortuitously and probably uniquely generated a form of life that is most unlikely to occur again, and in the broader scheme of things, is undoubtedly anomalous and strange. We are endowed with consciousness, intelligence, a mental life, and self-determination. This is strange: clearly, we are the outliers. We are the lucky winners of the lottery of life.

I do not know of a word that precisely captures this "eccentric" interpretation of human exceptionalism, but I will use one that comes close: *polytropos*. It is the Greek word used by Homer to describe Odysseus in the first verse of the *Odyssey*: *polytropon*, "a man of twists and turns", to use Robert Fagles' beautiful translation. The prefix *poly* means "many", but *tropon* has a variety of meanings. These include "way" (as in "manner") or "mode", thus describing someone clever, shrewd, able to understand and take advantage of an opportunity, or find a solution to a problematic situation. It can also mean "path", as in "journey" or "trip", thus describing someone who has seen the world and may be streetwise, much-travelled and much-wandering; in other words, a man of the world. We use the word *trope* to refer to commonly recurring rhetorical and literary stratagems, or clichés in creative works, which were once ingenious but have now become overly familiar motifs because they have been visited and revisited too many times. It is the same word used in the *Hymn to Hermes* to describe the god as creator of fire and bringer of dreams, emissary and messenger of the gods, intercessor between them and us, protector of literature and poetry, invention, and trade—but above all *polytropos*, the astute and tireless traveller. Even in the *New Testament*, God speaks to us *polytropōs*, "in many ways" or "in various ways" (*Hebrews* 1:1). The semantic richness of this word comes in handy for our present task. For our *polytropic* predicament, this unique combination and meeting of old intelligence with a new openness, makes us exceptional in many brilliant and varied ways. Our "eccentric" status in the universe explains and justifies both our dignity, as a unique source of rights, and our destiny, as a unique source of duties, in the following sense.

As travellers, we are in the hands of our hosts: others, nature, the physical world, but also society, culture, and the world we build, as well as the world we find. None of us ever belongs to the centre: each individual travels incessantly, from centre to centre, without being at the centre, like Odysseus travelling from place to place without ever being of that place. Ontologically speaking, we are all stateless persons. Thus, we should enjoy the universal *right* to be welcomed with hospitality and protection. As a beautiful glitch, we are all fragile, flexible, and malleable entities, inforgs whose lives are essentially made up of information and constantly reworked relations. Our dignity lies in our ability to be the masters of our journeys while keeping our identities and choices open to our control, preferences, decisions, and various influences. Any technology or policy that tends to close, shape, or fix perimeters around this inherent openness, as if we were just rigid interfaces, risks dehumanising us and degrading our dignity, not unlike the guests of Circe, who are forbidden to leave her island. Thus, conceived in terms of *polytropy*, human dignity provides an anthropo-eccentric foundation on which to build the right to privacy in terms of human dignity, and the individual control of, and responsibility for, our constitutive information. Most of our selves, understood as narratives, are written by other authors; we must carefully protect and uphold what remains private to us, with the awareness that we can strategically use this information to contribute to these various narratives about ourselves.

As travellers, we also have *duties* towards our guests when welcomed to a place: care and respect for others, whether human, animate, or inanimate. By this, I mean that we should uphold an ethics of care and respect for the whole network and all the nodes that welcome and support us. The universal trust (Chapter 10) implies a duty to care for the world we inherit from past generations and leave to future generations. This is the counterpart to our right to privacy. The duty of caring and the right to privacy turn out to be, somewhat surprisingly, two sides of the same coin. This is a distinguishing feature of being human: we can care beyond our own needs and impulses. A private life complements a caring life. This brings me to my last two comments.

First, compared with the other four philosophical anthropologies, it seems clear that only an anthropo-eccentric approach can provide an interpretation of human exceptionalism sufficiently robust to justify protecting privacy, which is directly grounded in the concept of human dignity. Consider the consequences of not respecting privacy based on the various interpretations of human dignity. They would all imply the violation of human dignity, but in what terms, exactly? In Greek and Roman philosophy, it would amount to a kind of harm to human beings' natural and unique ability to exercise virtuous control over themselves and their environment. This hardly seems to be the case today, however. In Christian philosophy, it would be equivalent to damaging a person's divine existence in the image and likeness of God. Yet this is clearly irrelevant to what we mean by protecting privacy today. In fact, Augustine speaks out quite firmly against privacy for the opposite reason: he argues that good people have nothing to hide from God or others. It sounds familiar. In modern philosophy, a violation of human dignity would be equivalent to attacking the rational autonomy of human beings and infringing on their ability for self-determination. This seems much more convincing, insofar as a *perceived* lack of privacy could influence individuals' choices and behaviours and constrain their autonomy. However, modern philosophy does not reveal anything about hidden (and hence unperceived) privacy violations, which also affect our *politics*. Indeed, autonomy would still be possible in a world without any privacy, precisely in the sense in which Augustine argued for a lack of need for privacy in a society where no person should hide anything from an omniscient God. In postmodern philosophy, the need for mutual recognition may even promote a *lack* of privacy, and this explains why sometimes we care so little about what we share online: to be recognised is to be public, and some people are ready to sacrifice any privacy to increase their public visibility and recognition. Privacy violations impact (an epistemological) ontology that understands human identity as *constituted* by information (i.e., inforg) and human dignity as a matter of *polytropy*. If, from an anthropo-eccentric point of view, human exceptionalism is based on the peculiar status of human beings as informational organisms—in essence, lacking permanent equilibrium, but constantly becoming themselves by reworking their constitutive information—then a complete lack of privacy inevitably dehumanises the individual in question. Such a violation would prevent the essential detachment (or "eccentricity") from the world that drives human life, makes it flourish, and puts us in a position to take care of the world. It would eliminate the special gap between the world and the mind, that enables the latter to construct a self-identity and a sense of reality. It would remove the grain of sand that gives rise to the pearl. It would pin down a life that is inherently open onto the fixed mounting board of a profile, like a needle used by a lepidopterist to pierce a once-fluttering butterfly. Zero privacy dehumanises.

This brings us to my last comment. Suppose our analysis remains at a level at which we talk about humanity as a whole, that is, as a single generalised entity. In that case, inevitably, human dignity is discussed in general terms that disregard individuals, Alice or Bob. The same happens with human destiny. However, a fundamental aspect emerges if we take a closer perspective and interpret persons individually, as open subjects, not just as a whole. If Alice and Bob meet and both place themselves at the periphery of their interactions, centralising each other, an endless and pointless dialectic seems to emerge, like two well-mannered people who, meeting in front of a restaurant, insist that the other should enter first. They could both remain outside. This sterile stalemate is a risk, but it is not inevitable, because we have seen that the decentralisation of agents can have the benefit of centralising their relations. In real life, we are all both agents and patients, not just one or the other, and thus our focus should be on relations, not on *relata*, as discussed earlier. Onto-centrism (the centrality of Being) should be interpreted—given an ontology that privileges relations instead of relata—as a Ratio-centrism (the centrality of relations, I am using "ratio" as "relation" not as reason, in this sense one could also speak of Logo-centrism, but this would have strong theological overtones). One cannot authentically place oneself at the centre, one can only be placed at the centre by the other. But from an external perspective, when it comes to the I-thou dialectic, the only element that remains central is their relation. So, at the core of an ethical discourse, we do not talk of the centrality of the spouses but of their marriage, to which they both "eccentrically" contribute. It is not one of the friends at the centre, but their friendship. Not one of the parties, but politics. Not any of us, but our society. The two people outside the restaurant can enter together as a couple. The centrality of relations is, in privacy terms, good news, because respect for personal information does not have to imply promoting secretive and solipsistic lives. Instead, it can be the basis of a society that supports and centralises the value of relations as the sum of the voluntary and fruitful contribution of those who constitute it from their peripheral position. Part of this contribution manifests itself in the experiential enrichment of one another. When this process is not only semantic but also economic, we can speak of an economy of experience. The next chapter analyses it in terms of leisure occupation.

Chapter 14
The Problem of Leisure Occupation

In 1930, John Maynard Keynes published a masterpiece that should be compulsory reading for any educated person, a short essay entitled: *Economic Possibilities for our Grandchildren* (Keynes 1930, 1972).[1] It was an effort to see what life would be like if peace, prosperity, and scientific and technological developments became increasingly prominent aspects of future human society. Obviously, things turned out differently from the ideas espoused in his essay. The Great Depression and the Second World War were soon to follow. Other disasters, conflicts, and crises awaited humanity in the following decades. The essay became recognised as a philosophical exercise relegated to collecting dust in libraries. However, the fact that history took such terrible and tragic steps following its publication does not detract from Keynes' brilliant insights.

---

[1] All references are from the 1931 online version of (Keynes 1930) provided by Project Gutenberg, so pages are left unspecified. I am sure Keynes would have found such free access to information coherent with the philosophy of the essay.

The Green and The Blue: Naive Ideas to Improve Politics in the Digital Age, First Edition.
Luciano Floridi.
© 2024 John Wiley & Sons Ltd. Published 2024 by John Wiley & Sons Ltd.

The essay has much to teach a generation that has never seen enemy tanks on the streets of Berlin, Paris, or Rome and will celebrate the centenary of the end of the Second World War, primarily in terms of what we want to achieve in the future, our *human project*.

According to Keynes, at roughly the time of the Renaissance, the combination of techno-scientific development, capital growth, and the mechanism of compound interest caused a sudden change in history, after which the rate of improvement in standards of living began to accelerate steadily and progressively. *If* left undisturbed (the italics is vital, because Keynes knew very well that this conditional was often a counterfactual, today we only need to remember the pandemic, the war in Ukraine, or climate change), those three factors were sufficient to solve:

> the economic problem, [that is] *the struggle for subsistence*, [...] the *primary, most pressing problem of the human race*—not only of the human race, but of the whole of the biological kingdom from the beginnings of life in its most primitive forms [my emphasis].

Keynes believed that the economic problem would not be eliminated for at least another hundred years, but that progress towards its solution was incremental, resilient, and relentless, precluding the possibility of return. So, he argued that society's economic problem, despite its magnitude and significance, is not humanity's "permanent problem". He was right, at least in principle. Nature and human foolishness may, of course, wreck any attempt to solve our economic problem. But, barring any major disaster, either accidental or self-inflicted, safe and sustainable techno-science, a sound economy, and decent politics may one day defy the curse so well formulated in *Genesis 3:17–19*:

> Cursed is the ground because of you;
> through painful toil you will eat food from it
> all the days of your life.
> It will produce thorns and thistles for you,
> and you will eat the plants of the field.
> By the sweat of your brow
> you will eat your food.

Neutralising Genesis' curse is a sound plan. In fact, it was always *the* plan, a crucial part of any human project. Because Genesis 3:17–19 can be interpreted as nothing other than the first step in a de-bugging strategy that explicitly identifies the problem inherent in Nature that needs to be fixed. Solving the economic problem has been part of the human project since day one. It was the plan when we invented the wheel and the plough. It was still the plan even when we plundered, pillaged, killed, raped, and enslaved each other. For millennia, we did not have the necessary resources to overcome society's economic constraints, and we often squandered the few resources we had painfully accumulated. We had to wait for the right breakthroughs in science, technology, and capital, and the investment and exploitation of billions of hours of accumulated human labour. These combined assets started bearing fruit at the beginning of the modern era, leading to Keynes' reflections in the 1930s. By then, as Keynes wrote, there was "no harm in making mild preparations for our destiny".

However, the economic problem is entangled with a second problem, which Keynes, with remarkable insight, called "technological unemployment". Solving this, too, has always been part of the human project:

> We are being afflicted with a new disease of which some readers may not yet have heard the name, but of which they will hear a great deal in the years to come— namely, *technological unemployment.* This means unemployment due to our discovery of means of economising the use of labour outrunning the pace at which we can find new uses for labour. But this is only a *temporary phase of maladjustment* [my emphasis]. All this means in the long run *that mankind is solving its economic problem* [emphasis original].

It should be remembered that Keynes wrote this in 1930. Turing was 18 years old at the time and had just failed to win a scholarship to Trinity College Cambridge (fortunately, he would be awarded one the following year to King's College, Keynes' same college, as it happens). The idea of a computer was not even on the horizon, let alone any fear that computers might eventually steal people's jobs. Robots pertained to the realm of science fiction. Yet Keynes was prescient. Today, the agricultural sector employs fewer and fewer people, and if employment in industry is still growing globally, it is decreasing or stabilising in developed economies and the EU. The picture is even starker in the USA, where the shares of employment in agriculture and manufacturing have declined sharply since the 1950s, to less than 2% and less than 10%, respectively, with close to 90% of jobs to be found in tertiary services and government.

As Keynes expected, almost everybody now deals with software, very few with hardware, and nearly nobody with bioware, in mature information societies. For instance, in the USA, between 2009 and 2019, 79.41% (increasing) of the workforce was employed in services, 19.18% (decreasing) in industry, and only 1.41% (stable) in agriculture. In the same period, the amount of leisure time grew steadily. On average, there is greater life expectancy and less poverty. Enormous and rapid shifts in the labour force from one sector to another, within a few decades, have turned "technological unemployment" into a macroscopic issue. However, following Keynes, we should be aware not to mistake this issue for the fundamental problem that deserves our greatest attention. Keynes envisaged this third and deeply embedded problem as a direct consequence of technological unemployment. Today it is more prevalent than ever and a most significant component of the human project. Let me call it the problem of *leisure occupation*:

> Thus we have been expressly evolved by nature—with all our impulses and deepest instincts—for the purpose of solving the economic problem. If the economic problem is solved, mankind will be deprived of its traditional purpose. [...] Thus for the first time since his creation man will be faced with *his real, his permanent problem—how to use his freedom from pressing economic cares, how to occupy the leisure*, which science and compound interest will have won for him, to live wisely and agreeably and well [my emphasis].

Today, we have the welcome, if painful, evidence that the economic problem is being solved, albeit with various costs. Technological unemployment is fundamentally what we have been planning all along, relying on animals, other humans' labour, science, technology, capital, compound interest, discoveries and inventions, entrepreneurship and innovation. We have been trying to make ourselves redundant since time immemorial so that we may devote our time to leisure. We have worked hard in order not to work anymore. But now that this historic opportunity is being enjoyed by, or at least within reach of, a growing number of people during increasingly extended periods of their lives, we have been caught remarkably unprepared. Those who enjoy free time the most are often the worst investors of it. We waste or even "kill" it, seemingly oblivious of previous generations' immense efforts and sacrifices to place us in such fortunate circumstances. The old and primal Adam does not know how to cope with his regained corner of paradise, as Keynes discusses:

> It is a fearful problem for the ordinary person, with no special talents, to occupy himself, especially if he no longer has roots in the soil or in custom or in the beloved conventions of a traditional society. To judge from the behaviour and the achievements of the wealthy classes today in any quarter of the world, the outlook is very depressing! For these are, so to speak, our advance guard-those who are spying out the promised land for the rest of us and pitching their camp there. For

they have most of them failed disastrously, so it seems to me—those who have an independent income but no associations or duties or ties—to solve the problem [of leisure occupation, my addition] which has been set them. I feel sure that with a little more experience we shall use the new-found bounty of nature quite differently from the way in which the rich use it today, and will map out for ourselves a plan of life quite otherwise than theirs. For many ages to come the old Adam will be so strong in us that everybody will need to do some work if he is to be contented. We shall do more things for ourselves than is usual with the rich today, only too glad to have small duties and tasks and routines. But beyond this, we shall endeavour to spread the bread thin on the butter—to make what work there is still to be done to be as widely shared as possible. Three-hour shifts or a fifteen-hour week may put off the problem for a great while. For three hours a day is quite enough to satisfy the old Adam in most of us!

In the leisure society, the risk is that countless people will be bored and demotivated, undecided about what to do with their free time, weekends, vacations, bank holidays, and retirement. We may turn into the "idle creatures" that Flavius describes in Shakespeare's *Julius Caesar* who, "being mechanical, [...] ought not walk upon a labouring day".[2] The mildly optimistic reply is that some people will learn to live a life of leisure worth living (education is the key here). Those who will not, may still be left with the opportunity of making the most of their leisure if they wish. Civilisation also means the freedom to be a couch potato. Unfortunately, two further problems will become increasingly pressing. Keynes does not discuss them in his essay, but they are clearly visible today.

In the long run, in the next century or next millennium, technological unemployment will progress into leisure occupation only if we successfully manage to decouple unemployment from a lack of income, from the consequent social unrest generated by unemployment (which is mainly a protest about the lack of income, rather than the lack of a job), and from the related erosion of personal dignity, insofar as having a paid job is still seen in our current culture as being indicative of having a role and purpose in society. Let us call this the *resource problem*. In other contexts, Keynes argued that solving the resource problem was possible and worth striving for. I agree unreservedly. A society in which a minimal and basic degree of financial independence and social welfare is guaranteed to all citizens will eventually shift the

---

[2] Shakespeare, *Julius Caesar*, Act 1, Scene 1, 1–4.

existential problem of purpose from the lack of occupation (unemployment) to inoccupation (non-employment). But for this to happen, the problem of inequality will have to be solved.[3] For as long as our society is organised in such a way as to promote and privilege rare "local maxima", i.e., a few immense accumulations of staggering wealth, the leisure society will remain a utopia for the vast majority. A cynic may then see the worrying growth in inequality as a way of saving the masses from having to deal with the genuinely permanent problem of existential purpose. In rhetorical and colourful terms: "make those idle creatures starve, and they will not wonder about the meaning of life". To argue thus is a silly idea that nobody should entertain, given its inconsistency with social justice, equality, and cohesion. The solution lies instead in finding and creating a better design of the mechanisms that facilitate the distribution of wealth. In other words, to make a leisure society truly possible, we need to base it on a better redesign of the labour and tax system that minimises the occurrence of local maxima, as witnessed by the current debates on inequality and tax reform in many developed countries.

Consequently, what emerges is the *political problem* that we need to address in order to make the shift to a fulfilling leisure economy possible. As "idle creatures", we risk transforming what could be a "liberal and leisure society" into an "illiberal lazy society", in which the Biblical "painful toil" is substituted by shallow entertainment as the ultimate source of existential distraction. It may seem a merely philosophical point, or even a problem worth having. But underestimating the risk of a society in which focused political engagement is discouraged means being less able to explain (and hence find an adequate answer to) why liberal and democratic improvements may not correlate to the economic growth of a society. "Bread and games" (*panem et circenses*) has been a successful strategy to instil political *appeasement* and mass distraction whenever those in power have had the means to afford it, way before its dystopian description in Huxley's *Brave New World*. Today, *panem et circenses* translates into a specific threshold at which unemployment ceases to be considered a problem when an acceptable level is reached in the growth of national gross domestic product (GDP), or

---

[3] For a short and very accessible criticism of inequality in the USA, the reader may wish to consult (Stiglitz 2011). The article is discussed slightly more technically in (The Economist 11 April 2011), negatively, and in (The Economist 15 April 2011) positively. I agree with the latter.

when living standards keep increasing, hopes for a better life for oneself or at least one's children are kept alive, if not fulfilled, and social unrest is avoided. This veneer of satisfaction means that democratic, liberal demands are postponed, and various forms of illiberalism begin to be ignored or tolerated, as China demonstrates. Democracy does not follow economic exchanges, trade, business relations and financial interdependence, as Germany (and EU in general) hoped when interacting with Russia, but rather economic discontent and social frustration, as China rightly fears. People take risks against autocratic regimes when they have nothing to lose and are desperate (i.e., hopeless), not when their future keeps improving and they are hopeful.

The human project that we have long been pursuing, to arrive at a liberal, democratic, leisure society, requires first solving society's economic problem through technological unemployment, sustainable growth, and equitable redistribution of wealth. In this new design for society, education supports people to use their time (encouraging them to stay in the educational system, and life-long learning experiences), to make the most of it (by learning and acquiring highly qualified skills for increasingly specialised jobs), and to enjoy it (by finding fulfilling activities and appreciating their leisure time). This is not a utopian blueprint, but part of the human project that deserves all our efforts and attention.[4]

If we have the wrong human project in mind, we end up misinterpreting technological unemployment as a curse, when, in fact, the true curse is that of having to eat bread earned "by the sweat of one's brow". When technological unemployment is misunderstood as the primary problem, the solution that emerges is to prevent it or mitigate its consequences at all costs.

Experts agree that, if properly designed, consumption taxes encourage savings and can contribute to economic growth. I would add that they can also shape more sustainable consumption patterns. For all these reasons, indirect consumption taxes, such as sales or value-added taxes, are ordinary in Europe and likely to increase. It is crucial that they are levied in a significantly progressive way. Even traffic fines reflect the recipient's income in Finland. However, it seems contradictory to propose tax consumption as an alternative to income or capital taxation when we need to find the right balance between the two to deal with economic growth and navigate towards a more equitable

---

[4] The idea is consistent with what has been argued in economics by (Brynjolfsson and McAfee 2014). For a philosophical approach see (Floridi 2014).

welfare system and a better redistribution of wealth. It is possible to reduce income inequality while stimulating economic growth. Both measures are needed simultaneously to progress towards the "leisure society" and the realisation of our human project. Keeping minimum wages so low that it is less expensive to employ human workers than robots, for instance, or taxing people solely on what they consume, rather than on what they earn, own, or inherit, would damage innovation (including technological innovation), and fail to improve the human condition.

We live in a world where digital systems are increasingly taking care of various tasks for us, often better than we can do them ourselves. We have seen that, like fish in water, digital technologies are the true natives of the infosphere, a space that is natural to them and in which they swim freely. We, as analogue organisms, dive into the infosphere, trying to adapt to a new environment of online and offline experiences, and often living in a hybrid *onlife*. This is particularly significant in the world of work, where we are joined and often replaced by increasingly flexible, effective, and efficient solutions, apps, robots, algorithms, and smart systems. The more we digitise the world, the more we share it with digital systems that behave as if we were not there. They are advancing, occupying, and performing tasks in more and more areas of work once considered impossible to automate: translating, writing articles, creating new images, reading X-rays, cooking, buying and selling shares, driving vehicles, cleaning floors, mowing grass, etc. At a superficial level, we seem to be on the back foot, in a seemingly futile and losing battle of resistance. In reality, things are different.

Work cannot be assessed as a finite quantity, as if it were a cake, such that, if a robot takes some of it away, then there will be less for people. Just think of housework: there is always work to be done, and, if we stop, it is because we have run out of resources, including time, energy, patience, and money. The threshold at which work is considered economically valuable—i.e., work worth doing because of a salary or some profit—is not fixed but shifts thanks to technology. Think of, say, how many new job opportunities eBay has generated. Rather than destroying it, digital technologies, including AI, are actually reshaping economically valuable work. Many jobs will continue to disappear, others will transition into different tasks and perhaps be reallocated—thanks to technology, I am now the one who scans the can of beans at the supermarket—and many others will doubtless emerge. The main problem is not the extent of this inevitable metamorphosis, which is difficult to predict, like its speed, but which is there for all to see. It is the fact that the digital revolution is causing these transformations to occur within a matter of decades, whereas the effects of the agricultural revolution took millennia to develop, and those of the industrial one centuries. Society is struggling to adapt to this unprecedented rate of change with the required flexibility in such a short time. It will need more time. As a result, social interventions will probably be necessary to protect those who will pay for the cost of the transition. We will have to anticipate some of these benefits today, borrowing from the future. This teaches us at least two important lessons about ourselves.

The first lesson starts with a recognition that AI is fundamentally an oxymoron. We saw that AI's success has not been attained because of the much dreamed of (or sometimes feared) marriage between biology and engineering, intelligence and machines, but because of the divorce it has instigated between the ability to perform a task successfully and the relative intelligence that would be required to do so. For instance, if I cut the grass, I need some intelligence to do it, but if a *robotic lawnmower* cuts the grass, then intelligence is not required, and I can get on with another job where it is still irreplaceable, like pruning the roses. For the first time in human history, we have put a permanent wedge between *acting successfully* and *acting intelligently*. As a result of this disconnect (another digital "cut"), we will increasingly need human intelligence to design, develop, use, and manage the digital. Sci-fi films such as *Terminator*, in which a superior *intelligence* comes to dominate the world and make us an obedient and submissive species, are just Hollywood entertainment. The real risk of the divorce set in motion by AI between agency and intelligence is that it dangerously dovetails with the laziness that is symptomatic of our *panem et circenses* politics. In this scenario, our unlimited capacity for adaptation may lead us to a society in which we are unable to cope or live fulfilling lives. We can avoid this scenario by ensuring that the design, control, and responsibility for digital systems and their operations remain strictly within the realm of human decision-making, and the latter is guided by the right values. This is, for instance, where the current debate on the EU legislation about data protection (the GDPR) and AI (AI Act) comes in. The GDPR, correctly interpreted, is supposed to guarantee the so-called "right to an explanation" for anyone affected by decisions made by fully automated artificial systems, as in the case of approval of a mortgage, or when the determination of a penalty is based solely on an algorithm. The AI Act should make auditing of AI systems the new normal.

The second lesson that the transformations caused by digitisation can teach about us concerns the idea of work as an ennobling activity, which identifies and shapes an individual. We define ourselves in multiple ways, but one of the most significant definitions is *homo poieticus*: the species that designs, builds, and modifies its habitat in boundless and ever more complex ways. The digital seems to steal this vital part of our essence through technological unemployment. Shakespeare, however, seemingly disagreed. When he speaks of "mechanical people", he always does so in a derogatory way. It is an ancient story: we must not confuse a *busy* life with a *working* life. We have seen that the Book of Genesis reminds us that while the sweat of the brow characterises us, it does so as a sign of punishment for our original sin. Ancient philosophy often sings the praises of *otium* as the best way for each of us to spend our lives. The story of work ennobling persons also has distant roots, but it only takes its form as a taken-for-granted idea, and becomes part of our uncritical modern *Ur-philosophy*, thanks to a mixture of Protestantism, the industrial revolution, new social classes of working-class and middle-class people, the decline of monarchies and their aristocracies, and the emergence of the world of business and productivity as values. Bourgeoise, consumerist modernity has convinced us that the *fruitful engagement* of our time is met in its *productive use*. Thus, we have become accustomed to thinking that a job or even a salary is the measure of a person's worth, without which that person is useless. Retiring becomes the end of our role, personal identity, and social value. We become irrelevant. Yet this is a flawed philosophical anthropology; after all, we never worked in Paradise. A positive effect of automation is that it pushes us towards the need to rethink these values. It is a lengthy process, which brings us to another crucial contemporary debate, that of the universal *basic income*.

Human history has finally reached the stage where it is possible to reason in a non-utopian way about the possibility that, one day, our work will not determine us and that everyone may be "pre-retired" from the beginning, in the sense that what we dedicate ourselves to will not be dictated by the necessity of survival, but by the life choices we want to make. In terms of a universal basic income, there are many reasonable objections. Some experiments have failed. So much so that, towards the end of this book, I will instead talk about *citizenship capital*. However, I am convinced that the universal *basic income* is not a dystopian vision. It would mean redistributing the enormous wealth accumulated (and that will keep accumulating) through the hard work and sacrifice of countless generations before (and after) us. The right to work may be part of the social contract but, eventually, we may see a right not to work as part of the universal trust. If this seems too far-fetched, consider that it may be because today we are still used to think that a salary is determined, among other things, by how many people can do a job, not how many people want to do it, and yet, in the future, things may change. If a job is rewarding, flexible, enjoyable, enriching, prestigious and so forth, it will no longer be counterintuitive to see it attract a lower salary than a job that is thankless, tiring, boring, unpleasant, and so forth.

Clearly, the scale of redistribution constitutes a vision of the future that cannot be realised immediately. We should ensure that we proceed equitably and gradually, for instance, by slightly reducing the number of working hours, granting a few extra days of holiday, or providing more flexibility in terms of smart working. This is reasonable, after all,

> the world's largest-ever trial of a four-day work week was a success, with most companies involved deciding not to return to the five-day tradition. Around 2,900 workers and 61 companies in Britain, ranging from banks to fast-food restaurants, said employee turnover and stress mostly fell while productivity remained flat or rose. Many bosses made workdays more efficient by cutting back on meetings. *The Economist*[5]

Nobody could convincingly argue that the *otium* generated by such a redistribution policy would be the father of all vices. In fact, the opposite is true: our leisure could easily be the condition that will favour our freedom from the contingent and idleness. It could offer a semantically richer and more authentic life in which we could place greater intelligence and care towards managing an onlife that could otherwise be an alienating (in which people are seen only as interfaces) or inauthentic experience. This opportunity and the risks of a *proxy-based* culture are the topics of the next two chapters.

---

[5] https://www.economist.com/britain/2022/11/17/a-pilot-scheme-to-trail-the-four-day-workweek-in-britain.

Chapter 15

Homo
Faber, Sapiens, Ludens, and Poieticus

The time available to each individual is a most precious resource because its *quantity*, though unknown, is finite, not transferable, and can be incremented only minimally, in a measure that is utterly insufficient compared to its high demand. Despite its fixity, however, the *quality* of one's own time and the *degree of intensity and freedom* in which one can enjoy it can be increased. Equally increasable are the number of potential packets of "(payable to) bearer time" represented by money, the "frozen time" with which it is possible to buy other people's real time and thus liberate or ameliorate one's own (money as time). The management of these variable features of time— quality, freedom and intensity of time, capitalisation of time-money—is at the roots of many technological innovations, which can be organised into four groups, listed in a loose order of logical dependence:

The Green and The Blue: Naive Ideas to Improve Politics in the Digital Age, First Edition. Luciano Floridi.
© 2024 John Wiley & Sons Ltd. Published 2024 by John Wiley & Sons Ltd.

1. materials technologies, which deal with the structure and properties of the physical world and provide the following three technologies with useful applications, essential to designing, modifying, or creating new realities;

2. "sanitary" technologies, whose aim is to sanate (heal) time, that is, to protract time, and to reduce or alleviate the time spent in spiritual and psycho-physical suffering;

3. time-saving technologies, whose aim is to liberate sane/sanated time;

4. entertainment technologies, which let us enjoy, or simply while away, our sane/sanated and liberated time.

Thanks to these technologies, humanity has been able to improve its status. Of course, we all die despite our best effort to manage our time. And since we are all necessarily more greedy (accumulation and conservation of time) than hedonistic (consumption of time), future generations always inherit part of the time liberated by their ancestors and solidified in material, financial and intellectual goods. The full utilisation of entertainment technologies leads to the transaction and consumption of free time and a blind alley. They hedonistically consume whatever amount of time has been liberated, and it is sane, producing amusement as "divertissement" and distraction in a philological sense, that is, as a moving away or diversion from the world. Television, cinema, video games, music, theatre, sport, and so forth can all be seen as vectors that transfer packets of condensed time from users to providers, in exchange for tokens of time disengaged from the quotidian, which allow the user to step away from time for a while. In a logical sequence, the technologies that kill or while the free time away occur in a second stage, when there are sufficient quantities of free time, both real and condensed. We can therefore disregard the entertainment technologies and concentrate on their condition of possibility, namely the time-saving technologies. The technologies that liberate time have a life cycle that is both circular and virtuous. Saving humanity's time, they eventually allow it to devote an increasing quantity of time to further discoveries and technological inventions, which can then liberate still more time, and so forth. Societies with powerful saving-time technologies at their disposal end up liberating ever more of it, thus determining the expansion of the entertainment industry, which helps to consume the enormous amount of free time now available to an increasingly large number of people. It is easy to see that the future industry will be an industry to sanate and consume time, that is, health, hospitality, and entertainment.

Within the group of saving-time technologies, we may distinguish two sub-groups:

3.1 energy technologies

These are technologies that deal with physical reality. They pursue the liberation of time through the increasingly efficient production, multiplication, and transformation of energy, at an ever-decreasing cost. Think, for example, of the lever, the wheel, the plough, the mill, and the various kinds of engines. From the perspective of a philosophical anthropology, these are the technologies of the *homo faber*.

3.2 information technologies

These are technologies that deal with the world of mental creations. They pursue the liberation of time through the implementation of increasingly efficient processes of data management broadly understood, such as the creation, preservation, communication, elaboration and incrementation of all kinds of data and content. In this case, there come to mind examples such as the abacus, the printer, the mechanical clock, the telegraph, the radio, the telephone, the transistor, partly the television, the computer, at least in its primary use, the Internet, the Web, AI. From the perspective of a philosophical anthropology, these are the technologies of the *homo sapiens*.

If we simplify a little, and leave out of consideration all those cases in which the two types of technologies are merged indissolubly, this time, the temporal order of occurrence of (3.1) and (3.2) is not merely logical but historical as well. Many of the main steps in the production of energy at low cost have occurred before most of the corresponding transformations in the technology of information, because the enlargement of the information cycle—education, formation, training, research, communication—to a high percentage of a population requires vast quantities of time. However, time is initially made available only by the accumulation of some energy-related power, which can be exercised on the world of things, and some exchangeable "bearer time" (money). Thus, in its early stages of development, modern society has been strongly characterised by constant attention to the mechanisation of industrial processes and the corresponding generation of new energy sources and new means to exploit them. Humanity has been willing to gain free time in exchange for the massification of production and on condition that DIY ("do it yourself") would stop being a necessary self-imposed commandment, to become a simple third-person invitation (organisation of labour).

Once a society equips itself with a sufficient store of energy technologies, their continuous employment begins to generate an increasing capitalisation of time, both as real free time enjoyed by the generation alive, and as durable and financial goods, inherited by future generations. The very success of the industrial society soon results in a dramatic increase in the quantity of information generated and required by the proper functioning of the whole system of production, and the new society of services it brings about. The universe of organised information becomes such a rich and complex domain, and the various types of data and information such a precious resource—a good if not already a commodity—that managing procedures require, more and more urgently, a technology adequate to their scale and level of complexity. At one point, the quantity of wealth of time accumulated makes the industrial society so complex, and the energy technologies that should liberate additional time so refined, that the very possibility of continuing to free ever more time for an increasing number of people comes to depend on the technologies devoted to the management of information, the vital sap of the system. The time-saving process reaches a threshold of transformation, beyond which information technologies become at least as vital as those energetic, and the system is ready to evolve from an industrial to an information-based model. The only factor still missing is a technology that can make possible the management of information on a level with the efficiency with which the energy technologies liberate time. The arrival of ICT in the middle of the twentieth century fulfilled this role. Thanks to ICT and computer science as the engineering of codified information, the infosphere begins to produce the means necessary for its own self-management. This is the sense in which the computer has represented the right technology at the right time. Although the military needs that arose during World War II were crucial in providing the enormous resources, both human and financial, necessary for computer science to take its first significant steps, it should be clear that the "economic necessity" of ICT was already implicit in the industrial revolution. It was the accumulation of capital and the corresponding growth in complexity of the financial and industrial world during the nineteenth century that laid the ground for an explosive demand for a powerful information technology in the following century. IBM was founded in 1911 as the International Business Machines Corporation. Meanwhile, its "cultural necessity" was a natural consequence of the growth of the infosphere, and therefore partly the offspring of the invention of printing and the mass production of books, in the form of mechanised reproduction of written language.

Thinking is not only tiring but also time-consuming and becomes tedious when demanded by repetitive and stereotypical tasks, those usually involved in the use and control of machines. It is not surprising, then, that the second (or fourth, depending on how one may count) industrial revolution has consisted in the development and application of self-regulating devices to control and improve services in general as well as manufacturing production and distribution. The analogue mechanisation of industrial processes has been joined by their digital automatisation, as clearly shown by the car industry and the development of robotic warehousing. Consequently, in a few decades, the physical goods and their mechanical production have become financially and culturally less significant than what makes both possible, namely an efficient management of information. The industrial revolution has been followed by the digital revolution, and the industrial culture, still so keen on concepts such as ownership, material object-hood, perceivable qualities, and automatic processes, has been slowly supplanted by a manufacturing culture in which concepts such as control, information, algorithm, virtualisation, and interactive process play a more significant role. Computers, networks, data, and algorithms have displaced engines and the energy industry from their central position.

From the perspective of a philosophical anthropology, it is now useful to synthesise the previous analysis by saying that the passage from the energy technologies to the information technologies represents the passage from the *homo faber* to the *homo sapiens*. This perspective helps us uncover a paradoxical feature in contemporary "info-dustrial" societies. Humans differ from other animals also because they are sufficiently intelligent to wish they could stop working and reasoning, and free enough to toil harder than them to pursue both aims to enjoy their sane and liberated time. There follows that the *homo faber* and the *homo sapiens* are direct but only contingent consequences of the truly essential *homo ludens*. We saw in the previous chapter that different cultures at different times have always mythicised the cosmological beginning of a working-&-reasoning age as the loss of a paradise, in which physical and mental activities are neither required nor pursued. It takes a *homo ludens* to eat the only fruit forbidden by God, unthinkingly and playfully. No fancy of the afterlife ever seriously comprises a workshop, a factory, an office, or a farm. Attempts to regain a heavenly state of leisure—to regain a *mythical* status of *homo ludens* by evolving through the *homo faber* and *sapiens* into the *actual homo ludens*—have constantly led humanity to delegate both physical and mental toils to other agents of very disparate kinds.

The history of human emancipation has been, so far, not devoid of some suc-cesses. Nature, animals, technological devices, and the labour of other human beings have all been employed to transform energy into force and to manage information. The paradox of the industrial and the digital revolutions, how-ever, is that, in both cases, the fundamental anthropological project seems to have failed, although nothing should have been more successful than the engine and the computer in sanating and liberating human time, evolving the *homo faber* into the *homo sapiens* and then into the *homo ludens*. The industrial revolution and the automatisation of the industrial society have decreased the autonomy and independence of the *homo faber* without elim-inating its need. With its mind-consuming work, the digital revolution has constantly increased the demand for intelligence, removing the possibility of a naive state of playful insipience from the horizon of the *homo sapiens*. Since the end of last century, it has become ever more evident that increasingly more employees can work less—the average hours of work in the EU is now less than 40 hours—only on condition that at least some of them spend more time than their ancestors doing conceptual work. The management of the industrialised society has turned out to require increasingly well-educated, properly trained, skilful individuals capable of carrying on a growing number of intelligent tasks. If the industrial society could still hope for the evolu-tion of the *homo faber* into a *homo sapiens* that may then approximate the *homo ludens*, the information society seems to have decreed the failure of the *homo ludens*' project: the sanation and liberation of time, finalised to its full enjoyment, has brought about more boredom and sadness than engage-ment and joy. No matter whether one subscribes to Max Weber's suggestion that Protestant ethics had a significant influence on the development of capitalism (*The Protestant Ethic and the Spirit of Capitalism*), it seems that, in info-dustrial societies based on a "working culture", the increasing generation of free time and leisure exacerbate various forms of psychological depres-sion and the rate of suicides. Humanity has always hoped to emancipate itself from life's necessities, but now that a significant quantity of free time has finally become available for the first time in history, what to do with it has become a serious problem for millions of individuals, as Keynes had predicted.

Is there any reason to hope that the human fundamental anthropolog-ical project may be rescued? Modern technology is what has provided most of us with some time for leisure. The redistribution of capital in a Marxian sense is actually a better distribution of disposable time. It is only in this free time that the *homo sapiens* can philosophise at liberty; Aristotle knew that already. Philosophy, however, pre-empties the human right to be unreflective, so after philosophy, the destiny of the *homo sapiens* seems to be either to face ontological failure—to remain forever a *homo faber* or *sapiens* or, when this is no longer possible, to annihilate himself in endless forms of entertainment—or to move towards the development into a *homo poieticus*, creator of intellectual and spiritual realities. Such evolution cannot be achieved by attempting to regain an unreflective state of blessed insipience, a mythical, pre-intellectual condition of direct contact with reality. The very philosophical process that creates the possibility of a solution also impedes this simple way out of the problem. The exit lies only ahead, at the end of the process of reflection, in the form of critical constructionism, according to which the mind designs the world that it inhabits and within which it operates, and must be responsible for it by taking care of it. Critical constructionism does not while away the time sanated and liberated by technology, but employs it to emancipate the mind from reality semanticising the latter (investing it with sense and meaning, through an ontologically oriented interpretation of design), hence, to build and improve both the biosphere and the infosphere, and to develop the state of philosophical reflection into a state of playful mental enjoyment of construction. A simple (i.e., non-reflective) constructionist attitude and an ethics of achievement already unite all human endeavours. It is also the approach we have seen regularly surfacing throughout this book, as one of the overlying themes in the evolution of the world of information and ICT. So, there are reasons for hope. The project for a *homo ludens* may be rescued by upgrading it into a *homo poieticus*. What is required is conceptual excavation and unconcealment (to use a Heideggerian term) and then design: the constructionist trend in modern culture needs to become self-aware of its own nature and acquire a more prominent role in shaping human actions, if it is going to be the basis for a new philosophical anthropology.

An increasing gap between mind and reality has characterised the history of modern thought. It is a process of epistemic detachment which has been unrestrainable ever since it began, and quite inevitably so. Knowledge is the means whereby the subject establishes the minimal distance, and emancipates itself, from the object. It develops as mind's answer to the presence of the non-mental. The rise of dualism and the escalating interaction between traditional knowledge, as an object, and innovative knowledge, as a further reaction to it, has led to the emergence of a new world. Today the infosphere is a universe which is, to an ever-increasing degree, the very environment we inhabit, and the challenges of which we must answer. It is a domain as utterly autonomous from each of us, as individual minds, as the physical world is, and which, unlike the latter, is capable of infinite growth in extension and complexity. What is our relation to such a reality? On the one hand, our situation is one of potentially full understanding of something that bears the stamp of total intelligibility. It is only an apparent paradox that several centuries of constant growth of knowledge should have made us lose such closeness to the world of things, while providing another type of reality, an entire universe of codified information, which enfolds reality, and intentionally keeps it at a distance from the mind. The human mind has created such a new environment, and since we are entirely responsible for its existence, we may also be confident of its potential, and complete intelligibility. On the other hand, in studying the infosphere, the mind investigates its own product and is bound to be confronted with the inevitable dilemma represented by a self-referential assessment. A radical reflection upon the reasons that prompt and sustain the incessant construction of the world of knowledge is badly needed. However, no innovative theory capable of explaining and vindicating the phenomenon of the construction of the infosphere (viewed from a purely epistemological perspective) can ever be based merely on the still dominant, but too unreflective, assumption of a human desire for knowledge for its own sake and some anthropocentric exceptionalism. We saw that a more "negative" anthropology is required, which places humanity at the periphery, and relations at the centre. The dualism between mind and reality; the self-reflective nature of knowledge; the emergence of the infosphere as a habitat of mental life; the constructionist capacities of the mind, and the corresponding challenges and duties; these are among the most innovative matters confronting our philosophical reflection today. They are not entirely new, for at least since the Renaissance the mind has constantly moved away from reality, intentionally constructing, and refining its own conceptual and cultural environment as an alternative to the world of nature. These issues are also far from having reached their ultimate development, and this is what makes their understanding a pressing question. They have certainly become more and more clearly discernible in our century. It is with respect to such new features of our knowledge and culture that Greek intellectualism is no longer adequate, prompting the development of a new theory of the genesis of the epistemic relation between mind and reality. As I anticipated in the previous chapter, when this relation does not work properly, the risk is *an ersatz experience*: alienating and inauthentic, as we shall see in the next chapter.

Chapter 16
A Proxy Culture

How many of us no longer assess the quality of hotels in person, but first rely on TripAdvisor? We may never have met some people in real life, but we are "friends" with them on Facebook. We may click "like" on a post about a social protest, but we are involved only in a kind of slacktivism, a gesture of virtue-signalling that costs and achieves nothing but makes us feel morally good or even superior persons. It no longer matters if we do not know where a place in town is, as long as we can access Google Maps and follow the instructions to get there. Five stars on an Amazon review can be sufficient to convince us of the quality of a product, even if we have never tried or seen it. Being a "bestseller" on the *New York Times* list often becomes a self-fulfilling prophecy. In all these cases, something, the *signifier*, has also come to mean the *signified*, as in a Saussurean theory of language.

This process of "signifying" lies at the heart of every semiotic process. It is the fundamental relation of "standing for" something. There is no sense, reference, or meaning without a signifier and the signified. For this reason, humanity has always searched for and created different kinds of signifying means, to interact with each other and the world, and make sense of both. After all, we are a symbolic species, and twentieth-century philosophy—whether hermeneutically oriented or based on a philosophy of language and logic—can easily be interpreted as a theory of signification. All of this is well known, if a bit convoluted. The critical point here is that our culture, the one that characterises today's mature information societies, is evolving

The Green and The Blue: Naive Ideas to Improve Politics in the Digital Age, First Edition. Luciano Floridi.

from a culture of signs and signification to a culture of *proxies* (meaning something that stands in place of something else) and interactions. What is the difference? Why is this happening today? And what are the implications of such a critical transformation for the way we communicate and understand the world, also politically? To answer these questions, we need to understand better what a proxy (a kind of delegate or substitute) is, and what a "degenerate" proxy might be.

Let me start with the concept of proxy (see Figure 16.1). In the Roman Catholic Church, a vicar is a representative or deputy of a bishop. This role, and its historical familiarity, led to the word "vicarious", meaning "acting or doing something for another"; hence we have the adverb "vicariously". The idea of a "proxy" is like that of a "vicarious" actor. The main difference is that its roots are political, not religious. For it is a late Middle English contraction of "procuracy", which means "legitimate action taken in the place, or on behalf, of another", in the context of government or some kind of socio-political structures (e.g., one could get married by proxy). Today, the use of the term "proxy" is influenced more by a vocabulary of information technology than religious or political ideas. It is likely to signify systems (such as a website) that accept requests for some service and passes them on to another system (such as the Internet). However, the meaning and the underlying experience of "vicariously" and "by proxy" are very similar. They both qualify actions whereby something *both* represents *and* replaces (*acts* or *behaves* in place of) something or someone else.

Let us consider next the concept of a "degenerate proxy". By "degenerate" I do not draw upon the negative, value-related meaning that the term has more recently acquired. In this context, I use it in its purely mathematical sense, in relation to the fact that a case of degeneration is a limiting case in which an object changes its nature to acquire another, usually simpler, one. For instance, a point is a degenerate sphere of zero volume obtained when the sphere's radius reaches zero. We can now adopt this conceptual framework to clarify the concept of "degenerate proxies". We begin by defining P as a proxy of R if, and only if, P has the following, double relation with R: P refers to R and acts in place of R (instead of R), that is, both "stands for" R and "stand in for" R. Now, let us try to "zero out" (or "degenerate") one or the other of the two dimensions of the vicarious relation. If P has a vicarious relation to (i.e., is a proxy for) R, but its ability to act *in place of* R is zero, then P is a degenerated proxy, which simply points back to R, but cannot replace it. Such degenerated proxies are called signs. A sign refers to something, but

	Proxies	Degenerate proxies	
		Signs	Surrogates
P stands for R (refers to R)	✓	✓	
P stands in for R (acts in place of, instead of R)	✓		✓
Relation	vicarious	signifying	surrogate
Peirce's classification		Icons Indices Symbols	
Disciplines		Semiology	
		Proxiology	

Figure 16.1 An analysis of proxies.

cannot substitute it by acting instead of it. It stands for R but does not stand *in* for R. Let us now perform the alternative operation. Suppose P has a vicarious relation with (i.e., is a proxy of) R, but its ability to *refer to* R is zero. In that case, P is a degenerate proxy, which simply acts *in place of* R, but without standing for it. These degenerate proxies are called *surrogates*. A surrogate can work in place of something else but does not refer to it. It stands *in* for R but does not stand for or signify R.

Given these distinctions, we can now apply them to the world of *signs* and semiotics. According to a classical analysis by Charles Sanders Peirce (1994), we can distinguish between three types of signs:

- *icons* are signs that *resemble* what they represent; for example, a photograph of a black cloud is an icon;
- *indices* are signs *related* to what they represent, for example, black clouds indicate impending rain; and, finally,
- *symbols* are signs that *denote* a specific reality under some specific conventions; for instance, the word "cloud" is a symbol denoting a particular meteorological phenomenon or a digital service.

In each of these cases, the *signifiers* (the photograph, the black cloud, the word "cloud") have a more or less complex referential relation with their referents (the things to which they point and "stand for"). What they have in common is that none of them can act in *place of* or *instead of* them; they do not "stand in" for something. In other words, they are degenerate proxies which have a substitutive relation ("acting in place of") with their referents equal to zero.

In many cultures, there seems to be a unique stage in which degenerate proxies, as described by Peirce (icons, indices, and symbols), are mistaken for non-degenerate proxies, and the signs are interpreted as magical. Icons, indexes, and symbols are also given the power to *stand in for*, or *instead of*, that to which they merely stand for, and are therefore treated as if they were true proxies, or true substitutes, able to behave instead of their referents. For instance, what one does to a photograph of an individual (icon) is expected to influence the person portrayed. Bleeding a person, even in the very rare case where this is recommended because of hypertension (index) attributable to a chronic disorder, is imagined as curing an illness; or cursing a person's name (symbol) can be a way of harming them. The issue is far from trivial. For instance, the conversion of bread and wine into the body and blood of Jesus Christ performed in the Eucharist has provoked theological debates over the centuries about whether to interpret bread and wine as genuine substitutes (proxies) or solely as degenerate substitutes (degenerate proxies), that is, mere signs, of the bodily presence of Christ.

Semiotics, the discipline that studies signs, is really the study of only one kind of degenerate proxy. In other words, it is a branch of "proxiology", a neologism helpful to suggest a yet-to-be-developed discipline that would study the whole field of proxies, including degenerate ones such as signs and surrogates and proxies in social contexts (e.g., in signalling strategies).

We have seen that a different kind of degenerate proxy emerges when the vicarious relation has a zero degree of referral (*stands for*), as it turns the proxy into a surrogate *(stands in)*. Take chicory coffee, for instance. It is a classic ersatz coffee that does not contain caffeine or real coffee but is used to *imitate* and replace the taste of coffee. Chicory coffee does not have a *semiotic relation* to coffee, as a representation (icon), a smell (index), or a name (symbol) can have. It has a *substitutive relation* with coffee, in the theoretical sense that one may drink chicory coffee instead of coffee without even knowing that it is a substitute (for instance, if one has never consumed any coffee other than chicory).

To summarise, proxies are more than signs in practical terms, because they are signifiers that stand in place of the referent and interact as if they were the referent itself (recall that one can actually marry through a proxy). However, from an epistemological point of view, proxies are also more than mere surrogates, because they still allow one to perceive the difference between them and that to which they refer. Chicory coffee is not a sign because it does not theoretically intend to refer to real coffee; however, it could completely replace it, if the drinker does not know real coffee, has never experienced it, and is accustomed only to chicory coffee.

We have never had magical powers because signs are simply degenerate proxies that do not provide a means to interact with their referents. However, we may have the impression to have magical powers today because of our proxy culture. This is a risk for those who mistake magic effects—the possibility of interacting with proxies that now do *stand for* and *in for* their referents—for magic causes or explanations (the supernatural, the paranormal, etc.). Much of the hype about AI sometimes seems to be based on such magic thinking. Given that signs are degenerate proxies, it is legitimate to consider our *proxy culture* as a direct development of the modern semiotic, symbolic, or sign-based culture that the mass media has nurtured in the recent past. The difference is that, in the Newtonian ontology of offline analogue things and a consumerist model based predominantly on material goods, proxies were difficult to develop and less required for interaction with the environment. However, now that living *onlife* in the infosphere is increasingly common and unavoidable, we are fully immersed in an ocean of data in a context where renting and using services is as dominant as buying material goods. This has the effect that proxies are both necessary to use and easy to obtain because they share the digital nature of their referents and facilitate how we orient ourselves in, and manage the infosphere. It is easy to have some form of informational structure to *stand for* (refer) and *stand in for* (behave instead of) another informational structure, just as it is easy to have the same digital "stuff" working as both data and software. This digital ontological uniformity has facilitated and reinforced the emergence of a proxy culture and has made it vital for solving the problems it creates. It has been estimated that, by 2025, humanity will have created more than 180 zettabytes of data. This is a vast number. The extraordinary thing is that the current generation has created all these data. In its entire history up to 2009, estimates suggest that humanity created only one zettabyte of data. Admittedly, much of the data in question is probably useless or insignificant. However, there is still a staggering and steady growth of information available today on every subject and every aspect of it. This means it is progressively more challenging to navigate and manage the infosphere without relying on proxies. At the same time, proxies are not simply the solution but part of the problem, because they are an additional source of data, the manipulation of which will require other proxies. The result is that, while the gulf between us and the *signified* reality grows rapidly, this continuous growth necessitates bridging the gap through other *signifiers* with which we can interact effectively. Signs and signifiers have always been crucial phenomena for every culture. However, only ours is a culture of proxies because only now has the sheer quantity of data made a qualitative difference to it, while technology has created full and genuine (not degenerate) vicarious relations in the same way as ordinary experiences.

All this brings some risks. As I have already said, we can confuse signs with proxies and thus fall into forms of occultism or superstition. Or we can confuse surrogates with proxies and so instead rely on a kind of "superficialism" that turns our experience onlife into an inauthentic life, the *ersatz trap*. In the same way that a sign-based culture risks becoming a merely self-referential culture—in which words refer to words recursively without ever reaching their non-semantic referents—so a *proxy culture* carries the risk of becoming a culture of surrogates (*Ersatzes*). In such a culture, proxies become mere replacements that conceal their original references (in our example, the "real" coffee) and make it difficult or impossible to retrieve them. They are replaced and obscured entirely without any residual connection to the original referent (returning to our previous example, the existence of the real coffee is lost altogether). A world without chicory coffee is not necessarily a better world. Still, a world in which chicory coffee is the only coffee is far worse and more superficial because diversity, and the possibility to choose, have been erased.

However, a *proxy culture* also brings advantages. An *augmented* culture (as in *augmented reality*) can offer more and higher-quality opportunities for our society's development. For instance, proxies can enable experiences and interactions that were previously unimaginable or impossible, as in the case of virtual goods, services, or experiences. It is worth remembering that, in statistics, a proxy is a variable that is irrelevant but functions in place of another variable that is neither observable nor measurable. Proxies can bridge experiential spaces that are otherwise inaccessible or difficult to access. In that case, our proxy-based culture can be an *augmented*, *enhanced*, and better culture that enables a more authentic onlife experience.

We are the generation moving out of an entirely analogue world and into an increasingly digital one. No generation before ours has ever been forced to adapt so dramatically to such profound changes in such a short time. How we adjust to this will also depend on how we design the proxies that will populate the infosphere and mediate our life experiences, and how we will control those responsible for them, so that they do not harm us but reinforce and expand our opportunities. It is worth stressing that, in the future, more and more proxies will be artificial agents, standing and behaving instead of their referents. Any mature information society today faces the challenge of developing a more inclusive and authentic culture, rather than an impoverished, superficial one. Thus, we return to the issues of human dignity, our "eccentric" exceptionalism, the importance of relations, our crucial role as carers and stewards, and how we interpret ourselves as informational organisms and as interfaces.

The issue to be addressed next is how politics has, on the one hand, devolved into marketing to manage human attention while treating citizens as interfaces, and, on the other hand, exploited a proxy culture to shape and manipulate public opinion through simple messages that represent and stand for (i.e., are proxies for) far more complex and challenging issues. This is the topic of the next chapter.

Chapter 17
Politics as Marketing

Marketing, or more generally public relations and communication strategies from which marketing techniques are derived, is a way of controlling and managing human beliefs (hopes, expectations, fears, etc.), choices, and ultimately behaviours. Thus, marketing sees and treats people as interfaces. It aims to identify the most efficient and effective methods to manipulate human interfaces (see Chapter 12) to obtain the coveted resources to which those interfaces give access. In politics, we saw that these resources are, in the following logical order: *attention, consent*, and *votes*.

The fact that marketing strategies and techniques dominate today's politics, as opposed to merely the purchase and use of goods or services, is unfortunate and even confusing. However, given the analysis developed so far, it should come as no surprise. In a world where people are seen and treated as mere interfaces, politics is not *downgrading* to mere marketing, but rather marketing is *upgrading* to politics, in terms of applying its strategies to command and control successfully the human interfaces that we have now all become in the political arena. As I shall explain presently, the outcome is the same, whether through downgrading or upgrading. However, the process by which these two outcomes are achieved is different, and this difference is

The Green and The Blue: Naive Ideas to Improve Politics in the Digital Age, First Edition.
Luciano Floridi.

crucial in motivating a different problem-solving strategy. Because it is not where one is, but how one got there that sheds light on how to get out of it.

There is a further advantage. Understanding the phenomenon more insightfully can help eliminate another potential confusion between truthful and successful communication. The digital revolution has radically transformed and bolstered the power of marketing, hence enabling its upgrade to the political realm. This is clearly shown by the oceans of digitised personal data, the billions of people who are now connected and live onlife in the infosphere, by the fact that algorithms are increasingly sophisticated, that the cost of processing power is becoming negligible, and that digital technologies are increasingly mediating social interactions. However, focusing exclusively on these techno-social factors is insufficient to comprehend fully the phenomenon of politics as marketing. This is because such factors only explain some of the conditions necessary to understand how politics is morphing into marketing, and, thus, how political communication is a marketing strategy. Yet one essential element is still missing from the preceding discussion: all of this is symptomatic of the most profound transformation in our philosophical anthropology, namely the answer we give today to the ontological question about human nature. We have seen that the digital revolution has changed our self-conception, culturally and socially. It has transformed us all, ontologically, into inforgs, and hence, *functionally*, into interfaces. This has happened both on a conceptual level (how we perceive and understand ourselves) and a factual level (how we treat ourselves and interact with each other). It is necessary to understand this transformation to explain marketing's upgrade to politics, and the profound influence marketing strategies have on current political discourse. Once this is clear, it becomes apparent that it is too simplistic to talk about *post-truth* communication. Instead, we should speak of the *success* and *failure* of communication, irrespective of the veracity or falsehood of the message. The goal is to "type answers on" human interfaces and get them to behave as desired, thereby acquiring the resources that the interfaces protect and, in this model, provide access to. Marketing is a form of nudging, and *"pushing the right button"* is becoming less and less a metaphor, and more and more a technique to describe interactions with individuals who have been reduced to mere human interfaces. The "marketisation" of politics means that political messages are like simple passwords: short, easy to remember, always the same, and repeated whenever the same human interfaces are involved and need to be "unlocked". Above all, they are neither true nor false but operate on a dichotomy of their functionality or dysfunctionality. Recurring to the terminology introduced in the previous chapter, political messages are *proxies*, which represent and stand for far more complex and challenging issues. If you do not like the messages (proxies), the best thing to do is to try to change the interfaces they work with and how they are accepted. This is why arguing with all the truth and evidence in the world would consistently make little difference to supporters of Bolsonaro, Brexit, Putin, Trump, or anti-vax movements.

There is a prevalent frustration among voters who expect and wish to see truth prevail in politics—think of cases in which the lies of those in power are refuted with facts, or examples of scandalous behaviour being revealed that in the past would have ruined the career of any bad politician. All of this is understandable and reasonable, but ultimately anachronistic. For instance, Trump, while guilty, was never convicted of any crimes, despite two impeachment trials. The marketisation of politics is largely regrettable, and it has rendered obsolete and dysfunctional the true/false approach. This is not because insufficient truth is accessible or because too many political falsehoods, contradictions or lies remain hidden, but because the true/false dichotomy has no grip on human interfaces. It is like typing in letters of the alphabet when the password is numeric: inputting any sequence of letters is futile because letters cannot longer interact with the system. Post-truth politics is actually *nonalethic* politics, i.e., simultaneously post-truth and post-falsehood. As stated above, political messages can be understood as proxies, which either work or do not. It is a question of the success and efficacy of interactions, not factual correctness. Therefore, this same politics is also post-coherence/incoherence. Again, this is not because much more needs to be done. If anything, this is the age of information, and we have an overabundance of digital material that blatantly exposes bad politicians' false, contradictory, and opportunistic communications. Digital technologies have facilitated the personalisation of political messages, to the extent that, in theory, any human interface can receive a successful, functioning message, irrespective of other interfaces and, therefore, of different types of messages, even if they are mutually incompatible ones. It is as if one were to complain that the password that works for Alice is the opposite of the password that works for Bob. This makes no sense, because it is the mechanism's logic that makes such inconsistency possible and preferable.

Given that politics today is post-alethic, paraconsistent—a term indicating here that contradictions are allowed even if they are controlled, e.g., when two messages can contradict each other but can still function with different interfaces/people—and based on a proxy culture, it follows that the idea of a universal and identical political manifesto that is informative, true, and coherent for all potential voters is obsolete. Moreover, it is one that very few people (the voting interfaces) are interested in adhering to today. The tendency is rather going in the opposite direction, namely towards an almost tautological vagueness of generic statements that cannot be rejected by anyone—who does not want excellent and free education for all, high employment, low inflation, more growth, lower taxes, better health care, better pensions, safer cities, healthy environments, no pollution, and sliced bread?—an increasing specialisation of personalised messaging, and a "bubbling" of the target audience (i.e., a transformation of the audience into multiple and divided communication bubbles), with the ultimate aim of equating one human interface to one human bubble. Marketing is nominalist by choice but Platonist by necessity, because it cannot avoid dealing with large segments of the population who have been grouped in typologies to suit a specific purpose. However, marketing has a nominalist vocation because it would like to communicate only to separate individuals, and to each individual in a uniquely personalised way. There is no inconsistency in attempting to achieve a unique one-to-one relation with each human interface. Alice can use Bob-as-interface and Carol-as-interface by giving them different and even opposite messages (e.g., to get both to vote for her), in precisely the same way that Alice can use two completely different keys to open two separate locks, two passwords for two interfaces. The keys or passwords can be mutually incompatible and have no relation to anything else in the world. They just need to work with the relevant interfaces.

Once one recognises that politics and marketing are now intrinsically linked, it is crucial to understand not *whether* but *why* this is the case and what processes led to this outcome. It is not because the digital revolution has absorbed the political realm into the realm of marketing, as if, in a Venn diagram,[1] the political circle has progressively moved within the marketing circle. Instead, it is because the digital revolution has expanded the power of marketing to control and manage interfaces/consumers/citizens and has, thus, entered politics. We can simplify this by stating that the marketing sphere has expanded to include and encroach upon the political sphere, which has never moved. A proxy culture has facilitated this shift enormously. In a "dynamic" Venn diagram, politics has remained stationary. It has not

---

[1] Venn diagrams simply visualise relations between sets using circles. For example, the circle-set of red cars partly overlaps the circle-set of sports cars to indicate in the part belonging to both circles that some sports cars are red.

developed (if anything, it has involuted). It is the realm of marketing that has expanded enormously and now encompasses the realm of politics.

As I anticipated, the outcome is the same, that is, the resulting static Venn diagram is the same, but analysing the trajectory of how we reached this result is crucial to understand how to deal with the problem. Politics will not be improved by relocating it, as if politics were the mobile part of the system, moving in and out of the marketing sphere of influence, or as if politics had temporarily derailed and all that was needed to correct the situation were to get it back on the tracks. Marketing is the fundamental dynamic force here. And as marketing expands in scope and begins to include political communication and strategies as well, the only way to improve politics (including its management and how it is communicated) is to improve marketing itself. At least two consequences follow from this analysis.

First, Berlusconi, Bolsonaro, Maduro, Di Maio, Duterte, Erdoğan, Farage, Grillo, Johnson, Le Pen, Meloni, Orbán, Putin, Salvini, Trump, Zemmour, and many other populists capable of saying anything and respecting nothing are, initially, the symptom and not the cause of the expansion of marketing into politics. As in the simplest Darwinian environment, these populists are the organisms that have adapted to and benefited most from the change in the ecosystem, and the marketisation of politics. Their fitness can be understood in terms of optimal marketing. Still lacking the ability or means to customise political messages to single, individual human interfaces, populists seek to maximise the capacity to tailor generic messages individually by identifying points of common interest (e.g., lowering taxes) or by creating points of common fear (e.g., xenophobia) among the human interfaces. Their marketing seeks to be Pareto optimal[2]: it communicates messages to interfaces so that it is impossible to reformulate these messages to work better with one interface without working worse with at least one other interface. Or, more simply: populists seek to give the human interfaces what the latter want and make them want what they say they can give them. This is possible because public opinion on any issue does not pre-exist but is instead formed by the relations that constitute it. It is only after it is formed on *that issue* that it becomes

---

[2] I am adapting this from economics, where "Pareto efficiency or Pareto optimality is a state of allocation of resources from which it is impossible to reallocate so as to make any one individual or preference criterion better off without making at least one individual or preference criterion worse off". Wikipedia.

more difficult to modify it on *that same issue*. It is not easy to reverse the initial malleability of public opinion. Once populists are in power (consider Orbán or Putin, for instance) or have an influential platform (think of Trump), their actions have an endogenous ecological impact. They resemble extremophiles as they thrive in circumstances that are poisonous to any other form of politics,[3] but in a unique, non-biological sense. They also contribute to pollute even more the political ecosystem (e.g., encouraging more selfish interests, more shared fears, more antagonism), thereby reinforcing a vicious circle in which the worse the environment becomes, the more likely it is that, in such extremist politics, only the most extreme species will be able to survive, and so on. As long as the ecosystem does not improve, these extreme kinds of political organisms will continue to thrive, and, if they disappear, they will be replaced by similar ones, as the environment remains the same. Theresa May is replaced by Boris Johnson; Matteo Salvini by Giorgia Meloni. If one does not like them, one needs to improve the ecosystem that generates and feeds them, and that, in turn, is sustained by them.

I have now come to the second consequence of the dominance of marketing in politics that I wish to emphasise. To improve the political situation, one must improve the marketing of politics, by focusing on the interface process itself. One must start by improving the information sphere in which we live, and the political marketing processes that take place in it, not by trying to move politics a little more to the right or a little more to the left, as if it were a piece of furniture in a living room. The whole house needs to be revamped, so to speak. It is the improvement of the infosphere that seems to elude politicians like Corbyn and Starmer in the UK, or parties like the Democratic Party in the USA and in Italy ("Partito Democratico"). They do not pay sufficient attention to the new morphology of politics. Seemingly unaware of it, they do not represent a new future. Instead, they continue to represent and promote an old past trying to return, applying obsolete solutions, which worked in the past, to new problems, which they cannot address.

Better political forces could prosper in a healthier environment, leading to an inverse virtuous circle that would improve the environment even further,

---

[3] "An extremophile [from the Latin *extremus* meaning 'extreme' and the Greek *philia* meaning 'love'] is a microorganism that lives and proliferates in environmental conditions that are prohibitive for humans, for example in environments with extremely high or low temperature, pressure, pH, or salinity values": *Wikipedia*.

progressively weeding out bad political forces. This dynamic is best understood in light of the *Matthew effect* and the *network effect*.

In sociology, the *Matthew effect* refers to any process whereby, in specific situations, the new resources that become available are distributed among the participants in direct proportion to what they already have. In English, this is expressed by the saying, "the rich get richer, and the poor get poorer". The name is derived from verse 13:12 of the *Gospel* of Matthew, which reads:

> For whoever has, to him more will be given, and he will have abundance; but whoever does not have, even what he has will be taken away from him.[4]

In economics, the *network effect* refers to the phenomenon whereby the value of a product or service gradually increases as the number of users or demand grows. Think of the usefulness of a messaging app: the more people who use it, the greater its usefulness, creating a feedback loop that increases the number of people who want to use it, and so forth.

The Matthew effect and the network effect are at the core of how bad politics has superseded good politics. As in the analogy of environmental pollution, the worse the political situation is, the less people will want to participate in politics, making the situation even worse. Whoever wins, wins even more, and whoever loses has no chance of winning the next time. The Matthew effect and the network effect lead to the complete ruin of the political space. Fortunately, these are dynamic processes that can also work in the opposite direction. Remember that the more one loses, the more one continues to lose, as in the case of a bank crisis in which everyone goes to withdraw their funds at the counter. Eventually, the institution in question goes bankrupt. Similarly, the less useful a social network is, the fewer the number of people who participate in it and the less useful it becomes, and so on. The only good thing about a vicious circle (or a bad network effect) is that it can be reversed into a virtuous one (or a good network effect) that can grow equally quickly. This means that populists can fail as rapidly as they can succeed. Trump, Johnson, and Bolsonaro have been replaced.

How can the direction of the circle be reversed, from vicious to virtuous? The following chapters seek to answer this question, specifically Chapter 20 on representative democracy as structural democracy, and Chapter 21 on "stealth" democracy. Before addressing these themes, however, it is best to answer another pressing question on the nature of digital power.

---

[4] New King James Version.

Chapter 18
Digital Grey Power

In 1941, Aldous Huxley published *The Grey Eminence: A Study in Religion and Politics*. It was a biography of François Leclerc du Tremblay (Huxley 1994, the French Capuchin friar also known as *l'éminence grise*—the grey eminence; the colour is partly a reference to his grey habit—who served as a highly influential advisor to *l'éminence rouge* (the red eminence), Cardinal Richelieu. Du Tremblay did not operate within the official architecture of power, while Richelieu was himself prime minister to King Louis XIII. Still, the Capuchin friar profoundly influenced French and European politics and the course of the Thirty Years' War, an extremely protracted and destructive conflict in European history, which one could describe as World War Zero. Du Tremblay had an extraordinary ability to manipulate events and people's behaviour, influencing *influencers*, behind the scenes. It was he who gave birth to the expression "being a grey eminence" and hence, the idea of grey power.

Grey power, that is, a secret or behind-the-scenes power, exists in every society, and societies and grey power change together, as coagents. The process can sometimes be dramatic, even revolutionary, but it is rarely linear and lacks a consistent rhythm. Consider how European societies and their respective grey powers slowly changed owing to the complex interactions between mercantilism, colonialism, and the emergence of the so-called

The Green and The Blue: Naive Ideas to Improve Politics in the Digital Age, First Edition. Luciano Floridi.

Westphalian system of sovereign states. Another case in point is how the USA rapidly transformed during the Gilded Age, which lasted from 1870 to 1900, alongside the grey power wielded by wealthy industrialists and financiers, such as Andrew Carnegie, Andrew W. Mellon, John Pierpont Morgan, and John D. Rockefeller. The changes in society and the grey power within it do not follow a domino effect pattern. Instead, they are more like a complicated waltz in the ballroom of history, one in which society and grey power dance together, sometimes revisiting some corners, moving in alternating rhythms and taking turns leading the dance, always in ever-shifting pairs.

This long premise is necessary to clarify that asking *how* grey power has evolved to fit our current societies is a pressing question but also a potential trap. It is pressing because grey power in mature information societies is not the same as in industrial, mass media, or theocratic societies. Without a deeper understanding of the nature of grey power and how it is exercised—in short, its morphology—developing a better society will be even more challenging. As always, we need to know something exactly, if we want to improve. Indeed, an intellectual history of grey power would make for fascinating reading. At the same time, however, a discussion of grey power can become a trap if we are not careful to avoid superficial simplifications. Recall that grey power is like ivy: it grows on the wall of official authority and flourishes in full shade. So, you cannot see it very clearly. It is easy to get confused.

At a time of significant social transformations and widespread conflicts, it is tempting to identify some focal points as the driving force behind the morphology of today's grey power. This is the trap we need to avoid. Climate change, immigration and terrorism, globalisation and financial markets, the housing bubble and the reform of the banking system, inflation and deflation, *hacktivism* and *slacktivism*, cyberwar and the Second Cold War between the USA and China, the euro and the Greek crisis, the expansion of the EU, multinational corporations and American cultural colonialism, the Arab Spring, China's GDP and globalisation, the emergence of a new world order, the war in Ukraine. The list of potential focal points is long, and these are just some examples. It can also be a distraction because it meanders through contingent historical phenomena, while failing to identify the more profound shift in how control and influence are exercised over events and people's behaviours and hence how they are primed to relate with such historical phenomena within mature information societies. Using a different analogy, these focal points are the surface waves on the ocean of history. No matter how gigantic, fast, and even dangerous they might be, we need to focus on the underlying currents that will still be there when the storm is over. We need to dive deep to understand the new morphology of grey power. We must risk taking a plunge into the unknown.

As we saw with Du Tremblay, when Christianity dominated Europe, grey power was a religious business exercised through the creation and control of *beliefs*, especially *fear* and *hope* in the afterlife. Yet, following Marx, one may argue that, in industrial societies, grey power changed and became exercised instead through the *creation* and *control* of *things*. To be more precise, in an industrial society, events and people's behaviour can be manipulated not only through force and the monopoly on faith, but also, and then predominantly, through the control of the means of production of *goods* and *services* (as well as people as human interfaces) and the corresponding management of wealth or capital. The "grey" of the new *influencing* eminences is that of their business suits.

Before adding anything else, let me clarify what power means here. By looking at the most powerful of entities, God, and hence at God's omnipotence, we can see that there are three kinds of power over any reality. The first, is the power to create or annihilate something. Imagine God creating a stone. Using a Greek word already encountered in Chapter 15 let us call this *poietic* power. Then there is the power to transform something into something else, such as the stone into a bird. This is *metamorphic* (transformative) power. And finally, there is the power of controlling the behaviour of something, e.g., to make the bird fly in a preferred direction. Another Greek word can help here: this is *cybernetic* power, in the original sense we find in Plato of piloting or steering a ship. Socio-political power is mainly cybernetic, that is, a matter of control. Eventually, capitalism, competition, and consumerism end up eroding industrial-financial grey power by transforming goods and services into commodities, i.e., undifferentiated marketable elements, which become so generic as to erase any perceptible difference in value between brands or versions. At some point, industrial manufacturing no longer works as the grey power behind the throne but kneels before it. The decline of industrial-financial grey power has been a long process, but it reached its symbolic peak in 2009 when, facing bankruptcy and liquidation, General Motors and Chrysler were granted an $85 billion bailout by the US and Canadian governments.

In the meantime, another grey power had emerged, based on the control of the means of production, not just of things, but of *information* about things. As Orwell (1949) famously wrote twice in *Nineteen Eighty-Four*: "who controls the past controls the future. Who controls the present controls the past". A dictatorship is above all a monopoly on information.

It is important to remember that in *Nineteen Eighty-Four*, there are no computers or digital technologies. Instead, the novel depicts a dystopian society dominated by the totalitarianism of analogue mass media. In this society, those who control (the means of production of) information (about things) can control and influence people's behaviour and events. With its close ties to knowledge, information has always been power—even in Richelieu's time. Still, grey power became predominantly informational only later and as the result of several factors, including the growth of the mass media sector; the rise of public intellectuals and a technical-scientific intelligentsia; the development of propaganda and advertising; and the emergence of the press and journalism as a so-called "fourth power" in addition to legislative, executive, and judicial powers (television is sometimes referred to as the "fifth power" after the famous 1976 film of the same name). If I had to identify a pivotal moment when the form of grey power based on wielding information gained prominence, it would be 8 August 1974, when Nixon resigned because of the Watergate scandal, brought to light by the investigative journalism of the *Washington Post*.

Some experts think this is still the context in which we find ourselves today. They focus on identifying the source of power in the knowledge economy or the Internet, instead of considering it as something emerging from wealth or capital. Perhaps. But it would be a dangerous error to apply this interpretation to *grey* power today, as this approach is anchored in an anachronistic view of the information society as a mass-media society. In such a way, it focuses on the visible aspect of socio-political power (the blogging or tweeting community, networked individuals, citizen journalists, hacktivists, etc.), but it ignores what lies behind it. Conflating an information society with a mass-media society risks confusing those who sit on the throne with the ranks of the grey power who stand behind it and influence those who wield visible power. If information and the means of its production were the new grey power, then newspapers would not be in danger, journalism would not be a profession in crisis, and publishers, bookshops, archives, and libraries would not close. Wikipedia would be more powerful than Facebook or Twitter. Publishers would dictate their terms to Amazon. The music industry would revolutionise Apple, not the other way around. Hollywood would determine the future of Netflix. Newspapers would impose their will on internet search engines such as Google.

In the next chapter, I shall analyse some of the mechanisms that have enabled the new grey power to emerge and replace the old industrial one. Here, to understand who the new grey eminences are today, we must realise that information consists of both *questions* and *answers*. The *informational* grey power at work in the mass media society was exercised by those who controlled the means of production of *answers*. It was still a kind of power over things, as things evolved into informational things. Today, the new grey power has become much more relational and does not so much control the answers as it does the questions. Consider that controlling publishing or communication, such as advertising, means sending answers to people who have not asked any questions: it is called *broadcasting* because it happens even if nobody is reading or listening. Today, however, in mature information societies, the transformation of information into another commodity means that answers are no longer worth anything; they are cheap, and often free. Giving *answers* is no longer in the remit or interests of grey power, which has moved further behind the scenes, from controlling information about things to the relational control of *questions* that generate information about things. It is symbolically telling that, in 2013, the *Washington Post* was acquired by Jeff Bezos, the founder and CEO of Amazon. However, if I had to choose a date for the coming of age of this new grey power, I would opt for 4 September 2014: the day the White House announced that it had appointed Megan Smith, one of Google's top executives, as its new Chief Technology Officer (CTO), and assigned as her deputy Alexander Macgillivray, a lawyer who had worked for Twitter in 2009, after eight years at Google as a prominent lawyer.

The new and emerging grey power is based on the control of the means of production of questions that can be asked, when and where, how and by whom, and the range of answers that, in turn, are allowed, facilitated, and received. And since an unanswered question is another definition of uncertainty, one can say that, in mature information societies, *the morphology of grey power* is *the morphology of uncertainty*. Who controls the questions controls the answers. Who controls the answers controls reality. Digital grey power is today the "sixth power". This seems to be a more valuable way of understanding the widespread phenomenon of AI-generated content.

Issues such as transparency, privacy, freedom of speech, intellectual property rights, or the right to be forgotten *also* belong to a more profound debate on the new morphology and workings of digital grey power. The controversy surrounding an experiment undertaken in 2014, in which Facebook manipulated the balance between positive and negative messages displayed to 689,000 of its users without their consent, revealed the depth and influence of the grey power of Facebook (which is basically an interface managing the flow of questions and answers of social information). The damage caused by the Cambridge Analytica scandal is well known. The coeval debate on the so-called "right to be forgotten" was also a debate on the opportunity for the socio-political power of the EU to regain control over the grey power held by Google, which enjoys a virtual monopoly on the way Europeans find information online, i.e., by searching answerable questions. Nor is Google any less ubiquitous in its country of origin. According to the US government transparency organisation MapLight, during the first quarter of 2015, Google became, for the first time, the company that invested the most funds in lobbying the US federal government, surpassing both big defence lobbyists, such as Lockheed Martin, and energy companies, such as Exxon Mobil.

If the previous diagnosis is correct, we have two tasks ahead of us. One is to learn how to make a *prognosis*: we need to understand how the emerging new grey power will likely develop, as a form of control that manipulates uncertainty. The new grey power seems more akin to the old theocratic power in Europe in that it manages questions, albeit not the ultimate questions about God and the afterlife, than to the less similar grey power of mass media. Digital grey power does resemble the industrial grey power insofar as it tends to subordinate politics to economics. However, we should resist the temptation of considering it just another case of "business as usual". Partly, this is a narrative quietly promoted by the new grey power itself. So, the second task is to find a *therapy* to understand what can be done to ensure that control over the morphology of uncertainty can be exercised benignly, without ulterior motives, kept under control by legitimate socio-legal and political powers, and at least not be replaced by even less desirable kinds of grey power. These tasks are long and arduous but crucial, so it is good to start acknowledging and dealing with them immediately. To do so, it is critical to be clear about the value and indispensability of representative democracy and why direct democracy—exercised as it is by reliance on those who control the morphology of questions (i.e., platforms)—is not a good strategy. Adopting direct democracy means increasing the likelihood of a marketisation of politics and that multinational corporations will no longer merely exercise grey power but may even replace nations in the central management of political power. Let us see why in the next chapter.

Chapter 19
The Digital Gift Economy

Let me start with a parody. It is Christmas, and your aunt has knitted a scarf for you. It is beautiful, useful, and you needed it. In fact, you love it. You feel that she cares about you and understands your wishes. You are most grateful for such a thoughtful gift. It seems that everybody is happy. How can there be anything wrong with such a win-win scenario? This is the same rhetorical question asked by many defenders of free online services. The answer is supposed to be stronger than a mere "nothing". It is supposed to be a much more positive "there is everything right with this!". Indeed, the new rhetorical question becomes "what is wrong with you, killjoy?". For the digital gifts from Apple, Baidu, Expedia, Facebook, Flickr (Yahoo!), Google, Instagram (Facebook/Meta), LinkedIn, Microsoft, Tencent, TikTok, TripAdvisor, Tumblr (Yahoo!), Twitter, Yahoo!, YouTube (Google), WeChat, WhatsApp (Facebook/Meta) and all the other thousands of digital aunts we seem to have online ensure that we, the *giftees*, are part of the information society, that we live on the good side of the digital divide, that we enjoy all the amazing fruits of our technological developments. And all this is free of charge. They make every day feel like Christmas.

End of story? Not quite. Think more carefully and critically, and you will realise that "timeo Danaos et dona ferentes" may still apply. The Latin phrase

The Green and The Blue: Naive Ideas to Improve Politics in the Digital Age, First Edition. Luciano Floridi.

means "I fear the Greeks even when they bear gifts". In the *Aeneid*, Virgil makes the Trojan priest Laocoön utter this now proverbial line, in his attempt to warn the Trojans not to accept the famous wooden horse left by the Greeks as an apparent gift. We know how it ends, and yet we seem to be falling into the same trap. Let me explain.

Of course, the digital gifts are paid in kind, through our data, but this is not the point here. Instead, the digital gifts we receive have three features that should make us think twice before accepting them gratefully. I already mentioned the first: they are indeed *enabling* us in countless ways and vastly more so than a simple scarf. It is hard to imagine life without them, for anyone so used to relying on them daily. This is why, when they work, they become an essential part of our *onlife* experience. However, as gifts, they are also *disenfranchising* in a crucial sense. Digital services as temporary gifts need no justification or legitimisation, including the oldest form of legitimisation, namely ownership, now replaced by authorised use. When using a digital gift, Alice is neither a customer nor a citizen; she is merely a user. She can take it or leave it, but she has no right to complain about the gift, for she did not pay for the service and neither did she vote for it. There is no ownership contract, only disclaimers and terms of service by which Alice must agree to abide in order to use the service. A new kind of legislation needs to be formulated to protect Alice. Yet the reasoning is that, if she does not like the scarf, she can always stop using it; it would be preposterous if she were to engage in any legal action against her aunt for the poor quality of the wool, the awkward length, the hideous colours, or the fact that the colours are those of a football club, which will identify Alice as a supporter of a specific team she does not care about. Her aunt would be sincerely astonished and appalled by her ingratitude. It is a gift, and gifts, as opposed to purchased or tax-paid goods or services, have the particular property of removing the right to complain or choose (I am oversimplifying, such gifts are regulated, e.g., by the GDPR, but not as much and as well as if they were purchased services or goods). Likewise, if digital gifts are useless or unwelcome, the suggestion is that the market will take care of them; perhaps better ones will follow. If they are useful, they may become essential, generating dependency and grateful loyalty. However, the lack of any possible reciprocity may transform gratitude into resentment for an unequal dependency, and thus turn the gifts into poisonous ones, when giftees turn against the gifters. Consider how quickly many digital companies moved from hero to foe. Twitter *docet*. All this also explains why our digital aunts are determined to create monopolies. When it is freezing, and that is the only scarf Alice can wear, it is hard for her not to be happy and grateful for it.

So free online services as gifts both enable and disenfranchise their users. They also *disempower* those who produce and sell alternatives for a price, putting the competition out of business. This is the third important feature that I wish to highlight. Alice's aunt and her knitting skills undermine the shop that would have sold the scarf that Alice needed and wanted. By presenting Alice with a free scarf, her aunt is *disempowering* a previous business. Moreover, with that shift in "business," a shift in power follows. The aunt is now the free source to whom Alice turns, the one on whom she depends, perhaps for a new scarf and a matching hat next Christmas. Giving away a service or good for free means disempowering any other agent whose business is based on selling that service or good. This explains why our digital aunts tend to make any kind of offering dirt cheap.

We saw in the previous chapter that the production and control of information was the old business model of the mass-media society and its source of influential power. In mature information societies, information is *commoditised* (in the business theory sense of the term) into undifferentiated marketable items—sellable things so generic that customers perceive little or no value difference between brands or versions—primarily through increased competition. Such a *commoditisation* ends up decreasing prices until it becomes economically more profitable to produce and give information away for free in exchange for personal data, by relying on an advertising-based business model and the control of questions (the morphology of uncertainty, seen in Chapter 18). This *commodification* (a similar but different term, to be understood here in the Marxian sense) assigns economic value to something not previously considered in economic terms—such as user-generated content and data about users' purchasing power, patterns, and preferences—making them subject to supply-demand and price-value dynamics. A significant side effect is a self-reinforcing cycle in which the escalating need to differentiate products fuels the exact mechanism that tends to commoditise them. The more the digital business cannibalises the analogue business, the more the analogue business needs the digital to ensure that it is not entirely cannibalised, increasing the resources spent on advertising, that is, on signalling campaigns that seek to resist *commoditisation*. In more colourful terms, the analogue is like a medieval king who is constantly captured by a digital foe to whom he must pay a ransom to be freed until he is captured again. The digital cannot believe its luck. In this process, digital companies can further disenfranchise their users—more free goodies as gifts—while disempowering those who held power in mass-media societies based on the production of information rather than on its mediation, management, search, repackaging, free sharing, and so forth. Google disempowers the news industry, TripAdvisor and Expedia the travel industry, and so on. The process spills over into other companies with different business models: Apple disempowers the music industry, Amazon the printing industry, and so forth. As you can see, any Manichean interpretation of good vs. bad forces is utterly naïve. The new digital barons replace the old analogue ones. Old forces, such as newspapers, public libraries, and the journalistic profession, are collateral damages. They emerged as a consequence of the printing revolution, as a way of coping with the risk of monopoly on information *production*. Today, information is commoditised, there is no monopoly—consider the blogosphere, citizen journalism, online news and books—and so they are becoming solutions in search of a problem.

Not every digital aunt replaces a previous business and corresponding power from the old mass-media society. Some cases are borderline, like Amazon's policy to sell under-priced Kindles. The more they are subsidised, the closer they look like gifts for their users. Some other cases, like Facebook (still the social platform, not yet Meta), seem to have identified new sources of *commodification*, essentially gossip, socialising, and online communication. Others still are just entering the market of free gifts in exchange for personal data; think of the services associated with the Apple watch. In all cases, when the digital aunts clash with previous business models, they have the decisive advantage of free and enabling gifts on their side. Resistance is futile.

In some societies, gift economies are complex and finely-tuned modes of exchange, governed by social norms and customs in which valuables are not sold for money or some other commodity, but are presented without an explicit agreement for immediate or future rewards. Through the masterful leveraging of two-sided markets—in which two distinct user groups, which provide each other with network benefits, are enabled to interact by a platform—digital companies have hacked (repurposed) the gift economy as a competing strategy brilliantly. I just highlighted three main features of this new "digital gift economy". The whole mechanism is based on two variables. One is the absence of effective, local competition: there is really only one Facebook, one Google, one TikTok, and so forth (more on this *pax digitalis* in Chapter 23). By their nature, two-sided markets tend to be dominated by one platform. The other variable is the availability of an immense, renewable resource, namely the amount of money spent worldwide on advertisements yearly. This does not concern all digital companies, of course, but only those that rely on advertisement as a business model.

According to a recent report by Statista "the [advertising] market saw healthy growth in 2021 and is expected to continue on the path and surpass one trillion US dollars in 2026".[1] In 2022, it was worth $880.9 billion.[2] According to data provided by the International Monetary Fund,[3] if this were the nominal GDP of a country, in 2022 advertisement would have ranked number 20 in the world, just below the Netherlands ($990,583 billion). Both lack of competition and increasing advertising spending are largely self-regulated. The market, whether analogue or digital, takes care of them. This is also part of the *disenfranchising* nature of free online services: controllers control themselves in a close circuit of interactions to which all the Alices in the world are invited as mere users, who can no longer afford not to accept the offered gifts and be left out of the infosphere.

The cost of this macroscopic mechanism is twofold. On the one hand, there is an ever-increasing pressure to acquire and process more and more personal data, which are the only thing that the online industry competes to sell to those who must advertise their goods and services. The more efficiently the almost billions-dollar ads available yearly are allocated, the more privacy risks being eroded. On the other hand, there is an increasing escalation in advertising budgets. This leads to an inefficient and skewed allocation of resources, with few winners taking all. In short, the outcome is less privacy, more inequality, and more unproductive investment, three severe problems in mature information societies, which now emerge as being linked like distant branches of the same tree.

There is no simple solution, but socio-political institutions could do much to improve the situation, by promoting more competition, better taxation, and by regulating more strictly the advertising industry, perhaps by following some of the lessons learnt from the limits imposed on the tobacco industry, and addressing the problem of how much money can be wasted in this new arms race (imagine for a moment what life would be like if paid

---

[1] See https://www.statista.com/topics/990/global-advertising-market/#topicOverview.

[2] See https://whatsnewinpublishing.com/global-ad-spend-to-rise-by-8–3-to-881b-warcs-ad-spend-outlook-2022–23.

[3] See https://en.wikipedia.org/wiki/List_of_countries_by_GDP_(nominal).

advertisements were illegal). As long as it is rational to offer gifts in return for increasingly less privacy and higher advertising revenues, do not expect much improvement in the future. When the outcome of a logical mechanism is unwanted, it is the mechanism that needs to be changed, not what it delivers. In order to achieve this, a better democracy may be needed, one that empowers people as customers and voters, the topic of the next chapter.

Chapter 20
Structural Democracy

The British referendum in favour of leaving the EU was a disaster. However, it offers three lessons on the relation between democracy and digital technologies and shows that democracy is best understood in terms of *structured power*.

The first lesson demythologises direct democracy as the "true" democracy. *Representative democracy* is the (regulative) ideal, not a compromise attributable to practical constraints, as many today assume. The argument goes roughly like this. John Stuart Mill suggested in *Considerations of Representative Government* (1999) that, if we lived in a community where everyone could inform themselves about shared social issues, participate in debates, discuss potential decisions and their consequences civilly and reasonably, evaluate their advantages and disadvantages, and finally reach an intelligent and tolerant consensus on what to do, by universal suffrage and an individual voting majority, then *that* would be the best democracy. This belongs to the myth of the city-state, particularly Athens, albeit an Athens that never existed historically: think of the trial of Socrates. Unfortunately, the argument goes, delegating political power is a lesser but inevitable evil, because there are too many of us. So representative democracy is a compromise, a better-than-nothing position, a lesser form of democracy when compared to direct democracy,

The Green and The Blue: Naive Ideas to Improve Politics in the Digital Age, First Edition.
Luciano Floridi.
© 2024 John Wiley & Sons Ltd. Published 2024 by John Wiley & Sons Ltd.

which is unfortunately unattainable. This has been the narrative, the white lie, that we have repeated to ourselves throughout the modern era. Yet, today, this story no longer holds thanks to the arrival of digital technologies. The time has come to outline what democracy really is and what it can be.

In Chapter 2 I argued that some people today are wrong about two issues relating to the new forms of agency, i.e., the artificial and the political. AI is not a marriage (paste) but a divorce (cut) between agency and intelligence; and democracy is not a marriage (paste) but a divorce (cut) between sovereignty and governance. In that chapter, I explained why AI is a digitally enabled separation between the ability to fulfil a task and successfully reach a goal and the need to be intelligent to do so. I promised I would deal with the second mistaken idea of believing that the structural separation between those who possess power and those who exercise it is a fault and that they should be brought together. The erroneous idea holds that the *disconnect* between *sovereignty*—here understood as political power that voters legitimately have and can delegate—and *governance*—here understood as political power that is legitimately exercised in a conditional, transparent, and accountable way, and therefore can also be legitimately withdrawn—should now be repaired, glued back together, so to speak, by the digital. The hope is that the digital, through platforms, apps, and other technological solutions, will "restore" a direct democracy—one which never existed in practice, but was much praised in the past—that would guarantee a (theoretically) disintermediated, constant, and universal political participation of all citizens. It is like telling John Stuart Mill that he was right in his day, but that, today, we no longer need to compromise, because finally, despite our societies being so populous, digital technologies enable us to do what he thought was preferable in a city-state but unfortunately unfeasible in a modern context. This is the same promise made by the use of referenda, especially when they are binding rather than consultative. Finally, the argument concludes, the only task left to the political class would be to implement and administer the decisions of the voters, often described as "the people". The sovereign voters would delegate politicians not as their representatives, but as their public servants, in a literal sense.

To summarise the line of reasoning based on Mill: direct democracy is the best form of democracy, but it is not feasible in a large society, so we must compromise and accept the second best, which is representative democracy; however, now digital technologies enable the direct participation of any number of people, so direct democracy is feasible, so we do not need to compromise, we can abandon representative democracy and opt for the best form of democracy, which is direct.

A direct, digital democracy might initially seem to be a good idea. The old "passive" media, from the press to the radio and television, have accentuated the positive aspects of representative democracy (i.e., information and public debate) but also its negative aspects (i.e., disinformation and populism). Many people are aware and weary of this. The Web seems to have mainly contributed to the damage, but it could balance things out by conversely contributing to the health of democracy, enabling its direct management. In 2016, I attended a conference in Lisbon organised by the Champalimaud Foundation on "The Unknown, 100 years from now: A voyage of discovery". We looked at society's challenges, with Nobel Prize winners, former presidents of Brazil and Portugal, famous intellectuals, and managers from large companies. Many topics were covered that merit further discussion, but the issue that struck me most was political. Tim Berners-Lee and Manuel Castells expressed converging opinions, albeit in different ways. Let me summarise them, hoping not to misrepresent their thinking. To put their point simply: they argue that politics can be saved through a shift from representative to direct democracy made possible by the Internet. According to them, the rationale behind sovereign states and their institutions no longer meets the political needs of the information society. They argue for them to be updated, so they stop being the problem and instead form part of the solution again. The Internet can enable this, if the network leads to disintermediation and new forms of direct, socio-political participation, aggregation, and consensus-building on pressing problems such as growing social inequality, political corruption, and environmental disasters.

I am not convinced that the therapy prescribed is helpful because I fear it is based on a wrong diagnosis. Like John Stuart Mill, people still think that representative democracy is a compromise caused by limitations in communication. Because we do not live in a small and isolated Greek town, our large numbers force us to delegate legislative, executive, and judicial decisions to the corresponding, relevant representatives. If we were all entirely online, there would be no problem; but in reality, we now live onlife, so the problem is already solved. We only need to take the next, reasonable step forward. Welcome to the digital agora, an allegedly open, public space. I disagree, becasue the situation appears to be very different. Apart from the fact that even the smallest municipality has a mayor and a council, and that digital technologies are also subject to monopolies, manipulation, intermediation, and exploitation of position no less than was the case with the old mass media, we shall see in a moment that the *structural* separation between those who possess and legitimise political power (i.e. popular sovereignty) and those who exercise it legitimately (i.e. representatives) is *a necessary* and *vital property* of democracy, not *a contingent limitation* to be overcome by representation. Representative democracy has always been plan A, never plan B. The "divorce" (a cut) between *sovereignty* and *governance* is a *feature*, not a *bug*, to use a common phrase from computer science. This separation precedes and logically underpins the distinction between a democracy based on values and one based on procedures (Bobbio 2005), and the equally fundamental, classic separation between the three powers, legislative, executive, and judicial. The absence and elimination of such a separation characterise autocracies, which are literally the union of (paste) the possession and exercise of power. In them, those who exercise power legitimise themselves, be they an absolute monarch, a tyrant, a "Duce", a dictator, a generalissimo, a Führer, or even a party, or an ethnic majority that imposes itself on minorities, understood as individuals. Digital technology should enhance and uphold, rather than reverse, this disconnect between the legitimator and the legitimised, by making it work successfully, not by removing it.

Why is this separation fundamental? Here the second diagnostic error arises. Representative democracy is not just the least-worst political system, as Churchill characterised it correctly. It is the political system that fails better than any other because it "breaks down" in the most socially secure and practical way possible. In other words, it is the most "elastic" or resilient political system—not the most effective. The best, most enlightened autocracy— understood as any political system in which there is no separation between the legitimator and the legitimised—works better than the best representative democracy, until it falls apart. When it does not work, it creates an irretrievable disaster. And given that mistakes or external catastrophes are inevitable in human affairs, we must design our politics for the worst-case scenario, not the best.

Politics is inherently fragile: what is needed is a form of governance that is best able to heal when it is harmed or breaks down. That is why the worst thing that can be said in politics is not "nothing works", but "there is nothing to be done". However, it is precisely this mechanism of self-repair that has broken down in many liberal democracies: just think of the problem of the *casta* (a term used in Italian by Castells in his report, it means socio-political caste or ruling class[1]) and its immovability. Therefore, we should focus on repairing the self-healing mechanism, by leveraging all our resources, including technological ones, for instance, by facilitating participation in democratic life and increasing accountability and transparency in the exercise of political power. The mechanism of separation between the legitimisation and the exercise of power should be safeguarded, because it is necessary and works well. Eliminating the separation, and thus representation, confuses democratic procedures, i.e., the free formulation and discussion of political issues by majority vote, with the wrongly targeted fundamental structure of democratic power, i.e., the separation between those who possess and legitimise it and those who exercise it legitimately. To understand the error, consider that any direct democracy risks becoming a "tyranny of the majority" (Adams 1788), and can be interpreted as an autocratic regime in which those, including a majority of voters, who have power exercise it directly through self-legitimisation. This mutually dependent identity between the source, management, and legitimisation of power is prone to risk, not because it is necessarily inherently malevolent, but because it is a fragile mechanism that lacks the flexibility to recover. Owing to human fallibility and weakness, errors occur and are, in this system, irreparable. In contrast, in a representative democracy, those who have and legitimise power do not exercise it and can correct it more easily. A representative democracy is the best system for dealing with risks, mistakes, and crises, not for guaranteeing successes. This is how I interpret the famous phrase, attributed to Jean Monnet, one of the key architects of the European Union: "Europe will be forged in crises, and will be the sum of the solutions adopted for those crises".

Those who have power (i.e., the citizens) must be able to delegate, control, criticise, and re-delegate it through debate and by voting freely. If they exercise it directly, however, they fall into dictatorship, this time of the majority. The risk is to end up like Jesus and Barabbas (or Brexit): a catastrophic choice resulting in irrecoverable damage.

It turns out that democracy is, primarily, a question of relation, the *structure of* power, even before it is a question of the *semantics* (i.e., values) or *syntax* (i.e., procedures) of power. Or, simply put, a democratic regime is not only a way of *exercising* power, but, primarily, a way of *structuring* it, by making sure that those who hold power do not exercise it, and those who

---

[1] https://foreignpolicy.com/2009/10/12/italys-untouchable-caste.

exercise it do not hold it. The fusion (nowadays, the digital integration) of the two sides leads to fragile forms of dictatorship or mob rule masquerading as democracy. Brexit, Le Pen, Putin, Salvini, Trump, and other populist disasters are sufficient proof of this. We must consider how best to design and use the structural divide between sovereignty and governance, not how to erase it simply because it has been eroded and no longer functions as it should. For this reason, *consensus-building* is the real difficulty in any decent democracy. Once the possession and the exercise of political power are separated, they still need to be bridged, but the challenges in doing so cannot be overcome by erasing this vital separation without falling back into autocratic governance.

To conclude this first lesson, representative democracy is not a compromise but the best option. The story we have been telling ourselves was necessary for it to be accepted and appreciated by everyone, but it is part of the "democracy by stealth" strategy, which I will discuss in the next chapter. Some pills are good but may be bitter and need to be sweetened. John Stuart Mill's was a white lie.

This brings us to the second lesson, which deals with the importance of information and its role in shaping politics. As Rousseau already knew, citizens can better fulfil their political role the better informed they are, not only about the issues under discussion, their order of priority and possible alternatives, but also about those they are electing and how they intend to manage the power delegated to them for the benefit of the *res publica* (or rather the *ratio publica*, as I shall argue). Digital technologies can be a great engine of civic information, consultation, and deliberation: to get an idea of how things are, eliminate lies, and expose the buffoons. Unfortunately, this proved not to be the case in the United Kingdom, where the political class, by re-delegating political decision-making to the citizens during the 2016 United Kingdom European Union membership referendum, resorted to demagoguery and polemical discourse to influence the public, creating media sounding boards devoid of reasoned dialogue or factual information. Once the mistake was made in favour of Brexit, no politician dared to remind the (small) majority, elevated to the status of an indisputable source of choice, that the final decision lies with parliament. It would have been legally possible to ignore the referendum, an event that in the UK is merely advisory. However, the political class that shirked and offset its responsibility by invoking the referendum was unable or unwilling to regain the necessary courage to retake responsibility by overriding it. The fear of taking such a decision led to decisions favouring fear. This process is visible in the case of Brexit and permeates many other political dynamics in countries, such as the USA, that have seen themselves as champions of democracy in the past.

We now come to the third lesson, namely that the relational logic of any union means that Brexit could encourage the EU to focus on its human project. To begin with, it is *plausible* (I am carefully avoiding the word "probable") that, following Brexit, Scotland, who voted in their majority to remain, could demand, and win an independence referendum and later apply to join the EU. As a result, England, Wales, and perhaps Northern Ireland (but even this is now in doubt) would be all that remains of the former British empire, a United Kingdom that will have preferred to commit suicide in the name of Victorian nostalgia rather than come to terms with its own history, accepting the end of the empire, and acknowledging its non-exceptional status as a mid-sized power and ordinary European country, leveraging its unique position, within the EU, as an interface between the EU and the rest of the world. The incoherence is apparent: a union, the *United* Kingdom, which has been successful for centuries because of a relational policy between different nations (mainly England and Scotland), and their equilibrium within an even larger union (the EU), has decided to abandon the relational logic only halfway. While it rejects the one in which it formed part of a larger system, it endeavours to maintain the smaller system of which it is composed. If your country is called the *United* Kingdom, it is inconsistent to reject the European *Union*, to keep thinking in terms of a local *Union*, but then deny Scotland an independence referendum. What could lie ahead is a break-up of the UK with parallels to Czechoslovakia. Ironically, such a tragic implosion could bear the advantage of conversely enabling a viable and improved European political project. Politics is not only a product of the economy (a necessary condition) but, above all, a human and social project (a sufficient condition). The EU should not be just a matter of laws and the common market. It must primarily be a project of social cohabitation with added value, in which being together is far preferable to being alone. The form will have to be designed, but without the "British brake" to hinder the process, constructing the European mosaic may now prove less difficult. Here again, digital technologies will be essential to coordinate everyone to contribute and reap the benefits of an enlarged EU. The post-Brexit EU could re-commence from the "networked Europe", for a Europe united by values and not merely geographical borders, as discussed in Chapter 3.

As we have seen in the previous chapter, all of this presupposes that it is possible to reverse the current vicious circles, in which the *Matthew effect* and the *network effect* are creating an ever-worsening deterioration in politics. How can this be done? The next chapter is dedicated to answering this question, and explaining what I meant by saying that Mill's position about representative democracy might have been a case of *stealth democracy*.

Chapter 21
Stealth Democracy

I have argued (Chapter 17) that the vicious circles caused by the *Matthew effect* and the *network effect* can be reversed. Let us now focus on exactly how to transform these two effects into virtuous circles, to eliminate rather than promote bad politics. From the point of view of simple logical analysis, there are three ways to eliminate a polluted political environment, in which the harmful marketisation of politics makes toxic politics the only kind that can thrive and pushes out healthier alternatives. The polluted environment can fail by:

1. collapsing on its own, or
2. being devastated by external forces, or
3. being reformed, to prevent collapse or devastation.

Let us simplify this by assuming that the two "ors" are exclusive (either/or), and not inclusive (and/or). In (1), bad politics collapses under its own weight, so to speak, when it has become so polluted as to lead to systemic failure. This is the case in Venezuela today, for example. Its current crisis as a failed state appears to be predominantly self-generated. Some anticipate a similar collapse in the case of North Korea. Waiting for (1) to happen may be a strategy, but as the two examples show, collapse may take a very long time, and cause huge human suffering.

The Green and The Blue: Naive Ideas to Improve Politics in the Digital Age, First Edition. Luciano Floridi.
© 2024 John Wiley & Sons Ltd. Published 2024 by John Wiley & Sons Ltd.

In (2), bad politics and its polluted environment can be devastated by external factors, such as revolutions, wars (civil or otherwise), public health, or ecological disasters. This lesson is frequently taught by history, through tragedies and catastrophes (see Chapter 26). Bad politics combined with populism lead to an often-repeated series of steps: simplistic solutions characterised by intolerance are followed by xenophobia, then hatred, which leads to the targeted identification of imaginary enemies, and finally conflict, external and internal. Black shirts, brown shirts, red shirts, and so on, lead to unimaginable suffering, which ultimately causes a reaction of total rejection of them and their violence. The history of the twentieth century is full of tragic examples, from fascist to communist dictatorships. Even recently, politicians escalate conflicts (armed or not) when they struggle to maintain power domestically, and they mobilise human interfaces to do so. Such conflicts serve to distract the human interfaces from the problems that could be attributed to bad governance and instead summon them against an enemy that acts as a proxy (Chapter 16) for all the nation's troubles. The problem shifts from *us* to *them*. For example, in 1981, the Third Military Junta of Argentina ordered the invasion of the Falkland Islands (Malvinas) and South Georgia, seeking to establish the sovereignty that Argentina has claimed over them since her brief possession of the islands from 1820–33 following its independence from Spain in 1816. This led to a conflict that "remains the largest air-naval combat operation between modern forces since the end of World War II".[1] Jorge Luis Borges aptly described it as "a fight between two bald men over a comb".[2] Vladimir Putin continues to use similar strategies to distract public opinion in and about Russia and to strengthen his power by promoting a nationalistic image of the country. The recent invasion of Ukraine is the tragic, coherent outcome of such a strategy.

In both cases, whether collapse or devastation, politics fails to be its own cure. The spiral of bad politics that exploits human interfaces begets the increasingly harmful marketisation of bad politics that can only end in disaster.

In (3), we find a healthier alternative, namely the democratic replacement of bad politics to prevent the first two scenarios from occurring. Unfortunately, this is far more difficult in practice because, as we have seen, the toxic agents in

---

[1] https://en.wikipedia.org/wiki/Aftermath_of_the_Falklands_War.
[2] *The Guardian*, "Falkland Islands: Imperial pride": https://www.theguardian.com/commentisfree/2010/feb/19/falkland-islands-editorial.

power continually poison the environment in which they thrive, to such an extent that they may eliminate the healthier alternatives that threaten their political ecology. This is why, when bad politics prevails, civil society does not react with greater involvement but rather with increased apathy. It distances itself from politics, which is seen as a menu of hopeless choices between bad options. If change does not ensue from either (1) the effectively suicidal logic of pollution, or (2) external catastrophic events, and if good, democratic politics becomes ineffective, what remains is a covert change, which I will term democracy by stealth, or stealth democracy.

An example of stealth democracy could be to reform the voting age or to replace the current First Past the Post voting system used to elect MPs to the UK parliament with a proportional system. These are entirely conventional and contingent features of the current situation in British politics. To use Machiavelli's terms, we must recognise the dependence of British politics on *luck* (accidents) and then identify what must be done accordingly as a *necessity* (stealth). Thus, stealth democracy can be implemented by appealing to external pressure, as many European politicians have done, i.e., by referring to Brussels whenever they needed to justify some positive and necessary but unpopular changes. We saw in the previous chapter that, perhaps, when Mill presented representative democracy as an inevitable compromise, his strategy was just a case of "stealth democracy". The typical reasoning, in this case, is as follows: you do not want A, you really want B, but as B is not accepted by public opinion, you present A as preferable but impossible and B as the best compromise: "if only we could do A, but unfortunately..., so let's do B". Today, in a world where citizens are seen and used as interfaces, changing politics by stealth would mean employing the same marketing strategies to gain attention, approval, and votes, using topics, policy suggestions, promises, and rhetoric that resemble those of the polluting politicians but ultimately have no real intention of carrying out the corresponding actions once in power. For years, blaming Brussels for good yet unpopular policies that had to be implemented has been a typically European instance of stealth democracy. A risky approach, but often a successful one.

To effect change through a stealth democracy is a temporary and extreme measure, to be adopted only when extremisms are in power. It is not Machiavellian in the sense of the *Prince*, but only in the sense of the *Discourses*. It may be an extreme (because it is also paternalistic) but necessary solution (the *necessity* of which Machiavelli speaks) to remove the rampant polluters of populism, nationalism, and xenophobia (all aspects of *fortune*) when social and environmental crises are in a critical state. As I argued above, what is needed is not an outright rejection of marketing strategies but a much-improved use of them to reach much better ends. The success of the Greta Thunberg phenomenon is a strong example that this can work. The message is no less populist than other current forms of political communication, but it serves a good end. And while a good end may not justify bad means, it can certainly motivate an improvement of them to serve a better end.

Many democracies are afflicted by populism. The populist epidemic is exhausting many liberal democracies, including those with the most historic roots, from post-Johnson Britain to post-Trump USA. We live in an interdependent world, where it is increasingly common for positive or negative sentiments to be shared altogether. Yet this is not a case of "fellowship in woe doth woe assuage" (Shakespeare, *The Rape of Lucrece*) or "two in distress make sorrow less" (Beckett, *Murphy*). Unfortunately, the opposite is the case, the worse off liberal democracies are, the more difficult it is for each of them to recover. The cure for democracy will not come from a new Marshall Plan or the EU. For each democracy to heal, the first step is to understand that, in this populist epidemic, every liberal democracy is sick in its own way, like "every unhappy family is unhappy in its own way", to quote the famous *incipit* of Tolstoy's *Anna Karenina*. Each sick democracy manifests its illness in multiple ways, but it is not worth dwelling on this because the second step is to realise that diagnosing how each democracy has fallen ill will not provide the remedy to cure it. Understanding how we got to this point is important to avoid a relapse, but it is also insufficient. New solutions are required to get out of the current crisis, beyond regrets, recriminations, or hindsight. Self-criticism—for instance by Labour in the UK, the Democrats in the USA, and the Partito Popolare in Italy—may be cathartic, but does not provide a way forward if it does not lead to constructive problem-solving. So, what can be done when populism is endemic, and democracy is in crisis?

Let us start with the most complicated problem, by continuing with the health metaphor: democracy now suffers from "antibiotic resistance" to democracy itself, in the following sense. When things go wrong in some countries, the therapy ascribed is usually democracy-based. North Korea's problems are explained by its lack of democracy. Are human rights being violated in China? The same solution is proffered again: a strong dose of democracy. And what can be done in Russia if not by increasing the same dose of democracy first injected in 1993? Since the Second World War, democracy has been used as an antibiotic to cure every political illness. So, when democracy itself is sick, in this case with populism, the temptation is to increase the dosage and implement direct democracy through online platforms, referendums, or tweets. We have seen that some people have vaguely articulated hopes for an unmoderated, unmediated sort of direct democracy, which is instantaneous and volatile, and where everyone has a say on everything. This leads to the tyranny of impromptu majorities that manage the state, flattening out all opinions through the logic of relativism, which erases the difference between true and false, and ultimately confuses politics (which at its best is supportive cooperation) with agonism (which at its best is fair competition). Not only is none of this effective, but it also aggravates the damage caused by populism. As in the case of excessive use of antibiotics, the solution becomes part of the problem: today, countries such as Italy, the UK, and the USA have become "treatment-resistant". We need to change the remedy because it is endangering us. And this is where we risk falling into the opposite temptation, illiberalism.

Illiberal democracies are all the rage, whether in Hungary, Russia, Singapore, or Turkey. There is a consistency in who sees illiberalism as a solution, noting that democracy is now resistant to further doses of democracy. The problem is not the effectiveness of the intervention per se, but rather that the patient is dead. While illiberalism can be highly successful in reducing conflict among the population and defending some kind of social law and order, it ends up suffocating tolerance, freedom, and justice, the three fundamental values that every democracy should protect and support, and without which no democracy can survive.

The therapy is not more democracy, which increases populism, or less democracy, which increases illiberalism, but instead, a better democracy, which is anti-populist, liberal, and political, to counter the tyranny of the majority and to represent, defend, and promote the interests of all, including minorities. So, a first prescription is: all goodwills (all people of good will, *bonae voluntatis*, to put it more Biblically) are needed.

We come to the second chronic problem. The worse democracy is, the less trust there is in politics, and the more civil society becomes detached from institutions and apathetic towards the management and steering of the *res publica*. Civil society tries to mind its own business, which further aggravates the health of democracy and politics.

All this exacerbates the problem, but, from another perspective, civil society's sense of detachment is also a sign of a healthy reaction. The social body is alive, and its pain bodes well for the therapy. Society hosts an enormous reserve of goodwill, skills, experience, and intelligence. According to global estimates, there are more than a billion volunteers worldwide, for example.[3] The trouble is that this reservoir of goodwill and intelligence is not directed towards politics because the latter is perceived as corrupt and something to be avoided for goodwill's sake. At best, goodwill adopts civic protest and, at worst, a protest vote, alternating between "every man for himself" and "to hell with politics and politicians". However, taking refuge in civil society is self-defeating, like ignoring a leak in the hull of the *Titanic* when everything seems fine on deck. And it is counterproductive because it distracts from finding a solution to avoid disaster. So, part of the therapy is to recognise, understand and use society's anger and disgust by redirecting it as strength and passion for promoting a better society. Hence, a second prescription is: all goodwills need to be involved in politics.

This brings us to the third and most serious problem: today, democracy lacks the oxygen vital for a human project for the twenty-first century. The past generation had a country to rebuild, a constitutional democracy to establish, an economic boom and widespread prosperity to pursue. Now that these goals have been *more or less* achieved, or have lost their motivating drive, we are disappointed by the *more* and frustrated with the *less*. We expect better. Not unlike the present, an uncertain and flat future may depress or irritate, but it cannot galvanise. We are missing something that really excites us, a world we aspire to and would like to build together. We are missing a collective call to action. Humanity does not live by mortgage alone. For this reason, fragmented fundamentalisms emerge that seem to be the best offer of a social utopia worthy of sacrifice. A teenager may wish to die while holding a Kalashnikov for a greater cause, but not for the next version of a mobile phone. Therefore, therapy for our democracy must start with creating a shared design of a common human project, worthy of our commitment. Here we get a third prescription: goodwills of all kinds must codesign the next shared human project.

The word that often accompanies "crime" is "organised". Criminal groups are generally organised because they share clear and strong interests and a lack of scruples in pursuing them. However, good people tend to be disorganised because they have multiple and often conflicting interests and are inclined to respect them. How, then, do we make it so that the good people

---

[3] https://unv-swvr2018.org.

win? What is needed is a *force* more compelling than self-interest, and an *urgency* that causes disagreements and divisions to be not only respected and appreciated, but also relinquished and overcome. Such a force is called *hope*, and the rampant disease of populism provides the urgency. The time has come to organise goodwill, to help defeat unchecked populism, because we know that the maxim "every little effort helps" is often false. It certainly does not apply when global challenges are in question. Only an organised whole can provide the crucial difference: remember the angels pushing the broken-down car, cooperating in Chapter 11. So, the fourth and final prescription is: make divergent forms of goodwill cooperate for a common goal, sharing a human project worth their hopes.

Hope, goodwill, and intelligence are everywhere, shared by hundreds of millions of people in factories, offices, homes, schools, professions, politics, any kind of organisation and *all* political parties. Above all, these qualities may be found most among young people, who should vote to replace the politics of fear, discord, and self-interest with the politics of hope, solidarity, and altruism. I do not know whether new "open parties" are needed to help unite divergent forms of goodwill and make them cooperate, or whether it is sufficient to reform existing ones. But I believe that quarrelling is futile and depleting our precious political oxygen, and that we need to focus instead on creating a political interface that welcomes and engages all forms of good-will and the many competencies associated with them, to make civil society interact with political life and the management of the *res publica*. The ill-ness is severe. The treatment is urgently needed. Some stealth democracy may help. The cure will doubtless not be easy to administer or quick to take effect, so the sooner the goodwills get together and serious, the better. The question is how to facilitate such cooperation. This is the topic of the next chapter.

Chapter 22
Nomos and *Paideia*

Humanity has always wondered about good and evil but especially about evil, seen as made up of abuse, atrocity, betrayal, disappointment, fear, horror, humiliation, injustice, offence, sorrow, suffering, vices, violence, and anything else negative that life has in store for us. Evil plays a leading role in all cultures and civilisations, from the first cuneiform tablets, which speak of unpaid debts, to the Epic of Gilgamesh and the Odyssey. There is no Dante or Shakespeare, Cervantes, or Goethe without evil as a great actor in human affairs.

Evil is a constant in history. It is also the object of study of ethics, which investigates its nature and causes, why it exists, and how it can be countered. Philosophers agree on the nature of evil insofar as they distinguish two kinds: the *nature-based*, called *natural*, and the *human-made*, called *moral*. An example can clarify the difference. In December 2021, many tornadoes caused deaths and injuries in various states of the United States, especially Kentucky. Pain, suffering, fear, losses of all kinds … these were all aspects of *natural evil*, something that even the legal system, no matter how secular, still calls "an act of God", for which nobody can be held responsible. Still in December, still in the United States, a student killed four people and injured seven others at a Michigan school. Equally devastating effects, but a very different cause, which

The Green and The Blue: Naive Ideas to Improve Politics in the Digital Age, First Edition.
Luciano Floridi.

in this case is entirely and exclusively *moral* because it is made up of human choices and responsibilities. It was an (evil) act of Humanity.

If you rely on similar examples, or consult an ethics textbook, the distinction between natural and moral evil seems clear and uncontroversial. But things soon become complicated. Natural evil has always been a major headache for many religions, especially Christianity, which sees God as omnipotent, omniscient, and infinitely benevolent. If God can do anything, knows everything, and always wants the good, how do we square that with the sufferings in Kentucky? God's will? Did people deserve it? Or could God do nothing about it? Whichever way you turn it around, it is a thorny problem that goes by the name, made famous by Leibniz, of *theodicy*: how to reconcile the existence of God (as described above) with the existence of natural evil.

Leibniz thought that the theodicy problem could be solved by arguing that our world, as a whole, is the best of all possible worlds, despite all its limitations. A little bit like saying that things may not be great, but they cannot get any better. Voltaire thought Leibniz's suggestion was a bad joke, and he famously mocked Leibniz and his philosophy in his classic satire *Candide, o Optimism*. The novella was published in 1759. In it, we find references to historical events, such as the Lisbon earthquake (1755), a natural evil that killed between 12,000 and 50,000 people, one of the worst outcomes in the history of earthquakes; and the Seven Years' War (1756–1763), a moral evil that caused between 900,000 and 1,400,000 deaths and is often considered the first global conflict in history (but see the Thirty Tears' War for a competitor). As Voltaire might have said, imagine if this were *not* the best of all possible worlds.

The story seems to end here, but in reality, over time, another factor takes over. Could the suffering and losses in Kentucky have been prevented? Tornadoes today remain unpredictable. Too sudden and chaotic, they generate too much data, and there is too little time to do the necessary calculations. Nevertheless, we can already run simulations, assign probabilities, and play the precautionary card. Most importantly, one day, we may have the data, the models, and the computing power necessary to predict them in time, with sufficient accuracy and reliability. And then there are the buildings. We should build them tornado-proof, as we do with anti-seismic measures in earthquake-prone areas. In other words, as science and technology advance, natural evil does not remain fixed but is translated increasingly into moral evil. That is, if things end badly, it is no longer God's fault, but Humanity's alone. For example, Hegel died of malaria, like Dante. It was a natural evil at the time, but today dying of malaria is an entirely human responsibility. It has morphed into a moral evil. In 2020, there were 241 million malaria cases worldwide and an estimated 627,000 deaths.[1] Like them, the deaths caused by the Lisbon earthquake today would be a human crime, not something over which to doubt the existence of the God of Christianity. As *The Economist* wrote about the 2023 earthquake in Turkey:

> The real culprit. Shoddy building methods, corruption and bad policymaking components of an economy powered by construction and rent-seeking, may have caused the most deaths, however.[2]

So, Leibniz's idea could be updated in the following version: this is not yet the best of possible worlds, but we are getting there, and in the future, natural evil could be a memory, leaving only human intelligence, freedom, and responsibility to prevent, avoid, minimise, or eradicate evils in the world. In the presence of moral evil, the theological solution is to excuse God and charge humanity with the mistaken use of its freedom. Evil would be an utterly immanent problem, a human problem. Perhaps this is the best of all possible worlds, after all, because it offers humanity the opportunity of removing any natural evil. Politics, and the management of human affairs, replaces Theology and the management of God's intervention (or lack thereof) in them.

Over time, on the ethical scale, the plate of natural evil is becoming lighter and that of moral evil heavier. Human responsibilities are increasing, not only for the many wrongs we cause—just think of climate change—but also because of the natural evils we can but do not prevent, minimise, or eliminate. Here too, science, technology, and, more generally, human intelligence make a considerable difference, for better or for worse. If the student in Michigan had not had a gun, he would not have been able to kill and injure so many people in an instant. Mass shootings, defined as at least four people shot, plus the shooter, are so common in the United States that there is an entry *for each year* on Wikipedia. That of 2020 lists 703 people dead and 2,842 injured, for a total of 3,545 victims. Proof that human stupidity and responsibility are immense because good legislation would be enough to eradicate an evil that is entirely and only moral. Everyone understands this, except some American voters.

---

[1] https://www.who.int/news-room/fact-sheets/detail/malaria.
[2] https://www.economist.com/europe/2023/02/12/turkeys-earthquakes-show-the-deadly-extent-of-construction-scams.

This path of translating natural evil into moral evil seems like bad news, but it is not. Because as far as natural evil is concerned—think of the pandemic—there is little to do except transform it into a subsequent human responsibility, for example, in the production and distribution of vaccines to everyone. But as far as moral evil is concerned, one can work to eradicate it, for instance, by getting vaccinated. So, the first step is to transform natural evil into a moral one, from acts of God to human shortcomings. The next is to fight moral evil itself. To do so, one must understand it. Hence the crucial question: why are we evil? Or, as some ethicists would rather say, why do we behave in evil ways? Ethics has done much work on this too, but in the end, there seem to be two prevalent interpretations of human nature that explain moral evil. Neither is flattering, but I believe each usefully captures part of the story, as often is the case. Both ground much political thinking.

The first dates to Socrates. We also find it in the Stoics, Rousseau, or Arendt. We do evil not because we are immoral by nature, but because we do not understand what good is for ourselves and others. Vices, wickedness, and horrors of all kinds result from human stupidity, moral ignorance, or some other *epistemic shortcomings*. Then there is another tradition, attributable to Hobbes as its best-known supporter, but which also includes Kant, for example. According to it, moral evil is the fruit of human intelligence at the service of human, intrinsic immorality. Each of us pursues our selfish interests and goals as much as possible, and if we stop, it is only because the outcome no longer suits us. The *shortcomings are moral*, not epistemic. Famously, Kant made this point by saying that "out of the crooked timber of humanity no straight thing was ever made". This echoes *Ecclesiastes* 1:15 "what is crooked cannot be made straight", but is more pessimistic than *Luke* 3:5 "[...] and the crooked shall be made straight".

In summary, and simplifying, there is moral evil because humanity is either good but stupid—let us call this the *Socratic anthropology*—or intelligent but evil—let us call this the *Hobbesian anthropology*. From these two philosophical anthropologies derive different ethical and political theories and practices, but above all, different answers to our previous question: how moral evil can be at least limited, if not eliminated. If we are good but stupid, then we must invest in our education: to make people understand more and better what is authentically good for themselves and others, for society, and for the environment. In this case, the Socratic solution to moral evil is called *Paideia*. Using a trivial example, warning messages on the packaging of cigarettes and other tobacco products concerning their harmful health effects are typical of a

Socratic approach: more information should lead to better behaviour. These messages have been implemented since 1969. In 2011, a systematic report concluded that "prominent health warnings on the face of packages serve as a prominent source of health information for smokers and non-smokers, can increase health knowledge and perceptions of risk and promote smoking cessation. The evidence also indicates that comprehensive warnings are effective among youth and may help to prevent smoking initiation. Pictorial health warnings that elicit strong emotional reactions are significantly more effective" (Hammond 2011). The Socratic approach may have its merits.

In contrast, if we are intelligent but evil, we must motivate through incentives and disincentives, which rational and selfish agents will find more or less compelling. Forget about Madison's angels: even devils incarnated can be coaxed into doing the right thing if properly nudged. In this case, the solution to moral evil is called *Nomos*, the body of laws and rules that make things work as they should. From a Hobbesian perspective, that is where society must invest in terms of designing its preferred forms of civil cohabitation and competition. Using the previous, trivial example, increasing the price of tobacco is a Hobbesian solution to motivate a rational choice and more virtuous behaviour. According to a recent study, it does have an impact, especially when you do not have much money and you can still give up smoking: "taxation is an effective means of socially-enacted preventative medicine in deterring youth smoking" (Ding 2003).

The history of civilisations oscillates between *Paideia* and *Nomos*, preferring one or the other depending on the context. But the approaches are not incompatible. Except for a few cases of pure holiness and utter wickedness, we are almost all a little bit good but stupid and a little bit evil but intelligent. For this reason, innovation and development must support both *Paideia* and *Nomos* to make us Socratically intelligent and Hobbesianly good. The tricky bit is to reach an equilibrium that is also *tolerant* of individual preferences and choices. Which is a somewhat philosophical way of saying that society can hope to improve only if it invests in science and technology, to eliminate natural evil or translate it into a moral one, and in education and rules, to reduce moral evil, and perhaps even eliminate it one day, to make any negative impact of an act of God a thing of the past.

Both Nomos and Paideia are necessary to implement fair competition and voluntary cooperation. To implement both, a society needs to have control over itself; in order words, it needs sovereignty, the topic of the next chapter.

Chapter 23
Digital Sovereignty

The popularity of *digital sovereignty* today suggests that it is a significant issue. True. But it also sounds like a technical issue that would concern only specialists. False. Digital sovereignty, and the fight for it, affect everyone, even those who do not have a mobile phone or have never used an online service. To understand why, let's look back at four episodes. I shall add a fifth shortly.

On 18 June 2020, the British government, after having failed to develop an independent, centralised, coronavirus app not based on the API provided by Google-Apple,[1] gave up and abandoned the whole project (Burgess 19 June 2020). They then agreed to start developing a new app that would be fully interoperable with the decentralised solution provided by the two Silicon Valley companies. This U-turn was not the first: Italy and Germany had done the same, only much earlier. Note that, in the context of an online webinar on COVID-19 contact-tracing applications, organised by RENEW EUROPE (a liberal, pro-European political group of the European Parliament), Gary Davis, the Global Director of Privacy & Law Enforcement Requests at Apple (and previously Deputy Commissioner at the Irish Data Protection Commissioner's

---

[1] Disclosure: I was a member of the Ethics Advisory Board for the NHSX app.

Office), stated that "Google/Apple can disable the system [i.e., the contact tracing app] on a regional basis when no longer needed".[2] This is *power as control*, as I shall explain presently, where it is abundantly clear who possesses it and can exercise it, as far as the coronavirus apps and the API are concerned.[3]

The second episode took place about a month later, on 7 July 2020. Mike Pompeo, the US Secretary of State, announced the intention of his government to ban TikTok (Clayton 7 July 2020). India had already banned it (Singh 29 June 2020) together with tens of other Chinese apps, including WeChat, following clashes at the India-China border in the Himalayas. TikTok is a China-based app used to create and share amateur music videos that are between a few seconds and three minutes long. Available in 40 languages, at the beginning of 2023, it had over 800 million active users every month, a total of 1 billion users and was available in over 150 countries. An app to share and enjoy singing, dancing, comedy, and lip-syncing short videos would seem harmless enough. However, the app can be used as a vehicle for social or political messages, for instance. Coupled with this is the fear that the app can collect personal data, including sensitive metadata, such as user geolocation, and may be used to support China's espionage and infiltration, hence Pompeo's announcement on a possible ban. However, things may change. For example, in 2020, Microsoft announced that:

> Following a conversation between Microsoft CEO Satya Nadella and President Donald J. Trump, Microsoft is prepared to continue discussions to explore a purchase of TikTok in the United States. Microsoft will move quickly to pursue discussions with TikTok's parent company, ByteDance, in a matter of weeks, and in any event completing these discussions no later than September 15, 2020. During this process, Microsoft looks forward to continuing dialogue with the United States Government, including with the President. The discussions with ByteDance will build upon a notification made by Microsoft and ByteDance to the Committee on Foreign Investment in the United States (CFIUS). The two companies have provided notice of their intent to explore a preliminary proposal that would involve a purchase of the TikTok service in the United States, Canada, Australia, and New Zealand and would result in Microsoft owning and operating TikTok in

---

[2] See YouTube video at time point 1:14:13, https://re.livecasts.eu/webinar-on-contact-tracing-applications/program.
[3] Part of the failure was also a failure of trust.

these markets. Microsoft may invite other American investors to participate on a minority basis in this purchase.[4]

Microsoft Corporate Blogs, 2 August 2020

And at the time of writing, in 2023, TikTok was banned on Canada, EU, Hong Kong, and USA government devices because of growing privacy and cybersecurity concerns about the app.

The third episode occurred a week later, on 16 July 2020. The Court of Justice of the European Union concluded that the USA did not offer sufficient guarantees about the surveillance and the security of personal data they handle. Therefore, they invalidated the *EU-US Data Protection Shield*, the agreement regulating the transfer of the data of European users to processors in the USA for commercial purposes. Days later, on 20 July 2020, Huawei, a leading Chinese company in the production of 5G networks and systems, threatened to retaliate against two European mobile communication companies, Nokia and Ericsson (Mukherjee 20 July 2020), if the EU were to ban its technology for security reasons, following the example of the USA and Great Britain.

These are just four examples from some ordinary weeks in the life of the digital revolution, albeit one taking place during a global pandemic. They are a mere snapshot, and they will age. The point is not their novelty. There are many more. Indeed, the reader may have others in mind, and I shall refer to one more in a moment. Their purpose is to make evident the common thread that unites them. These episodes all reflect the fight for *digital sovereignty*, that is, for the *control* of data, software (e.g., AI), standards, and protocols (e.g., 5G, domain names), processes (e.g. cloud computing), hardware (e.g., mobile phones), services (e.g., social media, e-commerce), and infrastructures (e.g., cables, satellites, smart cities), in short, for the *control of the digital*. Recall that in Chapter 18 power as control was defined as the ability to influence something (i.e., its occurrence, creation, or destruction) and its dynamics (e.g., its behaviour, development, operations, interactions), including checking and correcting for any deviation from such influence. In this sense, control comes in degrees and can be shared and transferred. This

---

[4] https://blogs.microsoft.com/blog/2020/08/02/microsoft-to-continue-discussions-on-potential-tiktok-purchase-in-the-united-states.

is crucial, as we shall see that today the ultimate form of control is individual sovereignty, understood as autonomy (self-ownership and self-control) and privacy, especially over one's own body, choices, and data.

The fight for digital sovereignty is an epochal struggle not only of all against all but also of anyone allied with anyone, with variable alliances changing according to interests and opportunities. The most visible clash is between companies and states, who vie for control with their asymmetric types of power over the digital. On the one hand, companies *design, produce, sell,* and *maintain* the digital. This *poietic* (creative) power over the digital means that states depend on companies for almost anything digital, to the extent that, for instance, in some contexts, companies are given responsibility for being the first line of defence against cyber-attacks. On the other hand, states have the power to *regulate* the digital, and this is a powerful form of *cybernetic* control (as we saw in Chapter 18 when discussing grey power), exercised by determining what is legal or illegal, incentives and disincentives, kinds and levels of taxation, policies for public procurement, as well as modalities and costs of compliance. The commonplace narrative that regulations could stifle or even kill innovation and destroy whole industrial sectors is also an implicit acknowledgement of the power of the cybernetic State. It is a significant counterbalance to the other narrative, which asserts the impossibility of regulating the digital because states and regulations always arrive too late compared with fast-moving companies and their nimble operations. Reconciling these two narratives reveals the real point: that between companies and states, the former can determine the *nature* and *speed* of change, whereas the latter can control the *direction* of change.

In this asymmetric dialectic, states sometimes use domestic companies to fight other states for political ends. Companies may try to deceive or circumvent states and their legislation, while relying on their "home" states to defend them against foreign states that oppose them. Moreover, companies sometimes even fight with their own "home" states, as was the case in the Twitter-Trump clash (Posner 29 May 2020). Finally, companies occasionally fight each other in the same country. For instance, Microsoft lost against Google in the competition for hegemony over the *search business* (they held 2.44% and 91.54% of the market share, respectively, in 2020[5]); but won a significant victory against Amazon, IBM, and Oracle for hegemony over cloud

[5] https://www.webfx.com/blog/seo/2019-search-market-share.

computing by securing the cloud computing contract of the United States Department of Defense (Joint Enterprise Defense Infrastructure or JEDI), worth up to $10 billion over ten years (Lardinois 26 October 2019; Tsidulko 30 July 2020). Facebook beat Google repeatedly in competition for hegemony over the *social* business: Orkut, then Google Buzz, and finally, Google Plus all closed down (Vítečková 22 June 2020). It would be interesting to write a history of how challenged multinational giants have failed to beat other multinational giants at their own game, or have learnt to avoid competing against each other. It would be a history of *de facto* monopolies and how a *pax digitalis* of non-belligerence emerged among these colossal actors. While waiting for such a history, let us return to the topic of digital sovereignty. We have seen that it generates some confusion. To orient ourselves, let us take a step back.

Sovereignty is a form of legitimate, controlling power. It is the power of the captain of the ship, to adopt and adapt Plato's cybernetic analogy. The debate about *who* can exercise it, *how*, *on what*, and *for what* purposes, has contributed to the shaping of the *modern age*. Conventionally, this period begins in 1492, with the "discovery" of America (in the sense of Europeans learning about its existence), but controversies about its exact end continue. A small-size (*S*) modernity ends with the French Revolution in 1789. Size *M* goes all the way to the Congress of Vienna (1814–15). Size *L* continues up to the outbreak of the First World War in 1914. I prefer using size *XL*, which runs until the end of the Second World War in 1945. This is the literal sense in which I like to use *post-modern*. I will justify this preference in a moment. Before doing so, we can now qualify *national sovereignty* as the controlling power exercised by the State on its territory, resources, and inhabitants. Such a phenomenon and concept are entirely *modern*, in the sense of the era beginning in 1492, and *analogue*, in terms of time, space, and the ontological primacy of physical things. It belongs to an Aristotelian-Newtonian *Ur-philosophie*. But the modern age is over, even in its protracted XL version. Our contemporary age is not just post-Westphalian and *post-modern*, in the chronological sense specified above. To characterise it in these terms indicates only what our age has ceased to be, but says nothing about what it actually is (note that XL is the only "size" of modernity that can accommodate *post-modernity* as a chronologically meaningful category). A more informative appellation for our period is, above all, the *digital age*. Nobody should be surprised by this taxonomy. Technology has always helped us date periods of human evolution, from the Stone Age to the Iron Age.

In the digital age, the infosphere is not a territory, data are not finite, scarce, rivalrous, natural resources like oil (so much the worse for the poor analogy), digital assets are mainly private (in terms of ownership, i.e. not publicly owned, not in terms of privacy) and constantly subject to market forces, and our profiles are created, owned, and exploited, as inforgs and interfaces, not just by states but also by multinational companies, which, as the word indicates, are globalised. For all these reasons, the digital age is forcing us to rethink the very nature of sovereignty. Modern-analogue sovereignty is still necessary but increasingly insufficient, exactly like the State, to deal with new kinds of power. Contemporary-digital sovereignty is also needed, to provide effective, democratic forms of control, through appropriate regulation. But who should exercise it *de facto* and *de jure*?

The first two decades of the twenty-first century saw the emergence of a sort of *de facto digital corporate sovereignty*. This is a form of controlling power supported by those who argue that corporate self-regulation is sufficient, that legislative intervention is unwelcome and hindering, and that any required checks and balances of corporate digital power will come from a competitive, *laissez-faire* approach, and market-based equilibria. We saw that this digital corporate sovereignty is built on hegemonic positions or *de facto* monopolies, which enjoy both poietic and cybernetic power over the digital, and rely on the shift from the individual as a voter-consumer to the individual as a follower-user. Let me comment on both points.

De facto digital corporate sovereignty leads to a situation where multinationals do not truly compete, as I have mentioned above. The logic of winner takes all, the so-called *Matthew effect* and *network effect*, dominate contemporary capitalism, especially in the digital industry and network economies. Once cumulative advantages create a monopolistic regime, there is no real competition, no authentic consumer choice, and, therefore, no real accountability of the companies that dominate specific markets. The time has come to introduce the fifth episode to elucidate this point.

On 29 July 2020, Jeff Bezos (Amazon), Tim Cook (Apple), Sundar Pichai (Google), and Mark Zuckerberg (Facebook) were questioned during a hearing of the House Judiciary Subcommittee on Antitrust, Commercial and Administrative Law on "Online Platforms and Market Power, Part 6: Examining the Dominance of Amazon, Apple, Facebook, and Google." Chairman David N. Cicilline gave the following opening statement, which is worth quoting at length:

[...]. Open markets are predicated on the idea that if a company harms people, consumers, workers, and business partners will choose another option. We are here today because that choice is no longer possible. [...] Because concentrated economic power also leads to concentrated political power, this investigation also goes to the heart of whether we, as a people, govern ourselves, or whether we let ourselves be governed by private monopolies. American democracy has always been at war against monopoly power. Throughout our history, we have recognised that concentrated markets and concentrated political control are incompatible with democratic ideals. When the American people confronted monopolists in the past—be it the railroads and oil tycoons or AT&T and Microsoft—we took action to ensure no private corporation controls our economy or our democracy. We face similar challenges today. [...] Their ability to dictate terms, call the shots, upend entire sectors, and inspire fear represent the powers of a private government. Our founders would not bow before a king. Nor should we bow before the emperors of the online economy.[6]

Corporate digital sovereignty is not just a philosophical idea, but a political reality. This leads me to the second point about the shift from voters-consumers to followers-users.

In the second half of the twentieth century, some people saw democracy and capitalism as two sides of the same coin. This can be explained partly by the general assumption that they were both accountable to people, through competition, which was based on political voting in a democratic society, and purchasing (buying) choices in a capitalist society, respectively. We just saw that Cicilline's statement assumes this same premise. It is also implicit in classic texts, such as (Von Mises 2005), for instance. So, it was coherently (but mistakenly) thought that exporting capitalism would have meant exporting democracy. In particular, it was erroneously believed that Russia and China would have become democracies through the Trojan horse of capitalism and its "free" (I write "free" because of the *pax digitalis* seen above) markets. This did not turn out to be the case. In some Western countries, the two systems merely travelled in parallel for a while. Whether the misleading narrative was a silly mistake, or a malicious plan depends on whom you ask and about whom they are talking. The fact remains that *popular sovereignty*, as the source that legitimises political power, including national sovereignty, was seen as the sovereignty of the paired voter *and* consumer, as if these two roles were

---

[6] https://cicilline.house.gov/press-release/cicilline-opening-statement-big-tech-antitrust-hearing.

intrinsically part of the essence of a citizen, as an indissoluble unity, empowered by competition for people's vote and money. However, since the end of modernity in 1945, following the XL concept introduced above, the progressive fulfilment (or at least the hope thereof) of the consumer's desires first stretched and then snapped away from the voter's needs, like two pieces of blue tack. Marx failed to see, or rather could not have seen, what is now easy to see, that capitalism flourishes by transforming the working class into the shopping class through consumerism. To promote consumerism, capitalism needs to guarantee a minimum amount of redistribution (or at least credit-worthiness) to create an increasing number of consumers who can (or at least believe themselves able to) afford a growing number of goods and services. This instils in those customers the hope that the future will always be better than the past. Tomorrow is not just another day; it is a better day wherein consumers may join (or improve their newly acquired status as members of) the bourgeoisie, to adopt Marx's vocabulary. And nobody wishes to face a gun if tomorrow is a better day. Likewise, liberalism did not see (or, again, could not have seen) that the progressive increase in relative prosperity and the hope of being better off in the future ultimately distract from political participation and deprioritise the demand for social change. Political rights can wait, while economic gains accrue. In both cases, one may quip that the worst enemy of democracy is a credit card. Theoretically, democracy should be more likely to represent the demands of the poor, or those who hope to become rich, than the rich minority. However, this cuts both ways, because democracy and capitalism are not two sides of the same coin: an economic future worse than the present simply motivates people to demand political change, and when this happens in a democracy, populism arises, and democracy is threatened. Our era provides plenty of examples, from Italy to the UK, the USA to Brazil, and Turkey to Russia.

In the past few decades, increasing prosperity made consumers consider democracy less and less essential, as long as the future continued to be economically better than the present. This coincided with the great decoupling of social sciences from ethics. After the end of modernity (the XL size), in liberal democracies, economics focused on *profit*, jurisprudence on *compliance*, and politics on *consensus*, while right and wrong began to be treated more as a matter of individual choices and preferences, in line with the political metaproject (see Chapter 9). Today, we know that it takes a lot of pressure (a kind of desperate courage), to rebel against a repressive and violent regime and overturn it, and that such pressure is relieved by economic growth. Thus, with an oversimplification (because there are various, complex factors in question), one may jest that, in China, the cost of rejecting democracy is a robust yearly growth in GDP. A weak growth and people may start complaining, and organise themselves politically en masse to demand an economically better society through better politics. When GDP grows, students, idealists, activists, and a few other politically minded people may be ready and have the courage to run grave risks for freedom, tolerance, and justice and protest for social reform and more democracy, but they remain a minority. More generally, autocratic powers will not be overturned by the masses who still hope that the next year will be more prosperous than the present one. This long argument should help to clarify that a fundamental shift has taken place in the role of the individual, who, in this century, has moved from being a voter-consumer, empowered by competition, to being a follower-user, disempowered by political and business hegemonies.

In an age when analogue reality is increasingly managed and controlled by digital reality, the socio-political sovereignty exercised on both appears to be essential for a better democracy and coordinated cooperation to tackle global problems, to make society fairer, and development at least sustainable. In Europe, this means asking who should exercise digital sovereignty, whether each Member State or the EU. The distinction is essential. When, years ago, Emmanuel Macron or Angela Merkel began speaking of digital sovereignty, did they mean the *national* one (France's, Germany's, etc.) or the *supranational* one (the EU's), as is the case when Ursula Von der Leyen referred to it? When supporting *national* digital sovereignty, the risk is supporting *digital sovereignism* or *digital statism*. These are culturally and economically anachronistic positions, which defend an autarchic and mercantilist version of the digital and serve as breeding grounds for populism. They range from the rhetoric of national champions, existing or expected to arrive, to the wishful thinking that foreign successes can be implemented at home with equal effect but no reforms. They should both be resisted. But the line that separates them from digital sovereignty can be easily blurred, even in the EU.

In the EU, analogue sovereignty is articulated on two levels. For example, *tax sovereignty* remains national, to the extent that multinational companies exploit the EU system and play national sovereignties against each other; think of the notorious Apple-Ireland case.[7] But, continuing with the example,

---

[7] https://en.wikipedia.org/wiki/EU_illegal_state_aid_case_against_Apple_in_Ireland.

monetary sovereignty sometimes has become supranational, whenever Member States have adopted the euro. Likewise, digital sovereignty should probably be articulated in equal terms, with implementation at both the national and supranational levels. In some fundamental cases, and in view of avoiding a fracture into digital sovereignism and statism, digital sovereignty could be exercised more easily by the EU, both in terms of feasibility and in terms of added value, resembling the case of monetary sovereignty and the situation in the Eurozone. We know, for instance, that *digital data sovereignty* is more feasible and effective at the EU level, through the GDPR. It may be reasonable to move in the same direction with AI sovereignty, Cloud sovereignty, 5G sovereignty, and Metaverse sovereignty, to mention some other critical, digital areas. Establishing a *de jure* and not only a potentially *de facto* supranational digital sovereignty at the EU level is probably the best way to respond to the multinationals' control of the digital.

The debate on digital sovereignty is not about replacing national modern-analogue territorial sovereignty, which is necessary but increasingly insufficient. It is about complementing it with a supranational, contemporary-digital one—which is often its condition of possibility—and providing a more comprehensive series of harmonised benefits, such as standards and requirements, and a level playing field to all actors and stakeholders, as well as enhancing opportunities of cooperation. But if this is the case, as I would argue it is, then at least one more significant problem remains to be solved: *legitimacy* (Schmitter 2001).

Recall that, if sovereignty generally understood (i.e., without accompanying adjectives) is the controlling power that legitimises other forms of power—by transforming power into recognised authority—and which requires no previous controlling power to be legitimised in its turn, then *national* sovereignty is usually based on *popular* sovereignty, which is understood according to the Aristotelian concept of the unmoved mover. To avoid the *regressus ad infinitum*, individuals pool their *self-sovereignties*—autonomous and self-determining control on themselves, their bodies, and their lives—through deliberation, negotiation, and voting, to create popular sovereignty, which in turn legitimises national sovereignty, which then controls individuals' legal exercise of their self-sovereignties. The "custodiendi" themselves answer the question "quis custodiet ipsos custodes?": who controls the controllers? The controlled themselves. This is not a vicious circle but a virtuous spiral, visible in the shift from individual sovereignty (self-sovereignty) to societal sovereignty (popular sovereignty). Understood not in terms of social contact but of universal trust (see Chapter 10), individuals, through their lives, join a polity, which is more stable than their independent existence, can achieve much more than their individual efforts, and can reconcile mutual interests. As they come and go, they strengthen and widen popular sovereignty. The question is now what happens when digital or analogue sovereignty are no longer national but supranational: how can supporting popular sovereignty be expanded to apply to supranational sovereignty as well? And indeed, is this even possible? There seem to be several alternatives, which are either defended or criticised in the EU under the general topic of "democratic deficit". In each alternative, popular sovereignty remains the constant and ultimate source of legitimisation of all other forms of sovereignty, including national and supranational sovereignty. How exactly this may work is a matter of controversy.

One way to approach the debate is to recognise that sovereignty is not like a coveted resource that, when given to someone, is no longer in the donor's possession and can be reacquired only by taking it back from that person. It is akin to a relation (control), in which one may engage more or less intensely and successfully. It is precisely because it is a matter of relational engagement that sovereignty is never "lost" when either exercised or delegated (no matter what the rhetoric of Brexit and "regaining sovereignty" said), and so it is not a finite or rivalrous resource: giving it to one person does not prevent the possibility of giving it simultaneously to someone else. Such a relational concept of sovereignty enables one to see that the legitimisation of sovereignty can be modelled in terms of the network's topology that seems to be the most appropriate for its structuring. In theory, many network topologies are possible, but three are of political and historical interest here.

In a *fully connected* network topology, each node enjoys both popular and national sovereignty, and the nodes are all linked together for a set of common purposes. Each node can leave the network at any time (secession) and self-legitimises itself through its own popular sovereignty. The network itself does not possess legitimacy over the self-legitimised nodes. This more *distributed legitimacy* is what some supporters of a *European confederation* of national states (the nodes), for instance, seem to have in mind when imagining the human project for the EU. It can be a robust version of intergovernmentalism, which can deal with fundamental issues such as currency, trade, or defence. Composed of a more or less strong network of Westphalian states (i.e., ones that have sovereignty over their territories), the political design of this network does not require innovation. As a modern concept, it is well established in terms of joint action among sovereign states that pursue shared goals and wish to further shared aims. It requires no changes in popular or national sovereignty, nor does it require the telling of a new narrative or story to gain popularity among voters.

In a *star* network topology (think of spoke-hub distribution), popular sovereignty is placed at the centre. It legitimises every other peripheral node directly, represented by different kinds of sovereignty, national and supranational included. The network operates according to its own supranational sovereignty. For instance, those who support a *European federation* seem to have this more *centralised legitimacy* in mind. It is classic and straightforward, in terms of political design, and represents an update of the Westphalian state to a federalised version. While centralised legitimacy may perhaps be easier to understand, it may not be popular among voters attached to nationalistic values, narratives, and policies. Language can be a significant barrier.

Finally, in a *hybrid* topology, an interrelated mesh, there can be nodes (i.e., popular sovereignties) that legitimise other nodes (i.e., national sovereignties), which in turn legitimise additional nodes (e.g., supranational sovereignties), possibly in a symbiotic legitimising relation. For instance, some supporters of a multi-speed Europe seem to have this *European congregation*[8] and more hierarchical legitimacy in mind for their European human project. Its variable geometry is less intuitive and more innovative in terms of political design. It is also more complex and challenging to implement effectively, and because it largely lacks a precedent, it requires a compelling story to be told to explain it and make it more popular. Despite this, it is not hard to conceptualise. It is fruitful to understand states today as individual but multiagent systems that pool and transfer their national sovereignties to create supranational sovereignty in some areas. We saw that the Eurozone provides an excellent example. The war in Ukraine has highlighted the need for more "EU" when it comes to energy and defence policies. So, one may argue that popular sovereignty (understood as the pooling of individuals' self-sovereignties) legitimises national sovereignty (now understood as the pooling of national multiagent systems' self-sovereignties) that in turn legitimises supranational sovereignty. This is how the "combined sovereignty" of the EU may be understood and promoted. Through the "enhanced

---

[8] I am adapting the term "congregation" from the terminology use by the University of Oxford to describe its sovereign body that acts as its "parliament".

cooperation" mechanism,[9] a hybrid network could support a core of more federal European states within a larger, more confederated EU called the United States of Europe.[10]

The EU currently has different solutions for different types of analogue sovereignty, and it is only beginning to have some kinds of digital sovereignty. The EU could streamline this by possibly opting, as a plan A, for a centralised, single form of analogue and digital sovereignty. However, this seems unlikely and, at best, possible only in the distant future, despite it being a preferable strategy. The good news is that a centralised design to manage sovereignty is not incompatible with the EU's continued preference for variable geometries of both analogue and digital sovereignty. For some people, this hybrid topology will remain plan B, with the advantage of feasibility and the shortcomings of representing a compromise. Still, I would like to argue that it should instead be the focus of a truly innovative design, which would transform it into a successful plan A. A partially connected mesh of individual, popular, national, supranational, and subnational (see, for instance, the case for indigenous data sovereignty in (Taylor and Kukutai 2016) sovereignties, both analogue and digital, could deliver full democratic legitimacy and great innovative flexibility, if they could be designed successfully. While it is far from an easy thing to achieve, if I am correct, one day, the *Congregated States of Europe* will not be an intergovernmental or supranational chapter in the history of the Westphalian state and its analogue/digital sovereignties, but a new book altogether, neither a confederation nor a federation, but a *differentiated integration* with its own design fit for the digital age. The EU could be one of the most significant political experiments in creating a new political body since the American Revolution.

But enough about a possible, more utopian, future. Let me close with a look at the past, and a not entirely inaccurate historical comparison. The fight for digital sovereignty may call to mind the Investiture Controversy, the medieval conflict between the Church/Pope and the State/Emperor in Europe over secular and spiritual power and, more specifically, over the prerogative to choose and install bishops. Of course, that controversy pertained to a very different set of circumstances from anything we see in the fight for digital sovereignty. But the comparison is not entirely inaccurate. That initial

---

[9] https://en.wikipedia.org/wiki/Enhanced_cooperation.
[10] See, for example, the proposal made by Guy Verhofstadt, MEP and former Belgian prime minister (Verhofstadt 2006).

medieval controversy marked a critical stage in the development of the concept of sovereignty, as the word's etymology makes it obvious. Today, the fight is not between secular and spiritual power but between corporate and political power for control over the digital. Yet, the roots of this clash are shared and very old. Most importantly, that medieval debate reminds us that whoever wins the fight for digital sovereignty will determine the lives of all people on both sides of the digital divide, precisely like the Investiture Controversy affected all people, no matter the degree of their religiosity. This is why I began this chapter by saying that digital sovereignty is not just an isolated matter of interest for some specialists. It is already affecting everybody. And therefore, it is essential to design it together, as best we can, in view of a shared human project, which is the topic of the next chapter.

Chapter 24

Green and Blue for a Sustainable and Preferable Future

In any discussion of the digital revolution, it is natural to wonder what equally radical transformation will be next. Human history certainly does not end here, and there will be other extraordinary technological, behavioural, and societal changes that we cannot even imagine. As I wrote in Chapter 8, just consider what someone would have foreseen in 1920 if they had been asked to predict the future in 2020. The correct perspective is that the digital revolution will undoubtedly bring other incredible innovations. Still, the transformation from an entirely analogue world to one that is also, and sometimes predominantly, digital has begun and is already maturing in some contexts. So, trying to predict the future is a bit like asking what else to expect after arriving on a new, uninhabited, continent and heading inland: we have "landed" on the digital, and we know only its shores and the route by which to

The Green and The Blue: Naive Ideas to Improve Politics in the Digital Age, First Edition.
Luciano Floridi.
© 2024 John Wiley & Sons Ltd. Published 2024 by John Wiley & Sons Ltd.

get to them, but the historic step has been taken. The most critical challenge today is understanding what to do with this new continent, which is yet to be explored, and effectively organised. In other words, the new digital challenges in the coming decades will, above all, be linked to digital policies, governance, social and environmental issues, and the development of the digital economy. We saw that much of digital *governance* is currently delegated to the (primarily American but increasingly also Chinese) corporate world, which implements its logic of profit and its entrepreneurial culture. It is an unsatisfactory solution to managing the digital realm, not necessarily in and of itself, but because it constantly risks giving way to colonising monopolies. To improve the present situation, we need the courage to make the right social choices and then political strategies. In other words, there is a great need for good politics.

In one of his *Sermons*, Augustine reminds us that "to err is human, but to persevere in error wilfully is diabolical". Today, we may not require references to devils or saints, but we should add that, although anyone can err, only the wilfully oblivious perseveres stubbornly in their error. Some readers will be reminded of some English (and I do not mean British) obstinacy over upholding a Brexit deal that is as damaging as it is anachronistic, but I am particularly thinking of Donald Trump's ill-advised decision in 2017 to withdraw the USA from the Paris Climate Accords. The inflammatory decision was much discussed, and owing to the level of debate, some people hoped that Trump would reconsider. He never did. If anything, he wilfully persevered, with the USA officially pulling out of the Agreement in 2020. According to *Vox*, a liberal American news website, during the 2016 election campaign, Trump had published 115 tweets denouncing global warming as a hoax, and condemning the Paris Agreement, supported by his predecessor Barack Obama, as an economic disaster for the USA. Trump's position was and remains nonsense, contradicted by every expert on the issue. However, Trump was impervious to facts and reasoning, and this allowed him a degree of perseverance in error that would have made the devil envious. It was an irresponsible and careless error, and there were (and still are) a thousand reasons to be concerned. An important one is linked to the digital.

America's biggest digital companies—including Amazon, Apple, Meta/Facebook, Alphabet/Google, IBM, Microsoft, and Twitter—publicly criticised Trump's decision on the Paris Agreement at the time. It is fitting that they did so. The digital blue is an excellent ally of the environmental green, and the two work best in tandem. Sustainable development and a more hopeful future for humanity will be possible only if both the green and the blue create a virtuous circle between nature and technology.

It is true that every operation involving data management consumes energy, most of which is still sourced from burning fossil fuels, thus contributing to global warming. For instance, already in 2011, Google estimated that each search on its website consumed the equivalent of a 60-W light bulb turned on for 17 seconds. Consider then that, at the beginning of 2023, Google managed, on average, 40,000 search queries per second, 3.7 billion searches daily, and 1.2 trillion searches yearly. The negative environmental impact of digital technologies is now levelling that of aviation, at about 2% of global greenhouse gas emissions. It is not surprising that subsidiaries such as Apple Energy and Google Energy exist to manage the energy consumption and costs of the affiliated companies.

However, it is also true that large information companies are increasingly environmentally conscious, opting for more and more renewable energy. Above all, according to the Global e-Sustainability Initiative (SMARTer2020), the positive impact of digital technology on the environment could be seven times higher than its negative impact, responsible for a 20% reduction in global greenhouse gas emissions by 2030.

The enormous contribution of digital technology to a significant reduction in ecological harm can be attributed to several factors. In the recent past, "dematerialisation" was a trendy talking point. People thought that printed books would decline, and e-books would take over; that transport of things (bits) would reduce, in favour of communication of bytes; and that remote working would predominate thanks to more online interactions, meaning less travel, and so on. Things have turned out differently. As a result of the digital revolution, we produce ever more paper, and printed books are more popular than ever (think Amazon); e-commerce has created whole new sectors for the movement of "new and used bits" (think Amazon and eBay and the corresponding postal services with all their packaging); and digital solutions have helped to bring down the cost of air travel, increasing aviation and low-cost flights as a result. Examples abound. It is sometimes forgotten that cryptocurrencies, such as Bitcoin, resemble small light bulbs. According to somewhat pessimistic estimates, the Bitcoin network consumed 14 gigawatts of electricity by the end of 2020, which is about the same as the energy annually produced by Denmark.

Of course, things could have been worse. Above all, the digital can help the analogue not because it replaces it, but because it rapidly expands the number of analogue operations by doing much more with much less and enabling new activities as well as ones that would otherwise be impossible. From this perspective, the digital can optimise resources, reduce waste, which has considerable energy savings, and make possible productive activities that would otherwise be financially unsustainable.

There are some reasons to be optimistic. In 2016, Google used its Deep-Mind AI system to reduce the energy consumption of its data centres, achieving a reduction of 15%. Much of the so-called share and circular economy would also be impossible without digital support. Before the Coronavirus pandemic, in 2016, for instance, 3.6 million tourists found accommodation in Italy through digital platforms and applications, creating a turnover of 3.6 billion euros, equivalent to 0.22% of the country's total GDP. Similar green-blue strategies could develop with promising results in many countries. In the *green* economy sector, the EU is already a global leader, and the environmental and cultural values of the Union are remarkable. The share, circular, and green economy should be seen as an excellent opportunity for economic and social development and growth, in coordination with a robust experience economy: wellness and health, culture, entertainment, and sport, leisure, hospitality, and tourism. This could start with meeting the targets of the Paris Climate Accords by investing in direct (infrastructure) and indirect support for the green and blue economy (whether as incentives or disincentives); implementing the UN 2030 Sustainable Development Goals; and adopting European directives on the circular economy, based on recycling and fully reusing materials. Above all, the development of digital technologies, services, skills, and investments could be accelerated and strengthened, to synergise strategically digital growth with environmental protection. The green and the blue alliance could play a vital role in supporting the development of sources of renewable energy, a critical issue in the whole process.

All this is feasible, and some of it is already happening. Still, Greta is right: some politicians, like Trump or Bolsonaro, were and are irresponsible and pushing us further in the wrong direction. They are doing little, nothing, or even the wrong things, to save the planet from global warming. That said, many politicians are neither devils nor saints. The famous bell-shaped Gaussian curve can be used to illustrate this. The line starts low on the left (few devils), rises gradually, gets longer and wider (many sinners), and descends symmetrically to the right, ending low (few saints). Most politicians and those of us who vote for them are in the middle of the curve. In largely functional democracies, resenting politicians means resenting ourselves who vote for them.

While we have known for decades that we are destroying the planet, it is tempting to place the blame entirely on the shoulders of today's politicians. They, too, live on this planet, have families, and know that we are about to pass the point of no return. However, they must juggle what should be done—which is difficult and often unpopular, as Macron found to his detriment when he tried to raise the price of diesel or the pension age—with what voters want, which is sometimes admirable but impossible, like squaring the circle: high living standards for all, low costs for all, more benefits, lower taxes, and no sacrifices for anyone, all the while supporting economic growth, protecting the environment, and respecting human rights. The equilibrium between the desired and the feasible is called "consensus". Consensus is not lacking in words but deeds, because the costs of saving the planet are immense, although those of not saving it are even greater. The figures vary, but not the scale. To put it bluntly, the bill ranges from 55 trillion $ for a global temperature rise of 1.5 °C, to 70 trillion $ for 2 °C, and up to 550 trillion $ if we reach 3.7 °C. We are leaving to future generations an immense debt, which is in some cases only repairable but no longer reversible (think about extinct species and destroyed ecosystems), with the consequences of horrendous human suffering and potentially terrible conflicts over remaining resources. It is the tragedy I discuss in Chapter 26.

Some people argue that each of us should change our behaviour because it will help to avoid this unfolding apocalypse: shorter showers, less meat or adopting veganism, fewer planes, fewer cars, more public transport, recycling, reusing, repairing, low heating or air conditioning, switching off the lights, not printing emails... As we saw in Chapter 22, all these factors are good but utterly negligible in the grand scheme of things. To use an analogy already encountered, it is as if each of us is pushing a car that will not start, if and when we can, with the idea that every little bit helps. We know this does not achieve results, even if we were all angels. There is a threshold below which any individual effort is pointless. Kant is correct: doing one's duty is not right because it is useful; it is right, *even if* it is not useful, to be able to look at oneself in the mirror in the morning and recognise oneself as human. And knowing that each little effort is futile by itself is vital because, otherwise, one would sleep peacefully at night thinking that turning off the lights and having a vegan meal actually contributed to saving the world. These are good things in themselves, but they are not useful, let alone being right because they are useful. Instead, the insomnia of reason generates ideas, and this is crucial because, to save the world, we urgently need to organise ourselves and cooperate.

The universality of behaviour (recalling Kant again) will make a big difference, and we urgently need consensus. How do we coordinate? With some sacrifice, good legislation, and an alliance between the public and private spheres. The only war we should fight is against the end of the world and an unfair society. We must make the most of the vast possibilities of digital technology, to know more, monitor better, and coordinate efforts to push the car together, to use the same analogy. How do we create a world that is welcoming to all? By radically improving the very systems by which we innovate, produce, and consume products and services, and then distributing the advantages of such innovations fairly. Here, too, the digital can help: to do better and perform more with fewer resources, in alternative or entirely unprecedented ways. The debt we leave to future generations will be lower depending on the quality of the marriage between the green of environmentalism, the sharing and circular economy, and the blue of digital technologies, to serve humanity and the planet.

In using the digital, we need to move from consumerist capitalism to a capitalism based on an ethics of care. It will not be easy to achieve, but it is the most viable human project for our century. The circular and green economy may well be a trendy topic, but it is also one of those debates in which there is still an immense gap between preaching and practising, promises and deliveries, intentions and commitment. It is a pity because the circular and green economy is an excellent idea. In a linear economy, resources are extracted, and goods are produced, distributed, consumed, and finally thrown away. For each product, one starts again from the first step. The waste is immense and accumulates. The circular economy, on the other hand, *repairs*, *reuses*, *reconditions*, or *recycles* products. In a linear economy, the problem is at the end of the process: it is called *disposal*. In a circular economy, the problem is at the beginning of the cycle, and it is called product *design*, which centres on *re*-purposing of products. Some time ago, I visited the world's largest military aircraft depot in Arizona, the 309th Aerospace Maintenance and Regeneration Group (AMARG), where surplus or out-of-service aircraft are stored, reconditioned, or partly recycled. Lined up were approximately 4000 aircraft from every recent war fought or planned for by the USA, extending as far as the eye could see. Wartime consumerism is a monument to human folly, but at least the AMARG is attempting to adopt a more circular approach to waste.

Up to the Industrial Revolution, the economy was always circular. Only recently has the age-old circular economy been gradually replaced by the mass production of disposable products and consumeristic capitalism. The old circular economy was poor by today's standards. Repairing or recycling was essential because there was little to waste. Nothing went to waste, if one could avoid it. In the 1970s, I remember that, in Guarcino, the small Italian village where my family originally comes from, people recycled glass bottles because they used them in the summer to bottle homemade passata in their backyard. It was tough work. So, people started buying the passata in the shop as soon as it became possible. And there is nothing wrong with that. Unfortunately, at that point, they also started throwing the bottles away: they were no longer needed, and they did not know what to do with them, until recycling collection became a possibility and the new normal today.

The whole story has three phases: circular but poor (repurposing bottles as containers for homemade passata); linear but prosperous (buying passata and throwing the bottles away); and now circular and prosperous (recycling the purchased glass passata bottles). The first transition from circular to linear witnessed a dramatic improvement in the quality of life of billions of people. The transition also damaged our planet profoundly and dangerously. The refrigerator is a good example: it is useful, scientifically advanced, and technologically sophisticated, but it was not recycled and polluting once disposed. That is why the science, technology, and innovation that made that first shift possible acquired a bad reputation. It is also why old-school environmentalism is often perceived as anti-technology and suspicious of innovation and entrepreneurship. However, the second transition, from a prosperous but linear economy to a prosperous and circular economy, can take place only by maximising the potential of new technologies and innovations, especially those based on digital solutions, including automatic and intelligent data processing. Used well, digital technology makes it possible to design products that can be reused and recycled, optimise the entire production and consumption cycle, and do more and better with fewer resources. Technological developments allowed us to enter the linear consumeristic economy. It is also technological developments that can pave the way towards a prosperous circular and green economy, where waste can become a resource, as we shall see in the next Chapter.

Today, digital technology can be nature's best ally. The trouble is that there is little time left to stop and reverse the damage done to the planet: we cannot rely only on market forces, which can take unlimited amounts of time and do not prioritise the world or humanity. Markets consume time, a resource they always need in abundance because "*sooner or later* the right balance emerges". Yet, even if proven right, the markets do not specify how "late" "later" is. This is why we need to assist markets with forward-looking policies of investment in innovation and STEM (science, technology, engineering, mathematics) training, legislation to promote the circular and green economy, and educating consumers to make smarter choices that are informed by the ecological impact of the products and services they purchase. It is not a small project, but it can be realised, and it must be realised urgently.

So, is the new alliance between the green and the blue all positive news? Not quite. The digital is not a panacea. It is a cure, and as such, has both costs and side effects. It can do a lot of good for the environment and the economy, but not without costs and risks, and it must be appropriately administered. The challenge is for the positive impact of the digital to save our planet and human society before other factors, including the digital's own negative impact, destroy it. This means that the countdown is well underway. We do not have centuries at our disposal, only decades. Maybe a couple of generations. There is much urgency. In the next chapter, I shall focus on a specific example: the economy of waste. But before moving to that topic, I need to introduce one more suggestion, the disappearance of externalities.

In pseudo-precise literature or pretentious conversations, an externality is a negative effect of a profitable activity. Call it a cost, paid by someone else, like what happens if Alice runs a profitable business that pollutes Bob's environment. Alice's externalities may be unintended, possibly avoidable. Still, whether they occur is not Alice's problem. And the fact that they may occur is unlikely to stop Alice from pursuing her activities, since the cost paid by Bob is not a sufficient disincentive to sacrifice her benefit. Sometimes, when people speak of "externalities" in this way, what they really mean is "collateral damage".

However, in economics, an "externality" is a neutral and precise concept. It refers to a *cost or a benefit* (negative or positive externality), due to the production or consumption of a good or service (and I would add here policies, regulations, or courses of action), incurred or received by a third party, which has *no control* (more on this in a moment) over the creation of that cost or benefit. For example, pollution may be an externality, but only if the polluted has no control over it, while the benefits of pollination caused by beekeeping are also externalities, but of a positive kind, even if one does not attach a reward to them.

Politics has always known the value of both kinds of externalities. Nobody is grateful for positive externalities (who does ever thank the keeper of the bees for the pollination they facilitate?), and the negative externalities of bad government today are paid tomorrow, by the next government, or another generation of citizens. Brexit jumps vividly to mind.

As for "control", this is an important clause. The lack of control may be due to a lack of information: the third party may not know. This might have been common during the industrial revolution, all the way down to the post-war reconstruction. Today, in an information society, this seems increasingly unlikely. More plausibly, the lack of control is due to a lack of power. In this case, an externality is both known and imposed. We need to remember this below, when "internalities" are in question. They are increasingly apparent, and if we do not deal with them, it is not for lack of knowledge, but for lack of power.

When considering the nature of externalities and that there is only one world, one can see that externalities are quickly becoming merely displaced (*elsewhere*) or delayed (*elsewhen*) *internalities*, that is, costs and benefits incurred or received by the very agents responsible for them, even if they did not consider them. We live in a single network, where there is no external space to dump one's own negative externalities and where positive externalities percolate more widely, building resilience.

If the disappearance of negative externalities has not become evident until recently, it is also because, despite all our holistic theorising, we practically keep behaving as if we had plenty of space and time at our disposal, plenty of *elsewhere* and *elsewhen*, so to speak. The growth of space debris and the recurrent suggestion that rubbish or even radioactive waste may be disposed of in Outer Space show how reluctant we are to take seriously the view that there is no disconnected, other reality where negative externalities migrate for good, never to return home.

The pandemic has made painfully clear that negative externalities are increasingly an untenable abstraction. What we do affects each other, *here* modifies *there*, *today* changes *tomorrow*. In an ever faster and more connected world, the time between doing something and its consequences coming back to haunt us becomes increasingly shorter. Brexit was possible not despite but because of the delay of its negative impact. If it had been immediate, its critics would have been right about the sudden pain it would have inflicted. This is also why the same political approach did not work with COVID-19, the effects of which have dramatically impacted the population almost immediately. Nothing better than a robust externality slapping one in the face to make one change behaviour asap (see Chapter 26).

Space and time have shrunk and keep shrinking. This is obvious. Therefore, externalities are disappearing. This should have been equally obvious. Better late than never. We should really speak only of internalities that, like boomerangs, seem to go away but always come back to the point of departure, faster and faster. Old externalities were only internalities with a very high latency. This may seem problematic, but it is also good news.

First, there is value in clarity. As long as we thought that externalities were alive and kicking, we could try to manage them. Now it seems we have been trying to manage phlogiston. It makes no sense to misbehave, thinking that the cost of such misbehaviour will be paid by someone else. Putting "anyone first", America included, is a head-in-the-sand approach because it is caused (also) by the end of externalities (in a smaller world, the "first" is, and sees itself as being, challenged by the second and the third) and yet makes such end even more dangerous by refusing to acknowledge it. Second, accepting the end of externalities means that we can start focusing entirely on internalities and design systems that handle them better. We need to become critically aware of them, and design policies to incentivise good internalities, which make the world a better place, and disincentivise negative internalities, which make it worse.

The end of externalities is the end of the delusion that we live in a disconnected world. It should also be the beginning of a better management of a connected one. As often in our age, this is a matter of good design: the right solutions are developed in the right way. Good design requires knowledge and intelligence, of which there is plenty. But unfortunately, its implementation requires goodwill and political leadership as well, of which there should be much more. Recall the lack of power to control the old externalities, not information about them. So, the simple conclusion is that the end of externalities should lead to society's more robust demand for better politics.

We are now ready to tackle the topic of the next chapter: waste, and how it could become a resource.

Chapter 25
The Value of Waste

It is often helpful to use different words to describe reality accurately. A precise vocabulary enables one to have a better articulated and detailed perception of the world, and one risks fewer approximations ("more or less"), generalisations ("throwing the baby out with the bath water"), and confusing idioms ("barking up the wrong tree"). This is why I envy people who know how to use colour names correctly, distinguishing, for instance, "bordeaux" red (#800000) from "burgundy" red (#800020). These people are correct; the colours are different, as further evidenced by the HTML colour hex codes in parentheses. To me, being abstract and absent-minded, they are both dark red.

Occasionally, however, it is helpful to have a single, common word to speak of distinct phenomena. The reason is that it can conversely help to perceive the similarities between different things and unify aspects of reality under a single concept (subsume) that otherwise might seem unrelated. This is the case with the English word "waste", which in Italian, for example, is translated in at least three ways depending on the intended meaning. "Waste" refers to different but related phenomena. Let us examine them with an example.

In *Tom Sawyer Abroad*, Huckleberry Finn quotes the saying "there ain't a-going to be no core". The sentence is not only a moral observation on the

The Green and The Blue: Naive Ideas to Improve Politics in the Digital Age, First Edition. Luciano Floridi.

lack of generosity but also a scientific fact, because there are apple varieties that practically have no cores. Let's assume then that, by producing apples *with* cores, we *wasted* the opportunity to produce them without. Furthermore, let us also assume that we have unfortunately adopted an inefficient production model, where we *waste* resources cultivating apples with cores. In addition, we have to count for the agro-industrial *waste* caused by the production. Many apples are also considered ugly and therefore not marketable and hence are *wasted*. Worldwide, approximately 45% of the fruit and vegetables produced yearly is *wasted* for aesthetic reasons. And of the apples that make it to market and are sold, a considerable proportion is not consumed, but *wasted*. In Great Britain, about 1.5 million "beautiful" apples are thrown away yearly: they occupy fifth place on the list of most *wasted* foods, after bread, milk, potatoes, and cheese. Finally, of the apples consumed, a part is discarded—the core that we did not avoid at the beginning—or ends up as undesired *waste* even if it is edible, as in the case of the skins. In Italy alone, the amount of food *wasted* yearly is worth 15 billion euros, almost 1% of the country's total GDP. It also poses a significant environmental problem. If world food *waste* were a country, it would be the world's third-largest producer of greenhouse gases, after China and the USA.

All these missed opportunities, scraps, avoidable costs, discarded parts, unused parts etc., can be summed up with one word: *waste*. The waste analysis, in the various phases just exemplified, is adaptable to any product or service. In terms of logical analysis, there is a triple waste of the *possible*, the *available*, and the *recyclable*. This vast and growing waste is a disaster but also an excellent opportunity. An economy that consumes waste is precisely what we should develop by conceiving new solutions, implementing those already designed, and bolstering, expanding and improving those that have already been implemented. The greater the amount of possible or actual waste available to "consume", the better the growth of the companies that can maximise its potential. This can go beyond the *circular economy* and represent *circular innovation*, because the "cycle" is not fixed but constantly expanded by new opportunities that did not exist before, were not taken advantage of, or were only partially or poorly exploited.

Unfortunately, we still conceive waste in twentieth-century terms, as the opposite of a resource and, therefore, only as an unwanted source of damage and costs. We do not see it for its opportunities, profits, and advantages. In the current prevailing paradigm, the consumption of resources is considered to be only and inevitably harmful to the environment, which it impoverishes, through extracting non-renewable resources, and degrades, through the discharge of toxic waste into the environment. Hence the apparent dilemma of the current human project and its consumerist development paradigm: either humanity suffers, but saves the environment by consuming less, or humanity flourishes, and is saved by consuming more (especially in developing countries), but the environment is destroyed. Humanity vs. Nature seems like an inevitable dilemma. In reality, there is a third alternative: reviewing our economy, its market mechanisms, and its business models, and revising the relevant legislation to exploit waste as a resource.

Considering waste as a resource highlights its unlimited and renewable potential, because waste will continue to be produced by opportunities that have not yet been conceived. In practice, we already know that countless untapped sources lie wasted and unused. The sun, for example, produces an estimated amount of energy every hour that would power 2.880 trillion incandescent bulbs. Waste can be considered, above all, as inefficiency. Fire and wood gave way to candles and oil lamps, after which we invented incandescent light bulbs, and today we have LEDs. An incandescent light bulb produces the equivalent light of 60 candles, for example, and LED consumes a fraction of the energy and none of the heat of an incandescent light bulb of yesterday. From the old technology of the candle to the new one of the LED, we are achieving more and more, improving our quality of life, and using proportionally fewer resources to power our energy use. The difference is made by human ingenuity, entrepreneurship, and technological innovation, all working in the right context of law and ethics.

Finally, consider waste as what is left unused. Today, fabrics for clothes and bags can be made from apple peels. The current quantity of food waste could feed double the number of starving people in the world. Carbon dioxide (CO_2), a greenhouse gas mostly generated by burning fossil fuels, is one of the worst types of waste we release into the environment. But we can turn even CO_2 into a resource if we know how to exploit it without generating even more of it in the process. After all, the gas contains "useful" atoms: one of carbon and two of oxygen. We already know how to transform the carbon in CO_2 into graphene, one of the most resistant and versatile materials, which consists of a layer of carbon atoms with a thickness of only one atom. And as my wife, a scientist, reminded me, diamonds are composed entirely of carbon. In fact, in November 2020, a company, Aether, announced the upcoming launch of diamonds produced using CO_2. Each two-carat diamond will "consume" about 40 tons of CO_2 in the process, equal to more than seven years of the carbon footprint of a person living in Italy. (P.S. Maybe my wife's comment was not just an editorial suggestion... I checked before the publication of this book. The company is not yet selling any jewellery).

An economy based on integrating and consuming waste represents a possibility of extraordinary growth. "Happy degrowth" is an analogue, pre-digital way of looking at development, because it primarily considers resources as a finite quantity of what can be extracted from the planet, like oil, not from outer space and certainly not thanks to human intelligence. "Happy degrowth" underestimates the fact that digital technologies, including AI, by managing data and processes in an increasingly innovative (novelty), efficient (less waste), and effective (more results) way, enable us to expand the realm of the feasible and multiply the possibilities of what we already can do, at decreasing costs. Innovation has always proceeded also by looking to waste as a potential resource. Today, thanks to digital technology, our economy can become an innovative waste-consumption economy. In this case, too, the digital blue is good for the analogue green of all environments. We must put our ingenuity to the task of designing how to reduce and exploit waste. The time is right for a paradigm shift: to view waste as a resource, an enabler of happy growth, for the benefit of all humanity and the planet. The alternative to a paradigm shift in our current form of consumeristic capitalism, is a slow-motion tragedy, as I argue in the next chapter.

Chapter 26

Climate Change and the Terrible Hope

Disasters are of many kinds, but at least two can be distinguished using Greek terms: *tragedies* and *catastrophes* (I know, "what joy", to quote a popular song based on Psalm 146, but it is better to see clearly than to ignore blindly).

Tragic disasters come gradually, taking time to develop their full harmful effects, progressively worsening. Often, given their incremental development, they are heralded. They have distant causes, one knows that they are coming and escalating. In this sense, for example, it is a tragedy to continue smoking, or have an unhealthy diet if one is obese. One is slowly committing suicide. Every day is a little worse, and every day is a day lost to stop the tragedy. At the level of humanity, the climate crisis is such a tragedy: foretold, worsening, not stopping, and leading to lethal consequences. The patient knows very well what is happening, but procrastinates and postpones, adapting rather than reacting.

True tragedy has an epistemic and a moral component: one knows that a disaster will happen but that there is nothing one can do to prevent it.

The Green and The Blue: Naive Ideas to Improve Politics in the Digital Age, First Edition. Luciano Floridi.
© 2024 John Wiley & Sons Ltd. Published 2024 by John Wiley & Sons Ltd.

Oedipus knows what he is destined to do, so he flees, but fate pursues him. They say knowledge is power. It should be, at least morally. It is certainly powerlessness that makes the knowledge of an incoming disaster tragic. Life is full of these tragedies; it is enough to have had a terminally ill person nearby to know it. But sometimes, a tragic disaster has nothing to do with "external" powerlessness. One *can* quit smoking, have a better diet, get some exercise, and lose weight. It is not powerlessness as fate (the *Moirai*) but powerlessness as *akrasia* or "internal" helplessness (weakness of the will, as Aristotle tells us insightfully) that makes a tragic disaster happen, assuming, of course, that one has eyes to see. It is because Oedipus knows that he knew, that, in the end, he will blind himself, for episteme is a visual business in Greek culture. Climate change deniers like Trump do not run this risk.

Avoiding a tragic disaster then becomes a matter of responsibility and goodwill. Humanity has the power (technical capabilities and financial resources) to halt and then reverse climate change, but it lacks the will. It is a case of *social akrasia*. It is as if Oedipus had a real chance not to kill his father and not to marry his mother. And wasted it. Humanity too flees in vain, like Oedipus, but in a different sense: not to try to stop the inevitable tragedy, but in order not to see the preventable one, which it could avoid if it wanted. We have robots on Mars, and we may have a human colony on the Moon. Wealthy people can holiday orbiting the earth. And with the agreement formulated at COP27, rich nations will reimburse poor ones for the unfolding tragedy and its costs. But COP27 did not lead to severe measures to reduce the use of fossil fuels. After many difficult discussions, people agreed on a sort of reimbursement of costs and damages, a bit like the richest sharing their material wealth with the poorest on the Titanic. We continue to burn plants and animals that died in the distant past, destroying other plants and animals living today and tomorrow, ourselves included. We burn dead organisms to engender living ones. Instead of going straight to the sources of that energy, which are renewable, we settle for using their outcomes: coal, oil, and gas. It remains a tragedy. The difference, to paraphrase Gibson, is that COP27 ensured that the costs of the future are somewhat more evenly distributed. Necessary but entirely insufficient.

There is a terrible hope, which could make humanity overcome its social *akrasia*, change its suicidal course, and start getting serious about preventing the tragedy of climate change. But to explain it, and understand why it is terrible, we must first understand the other kind of disaster, the catastrophic one.

Catastrophic disasters, as the etymology of the word says, are sudden, severe, shocking, or dismaying, to use a somewhat obsolete term. A vertical fall, a U-turn of events. It is the unexpected heart attack (myocardial infarction, to be precise), the unpredicted cerebral stroke that comes one day without any warning. For investors, the "collapse" of FTX, a major cryptocurrency exchange firm, was not a tragedy, it was a catastrophe: it seemed to be healthy until it was no longer. In July 2021, it was still valued at $18 billion. In November 2022, in a few days, it went bankrupt due to disastrous management errors and illegalities. The same goes for the vertical fall of Elizabeth Holmes, whose company, Theranos, was just a big hoax, an empty promise suddenly unmasked (miraculous clinical tests obtained through a non-existent app and a drop of blood, at home). After being one of the stars and darlings of Silicon Valley, she was sentenced to eleven years in prison in 2022. And coming to the most recent news, at the time of writing this book, the question is whether the demise of Twitter is near, and it will end. My hunch is that *if* it happens—a real hypothetical "if," because Elon Musk could straighten things out, although, so far, he has seemed stubbornly incapable of handling the crisis—it will be catastrophic, not tragic. Today nobody moves, because everyone is on Twitter, but if users move, it will not be a small trot, but a gallop to the next platform that can compete with Twitter. We saw that this is the nature of the network effect: all or none. This is why Musk did not spend 44 billion $ to create a new Twitter, but to buy the existing one, and Truth Social, the platform launched by Trump, is just a small echo chamber of little relevance. The technology to create a service like Twitter is within everyone's reach; just think of Mastodon (where you find your philosopher trying to emigrate from Twitter: @lucianofloridi@mastodon.world). No magic recipe. It is the mass of users that makes all the difference. The network effect seems to require quite a significant catastrophe to trigger action.[1]

Let's go back to the tragedy of climate change. Sometimes people give up bad habits due to a great fright. A non-fatal heart attack can make even the

---

[1] There is a branch of mathematics that studies the formal and quantitative aspects of catastrophic changes, rightly called catastrophe theory: https://en.wikipedia.org/wiki/Catastrophe_theory. It was made so popular by René Thom since the 1960s that even a philosophy student like me could not ignore it once, in the mid-80s, Thom's two books were published in Italian translation (*Stabilità strutturale e morfogenesi. Saggio di una teoria generale dei modelli*, Milano, Einaudi, 1980, and *Modelli matematici della morfogenesi*, Torino, Einaudi, 1985).

most inveterate smoker quit. In short, a major and more disastrous tragedy can be avoided thanks to a minor catastrophe. This is the terrible hope to which I refer. If climate change continues to make disasters occur gradually, humanity will get used to the tragedy, and will slipperyslope towards the end without ever radically changing capitalism, from a consumerist logic to one of caring for the world. Humanity will end up like the frog, which is said (in a fantastic but false tale) to die by gradually boiling, if the cold water in which it is immersed is slowly heated. So, one must hope for a catastrophe, as small as it takes to galvanise (I could not resist) humanity to change its course of action.

Of course, there is an alternative, more intelligent, more moral, and much less painful: understanding, and then acting based on what has been understood. We saw in Chapter 22 that Socrates thought we are like that. That errors, especially moral ones, are a consequence of our ignorance, of not having fully understood what is good or bad for us, and the related consequences, and therefore, that it is enough to explain things well to make people act well. Occasionally, Socrates is right. But he is often wrong, not least because Aristotle is right about personal (and I would add social) akrasia. Just think of the customers who buy at the same time a pack of cigarettes, on which it is written that scientifically they are killing themselves, and a lottery ticket, although they know that, statistically, they have no real chance of winning. We must be Socratic, but not because it helps improve things. The philosopher Jiminy Cricket knows how the story ends: no one listens, and maybe a shoe will hit his head. Socrates was killed by his fellow Athenian citizens, and the list of philosophers who have died for their ideas is long. As I tell my students, philosophers' job market has vastly improved since then. No, we must be Socratic because it is the right thing to do in a deontological sense, even if it does not help improve anything. We must understand and change wrong behaviours, because that is what reason dictates (Kant was right); because of some rare successes (why not, after all, I did not write that Socrates is always wrong); to prepare for the changes that will come and allocate responsibilities for what will go wrong; because, as a by-product, if everybody were to act decently, the world would be a decent place (this is the advantage of the universalisability of goodness); and finally to have at least the satisfaction to be able to say "I told you it was a big iceberg" when the Titanic sinks. But not because it is useful. This is not why we should turn off the light, take shorter showers, use public transport, avoid eating meat, recycle, vote for the least disappointing politicians, and so forth. If the justification for doing the right thing were its usefulness, then this is a *modus tollens*, and history should teach us to start misbehaving immediately, for a moral life certainly is mostly useless. So, the truth is that, *pace* Socrates, philosophy, as a clear understanding of what is right and good for us, is not enough to carry out significant, historically profound changes. It never was in the past, and I doubt it will ever be. History does not work this way. Usually, humanity changes course of action only after a disaster, not before. It fights to liberate Auschwitz, not to prevent it. So, something else is also needed: good legislation (as we shall see in the next chapter), as always, and a catastrophic slap from Mother Nature. Let us hope it will be small, effective, and well-intentioned. Or perhaps, even better, a fake, amplified by PR and mass media; we have begun seeing this whenever the weather causes some disaster. Maybe climate change will become the scapegoat of any catastrophe, even unrelated ones, and that will finally trigger a change in human behaviour. But this is a terrible hope. If we wish to have a chance to avoid the dialectics between tragedy and catastrophe, we need more and better regulation, the topic of the next chapter.

Chapter 27

From Self-regulation to Legislation

If I were to pick a year to mark the beginning of the commercial Web, I might suggest 2004, when Facebook was launched, and Google held its IPO (initial public offering). Before that, the debate on ethical issues—from privacy to bias, from moderating illegal or unethical content to the protection of IPR (intellectual property rights), from fake news and disinformation to the digital divide—had been largely academic. Not in the negative, metaphorical sense of practically irrelevant, but literally: most of us discussing these problems worked in higher education. They were predictable problems, and, since the end of the 1980s, at conferences, in specialised publications, or in university lectures and seminars, we discussed them as fundamental and pressing, both ethically and socially. At the first conference of the International Association for Computing and Philosophy, in 1986, among the topics on the program, we had: online teaching; how to teach mathematical logic with software that ran on DOS; and something that was called at the time "computer ethics", which later became "information ethics", and which today we call "digital ethics". But it was too early. Prevention is not applied but rather regretted during the therapy.

The Green and The Blue: Naive Ideas to Improve Politics in the Digital Age, First Edition. Luciano Floridi.

After 2004, concerns started spreading to public opinion. The commercialisation of the Web brought into everyday life ethical problems already present in specialised contexts, such as spyware, software that collects data without the user's consent. The term was coined in 1995. Soon the pressure began to build up to improve companies' strategies and policies, and update—or rather, upgrade—the regulatory framework. It was during that period that self-regulation started to appear as a strategy for dealing with the ethical crisis. I remember meetings in Brussels where it was common for managers, policymakers, legislators, politicians, civil servants, and technical experts to support the value of self-regulation, for example, in contexts such as free speech online. It seemed like a good idea. It certainly did to me. Already in those years, Facebook insisted on the opportunity not to legislate but to operate in a "soft" way (the expression "soft law" is used to refer to rules without direct binding effect), through codes of conduct which, for example, would have guaranteed the presence on the platform only of people over the age of 13. I objected, even at the time, arguing that the empowerment of parents should not be equivalent to a shift in legal responsibility. If a child buys alcohol from a shop in England, the parents may be reprimanded, but the shop is in legal trouble. The notion was circulating that the digital industry could formulate its own ethical codes and standards as well as request and monitor adherence to them, without the need for external controls or impositions. It was not a bad idea. And I use the double-negative on purpose, to endorse a limited and contextualised, yet still positive, assessment. In the past, I have often argued in favour of self-regulation. Not as a definite, complete, or unique solution, but as a good, complementary step in the right direction, to be followed by many others, including legal measures. Moral suasion should be given a chance.

Many international relations are based on soft law, for example. In particular, the Council of Europe promotes respect for human rights, democracy, and the rule of law through recommendations that indicate desirable behaviours and outcomes, but without sanctions for non-compliance. Recently, I introduced and defended the need for *soft ethics*, not just the hard one, which we learn in life, and which we study in the classics (Floridi 2018). Soft ethics respects but goes beyond mere compliance with the law in force. Thus, soft ethics is not only *post-feasibility*—in the three senses of avoiding sci-fi speculations, being overly demanding (non-supererogatory), and endorsing the classic "ought implies can" condition—but also *post-compliance*. It assumes that, if the law is morally acceptable (if it is not, then the hard ethics case applies), once one has complied with the law, one may not only follow the law, but also do more than is required and less than it is allowed. For example, paying employees more than the minimum wage, or not taking advantage of some legal loopholes, are cases of soft ethics.

In theory, through self-regulation, soft ethics, and soft law, companies could adopt better behaviour models and operate in ways better ethically aligned to commercial, social, and environmental needs and values. And they could do so in faster, more agile, and more efficient ways, an essential consideration for an industry evolving as rapidly as the digital one. All this could happen by anticipating and without having to wait for new legislation or international agreements. Self-regulation could prevent disasters, enable companies to seize more opportunities, and prepare companies to adapt to future legal frameworks, if developed and applied correctly. I had in mind the philosophy that had inspired one of the greatest Italian innovators of the last century, Adriano Olivetti. He had applied (what I call here) a soft ethics strategy to run his company, with extraordinary success. So much so that, today, Olivetti's factory, buildings, and residential units in the industrial city of Ivrea (Piedmont)—built according to his Community Movement ideal (Movimento Comunità)—are recognised to be a model of social project, and are listed as a UNESCO World Heritage Site.

Soft ethics could also contribute to the legislation itself, anticipating and experimenting with more easily updatable and improvable solutions. Soft ethics and soft law could work as sandpits. The EU also recognises this in the recent AI Act. I remain convinced that, in those years, it was realistic and reasonable to believe that self-regulation could help foster an ethically constructive and fruitful dialogue between the digital industry and society. As I have often argued, it was worth trying the path of self-regulation, not exclusively, but in a complementary sense to the evolving legislation. Unfortunately, things went very differently.

If I had to choose another year, this time to indicate the coming of age of the era of self-regulation, I may suggest 2014, when Google set up an Advisory Council (of which I was a member), to address the consequences of the ruling on the "right to be forgotten" by the Court of Justice of the European Union. It was the first of many other similar initiatives that followed. That project had considerable visibility, a lot of exposure, and I believe it managed to achieve some success. Yet, overall, the following era of self-regulation was disappointing. In subsequent years, the Facebook-Cambridge Analytica scandal in 2018—predictable and preventable—and the blatantly ill-conceived and very short-lived Advanced Technology External Advisory Council, set up by Google on AI ethics in 2019 (of which I was a member), showed how difficult and eventually ineffective self-regulation was. Ultimately, companies appeared reluctant or unable to solve their ethical problems, not necessarily in terms of resources, lobbying, and public relations, but in terms of top-level strategy, at the C-suite level, to improve mentality and wrong behaviours that were just too deeply rooted. When the industry recently reacted to the ethical challenges posed by AI by creating hundreds of codes, guidelines, manifestos, and statements, self-regulation appeared in all its embarrassing vacuity. The impression of "blue washing" was strong and widespread. Today, Facebook's Oversight Board, established in 2020, is an anachronism, a belated reaction to the end of an era during which self-regulation failed to make a significant difference. It is too late, not least because legislation has caught up (or it will soon) with the digital industry. In particular, in the EU, the General Data Protection Regulation (GDPR, in force since 2016) has been followed by legislative initiatives such as the Digital Markets Act, the Digital Services Act, and the AI Act, to name the most significant. It is a regulatory movement likely to generate a vast Brussels effect, replacing soft regulation, which never really took off, with legal compliance and penalties.

Companies have a crucial role to play beyond legal requirements, both socially and environmentally. And for this, soft ethics remains an essential element of competitive acceleration and "good citizenship", in contexts where the legislation is either absent, ambiguous and in need of interpretation, or clear and ethically sound. But the era of self-regulation, as a strategy for dealing with the ethical challenges posed by the digital revolution, is over. It leaves behind, as a legacy, some good work. It cleared up things, by identifying and analysing some problems and solutions. It improved cultural and social awareness. It helped develop new, ethical sensitivities. And it did make some positive contributions to legislation, at least indirectly. For example, the High-Level Expert Group on Artificial Intelligence (of which I was a member), set up by the European Commission, saw the participation of industrial partners, and provided the ethical framework for the AI Act. It was not a collaboration to regret. However, the call for self-regulation, which society aimed at the digital industry, was largely ignored. It was a great but missed historical opportunity, very costly socially, environmentally, and economically. One only needs to think of the vast and ramified consequences of online disinformation. The time has come to acknowledge that, much as it might have been worth trying, self-regulation did not work. So, to use the words of the Gospel, now that the invitation has not been accepted, the alternative is "to force them [companies] to enter" (Luke 14:23). Self-regulation needs to be replaced by legislation; the sooner, the better. *Dura lex*, sed *digital lex* is why the EU is at the forefront of the digital governance debate.

***

This chapter concludes the presentation of the conceptual framework that serves to introduce, in the following chapter, some naive ideas to improve politics.

Chapter 28

Hundred Political Theses for a Mature Information Society

Throughout this book, I have argued that political thought should move from a *thing-based* to a *relation-based* ontology, and that we should think of politics as a *science of relations*, as well as a means to guide and manage the *ratio publica* rather than the *res publica*. A relational paradigm can help us understand how a mature information society, in terms of its socio-cultural expectations, can articulate and pursue its own specific, complete human project—i.e., both individual, as a meta-project that enables personal projects, and societal, for group projects—by equipping itself with the right infraethics through which to organise and implement it. Adopting this

The Green and The Blue: Naive Ideas to Improve Politics in the Digital Age, First Edition. Luciano Floridi.
© 2024 John Wiley & Sons Ltd. Published 2024 by John Wiley & Sons Ltd.

paradigm makes possible, and at the same time requires, cooperation and the development of good ideas to formulate a better politics, in the sense of both creating favourable conditions of possibility—which aim to design and thus construct what is or should be a good democracy for a mature information society—and unfavourable conditions—which reveal the presence of bad politics that hinders the construction of what is or should be a good democracy. In this chapter, which comes last but is actually the heart of the book, I outline, in the form of 100 theses, some of the ideas that seem to me most important and relevant today. I hope many of them will seem uncontroversial, but I am afraid that a few may not. They can be read as conceptual explanations, or logical consequences of a single premise: how to define good politics for a mature information society, which intends to pursue an ethically desirable and fulfilling human project, through an effective infraethics that everyone can share, counteracting (stealthily if necessary) the bad politics rampant today, through effective communication (i.e., marketing), working on cooperation and not just competition, in favour of a capitalism of care and not consumption, leveraging the marriage between the green and the blue to save humanity and the planet.

I have tried to make this chapter more accessible by separating the various ideas schematically and numerically, so that it is easier for the reader to agree or disagree with each one, and perhaps identify where other ideas are needed, or which ones require upgrading or refining, or must be rejected. I have put some critical concepts in italics, when they are first introduced, before I discuss or explain them. I have also tried to make the text readable on two levels. The first level is a network that connects each numbered idea, readable as a node, separate from the underlying paragraph, serving as a slightly more detailed discussion. Reading only the numbered sentences should be sufficient for those in a hurry. For those with more time and patience, the second level is more detailed and sequential, requiring a linear reading instead of a networked one.

* * *

1. A *society* is not formed through the *social contract* but emerges through the *universal trust*.

   The idea of the social contract is based on an obsolete anthropocentric, atomistic, and mechanistic Aristotelian-Newtonian ontology. It should be replaced by the idea of *universal trust*, according to which all human beings begin their existence as only beneficiaries of the world; become responsible trustees of the world as moral, social, and political agents; and end their existence as only givers or donors of the world.

2. A society is the totality of the *relations* that constitute and pre-exist it.[1]

   Society is formed by, and not merely composed of, many individuals, who are not like stones gathered in a heap, or atoms, but interconnected individual nodes made up of relations. Thus, the model of a society should be based on a relational ontology.

3. A *good society* is a *tolerant* and *just* society, therefore *peaceful* and *free*.

   These four moral relations (values as valuable ways of interacting) are presented in order of logical precedence and are essential. They refer to the four conditions identified by Locke (*tolerance* is the foundation of *peace*), Mill (tolerance is the foundation of *freedom*) and, between them, Kant (*justice* is the foundation of tolerance). However, in this book, I have argued that tolerance and justice have this logical order (tolerance has priority over justice), even if they are co-necessary.

4. A *civil society* organises itself into a political *community*, called a *polity*.

5. A *government* is the executive leadership of the polity.

6. The best way of creating and maintaining the government of a polity is *democracy*.

   This is because democracy maximises the just care, and tolerant growth, of individual, social, and environmental relations, and attends to the satisfaction of the interests, needs, and reasonable hopes not only of all persons (both physical and legal) and groups of persons, but of all *relata*: human, natural, and artificial.

7. *Direct* democracy is not the best form of democracy.

   This is because direct democracy always and inevitably risks becoming a tyranny of the majority.

8. The best form of democracy is *representative*.

   This is because the necessary initial condition that makes democracy work is the *structural* separation between *popular sovereignty*—those entitled to vote hold political power and legitimately delegate those

---

[1] The indirect reference to proposition 1.1 of Wittgenstein's *Tractatus* ("The world is the totality of facts, not of things") is deliberate.

who exercise it—and *political governance*—those who govern receive political power from the people's votes and can legitimately exercise it or be removed from power through the exercise of popular sovereignty.

9. All forms of *autocracy*—including a tyranny of the majority—arise from the self-legitimising identity between sovereignty and governance, i.e., between the possession, exercise, and legitimisation of political power.

   Every form of government and governance is inescapably fallible: sometimes, governments do not work or work poorly. From this, it follows that a democracy is preferable to any autocracy, not because it works better, but because it is far more *resilient*. When it fails, it does so less severely than any autocracy because it causes less damage and is better able to repair itself. To put it more formally, any autocracy is incompatible with *Condorcet's jury theorem*.

10. A good democracy allows for a choice between *real alternatives*.

    This is because the multiplication or accretion of choices and the lack of alternatives with real content are clear indicators of the anti-democratic nature of a political regime, as they reduce rather than expand the space for political decision-making. Citizens end up choosing between predetermined *options*—as in a restaurant menu, or a referendum—but do not have a say or position to decide between *alternatives*—whether to go to the restaurant, and which restaurant to go to, to use the same analogy, or whether to have a referendum and how to formulate its questions.

11. A good democracy offers the right *granularity of alternatives*.

    This means that the more choices are packaged together and then collected into single blocks upon which to ask citizens for political decisions, the less good the democracy in question is.

12. A *proportional* system is better than a *majoritarian* system because it offers a better granularity of alternatives.

13. A good society requires a good *politics*.

    "Requires" here means both "asks for" and "needs".

14. Politics is not good when it does not allow changes in *starting positions*.

    The impossibility of reworking starting positions is an objective indicator of the undemocratic nature of a political regime, which reduces the available space to construct the human project relationally. Lack of, or low social mobility, for example, is an indicator of bad politics.

15. Politics is good when its aim is to care for the *prosperity* of the *whole* of society and its environments, not only individuals: the people in it, and public and common goods, including all the natural and artificial habitats that belong to it or in which it lives.

    The "whole" ideally means not only the society that expresses it, but the entire human society and the planet that hosts it (cosmopolitan prosperity).

16. *Prosperity* is a relation that includes the protection and promotion of civil liberties, education, security, health, equal opportunities, and the possibility of growth (an individual project).

    Following a relational rather than a thing-based, ontology ensures that politics is *reticular.*

17. The totality of the individual public fabric, the social fabric, and the fabric of public and common goods is the *ratio publica.*

18. Good politics is reticular if it recognises and takes care of the *ratio publica.*

19. A policy is no good if it tears the fabric of the *ratio publica*, thus failing to ensure a widespread minimum standard by which to live an individual and/or community life with dignity.

    For this reason, the violation of the dignity of individuals or groups of people is an indicator of the undemocratic nature of a political regime, which reduces the space for the development of individuals in society to construct their lives and a relational politics.

20. Good politics is *universally participatory* (political co-design).

    Good policy needs the input and active participation of all parts of society, including associations, companies, and administrative structures. A good policy is successful only if it involves all social partners and stakeholders, at all stages, from reflection to the elaboration of good ideas, to their discussion, implementation, and refinement.

21. Good politics is *cosmopolitan.*

    This is because networked (reticular) participation in politics has no natural or geographical boundaries, only historical and pragmatic ones, which are accidental.

22. Politics can develop into good governance only with the positive support of *public administration.*

    Failing to work in synergy with public administration is a strategic mistake because the public administration has the inside knowledge and control of the mechanisms and degrees of feasibility of political projects. It is also an error of perspective, because only the commitment of the public administration can guarantee the continuity and ultimate success of projects, even over the course of several governments.

23. Making good policy together with social partners and public administration means *designing* the underlying relational networks (*infraethics*) that facilitate good and desired behaviour, while hindering bad and undesirable behaviour.

This means operating with policies that shape *by design* the relational conditions of the possibility of the behaviour to be determined or modified. Creating the design is a question of creating relational mechanisms that function not only according to a logic of control and eventual sanction but, above all, according to a logic of flexibility and self-reinforcement, in virtuous circles that work better the more they do (the *network effect*). For example, the widespread preference of citizens for using digital payments instead of cash may lead to, as a beneficial side effect, a better fiscal control on the transactions themselves, and thus a lowering of tax evasion. This, in turn, would lead to a lightening of the tax burden, improving the economy, and a greater incentive to use digital payments, and so on. It is, therefore, a question of technically designing virtuous circles that improve society and become stronger the more they are used.

24. Good politics pursues its aims, including its human project, by promoting the *economic well-being* freely sought or enjoyed by individuals, not through *coercion*.[2]

---

[2] "Income capacity and economic resources are not seen as an end, but rather as the means by which an individual manages to have and sustain a specific standard of living. Variables that can help measure economic well-being include income, wealth, consumer spending, housing conditions, and ownership of durable goods. As in most other dimensions of well-being, one cannot limit oneself to studying the average or median levels of the chosen indicators, but has to take into account the distribution in the population: the judgement on the level of material well-being of a society may vary if the same overall average income is equally distributed among citizens or is concentrated in the hands of the wealthy few". This quote comes from a website that is no longer available (www.misuredelbenessere.it/). I subscribe to it, but I did not wish to appropriate the wording, which is not mine.

25. Good politics does not use coercion as a means but maintains a monopoly on *violence* to eradicate it altogether or replace it with a peaceful, equitable, sustainable, and productive *competition*.

Competition, like *coordination* (agents pursue their projects without interfering with each other), cannot replace *collaboration* (agents pursue joint projects, each taking care of separate parts or stages of them), and *cooperation* (agents pursue joint projects together) because both fail to mobilise the whole network, and can at most guarantee the success of the individuals (whether single individuals or individual groups it does not matter). In other words, competition and coordination have much higher opportunity costs than collaboration and cooperation. Imagine Alice and Bob cooking and eating their own meals when they want and as they wish, using the same kitchen. They coordinate their actions as long as neither of them represents an impediment to the other. Less metaphorically, when markets work correctly, they are good at creating coordination, e.g., through competition between Alice and Bob. Collaboration requires coordination, but it also includes sharing tasks: Alice may contribute the appetisers and the drinks and Bob the main course, in our example. Markets are significantly less good at creating collaborative relations without society's incentives. Cooperation needs even more, for it implies sharing the whole process: Alice and Bob do the shopping and the cooking together. They co-design, co-create, and co-own the meal, so to speak. Markets do not perform well at all when it comes to cooperation unless the law intervenes. This is where infraethics becomes helpful. For global problems require more than coordination or even collaboration, they require cooperation: a sharing of decision processes, choices, and implementations of policies that touch the lives of millions and sometimes billions of people. We only need to think about the pandemic or climate change. So, markets are necessary mechanisms, but they are largely insufficient without political will and normative incentives. The C in OECD is after all that of "cooperation", not "competition".

26. Good policy is guided by *good ideas* in satisfying, reconciling, and prioritizing, within its human project, the reasonable hopes and legitimate interests of individuals and society, with regard to personal, social, and environmental prosperity.

27. Ideas are good when they provide politics with *implementable* (feasibility), *efficient* (cost), *effective* (outcome), *shareable* (consensus), and *preferable* (ethics) strategies for taking care of individual, social, and environmental prosperity.

28. Good ideas are generated by good *deliberation*.

29. Deliberation is good when it is *rational* in its reasoning, *informed* about the facts, aware of its own *fallibility*, *tolerant* of different opinions, and open to *constructive dialogue*.

30. Political deliberation takes place in the *public sphere*.

31. The public sphere is part of the *infosphere*.

32. Good ideas are consolidated into good *practices*.

33. A practice is good when it is *transparent* in the sense that it is *accountable*, *auditable*, and *improvable*.

34. Good deliberation is promoted by a good *political debate*.

35. A political debate is good when it decides, in a satisfactory way, on the quality of the available ideas, their compatibility and priority, and how to implement them, giving rise to a tolerant and just market of ideas.

36. Good ideas are not partisan but, precisely because of their nature, *can and should be shared* by more than one political programme.

    Political parties should compete for votes by presenting good ideas, but then collaborate and cooperate for the governance of the *ratio publica* when in power, through the sharing and refining of good ideas.

37. Political involvement is increasingly *"on demand"* and *"just in time"* and less and less *"always on"*.

    We must be able to recognise and support good ideas, irrespective of their source and context, in an *on-demand, just-in-time* policy. Such a policy means that the marketing-based management of civil society's attention must be predicated on a forward-looking interest in the proposal of good, relevant ideas, and not guided by attention-grabbing alarmism, emergency, crisis, exceptionalism, or urgency.

38. Sharing good ideas, irrespective of political affiliations or programmes, means prioritising *ethics* over *ideology*.

39. Good ideas have the power to motivate politically (political psychagogy) through three factors: *hope* (which can also be altruistic), *interest* (typically only personal), and *reason* (from common sense to logic, from the correct use of facts to probabilistic reasoning).

40. Hope motivates more than interest.

    Hope can overcome any self-interest, including the fundamental interest in one's or others' well-being or survival, even to the point of justifying self-harm and suicide. For this reason, fundamentalist or ideological terrorism, which relies on hope, cannot be overcome by appealing only to interest. It must be opposed by offering better hopes.

41. Self-interest motivates more than reason.

    There is no reason, including in terms of mathematical certainty, that cannot be neglected or ignored for self-interest.

42. Reason can be reconciled with hope and interest, but it follows from the above that it motivates less than either.

    This is why the deepest-rooted greed, which is based on selfish interest, cannot be countered by appealing to reason. In particular, social problems—such as abuse, corruption, exploitation, fundamentalism, intolerance, violence, and environmental problems, including global warming, species extinction, pollution, animal abuse, and ecological vandalism—cannot be solved by leveraging reason alone. Good politics needs to appeal to self-interest and hope as well.

43. Good politics is successful if it motivates (marketing) primarily through hope, then interest, and then reason.

    Whether by Berlusconi, Johnson, or Trump, a winning election campaign devalues the current politics—which everyone should be interested in changing because it is always unsatisfactory—and overestimates the future, which everyone hopes will be better. Conversely, a losing election campaign, from that of Hillary Clinton to that of Remain versus Vote Leave in the Brexit referendum, assesses the present as already satisfactory—thereby disappointing the hopes of all those who wish for better—and predicts a possible future as worse or risky in its absence—promising only a reasonable *more of the same* (another Clinton presidency, the usual EU, etc.). This results in a political message that frustrates the hopes of the electorate and is bound to fail.

44. *Fear* motivates only indirectly, through hope, interest, and reason.

45. *Punishment*, understood as an instrument for managing fear, is not effective if it generates *despair*, which can be understood as a total lack of hope.

46. *Public opinion* consists of the hopes, fears, expectations, and interests of the public expressing it.

47. Public opinion can be reasonable (*nous*), but it is often mainly emotional, in terms of hopes, fears, and expectations, and instinctive, in terms of interests (*doxa*).

48. Public opinion does not pre-exist, it is formed.

    There is no such thing as public opinion as a given. Forming public opinion means creating and prioritising the hopes, fears, expectations, and interests of the public. Public opinion does not pre-exist, as if it were something external with which politics must deal. Instead, it is formed, also by politics. However, once formed, a given public opinion is "reified" (hypostatised, i.e., it becomes a thing), and subsequent politics must come to terms with the new political reality. In this dialectic, it is essential to improve every aspect of public opinion whenever possible, before it becomes too rigidly and immutably reified.

49. The shaping of public opinion takes place through the *marketing* (rhetoric) of ideas.

50. Marketing interacts with human interfaces to obtain their resources.

51. Political marketing aims to gain the attention, support, consent, and votes of the electorate.

    The electorate is the interface, and attention, support, consent, and votes are the desired resources.

52. Good politics transforms (marketing) good ideas into public opinion.

53. Good ideas alone are insufficient, they must be supported by appropriate marketing (rhetoric).

54. The *rhetoric* (marketing) *of reason* is the best way to form public opinion politically, but it is never sufficient.

55. Good ideas are *timely* (i.e., they work at the right time), not *timeless* (i.e., they work at any time). They are, therefore, *dynamic* and can always be updated or become obsolete.

This is because the solutions they propose are not immutable, like the laws of nature, but contingent, like human history, and must evolve in relation to the problems with which they deal. It follows that voting for the same party no-matter-what is a mistake unless the party is also changing and adapting to the historical circumstances (does not behave like the fly hitting the glass).

56. The timeliness of good ideas is *relational*.

This is because it depends partly on circumstances and changes interactively with them, while seeking to improve them. It is not *relativistic*—as if it depended entirely on circumstances and only ever changed with them—and it is not *absolute*—as if it did not depend at all on circumstances and never changed in relation to them—but it is *relational*.

57. *Consensus* must be built on good ideas, their priority, and feasibility.

58. Consensus is the cooperative and contextual convergence of social relations on what needs to be done and how (the agenda).

Consensus grounds the conceptualisation of good politics and the translation of the possible into the preferable. Equilibria, both socio-political and economic, are designed through consensus (including about rules and acceptable practices), they are artefacts and not natural states of socio-political and economic systems, which left to themselves are always dynamic and imbalanced.

59. The two fundamental values that characterise social and political relations are *solidarity* and *trust*.

60. Politics as praxis is the totality of *solidarity and trust relations* that organise and guide a society on what needs to be done.

61. *Solidarity* regulates needs in a society and is the basis for *green* (i.e., environmental, and ecological) *solutions*.

Solidarity means the care of relations towards the world and the present, past, and future generations (*universal trust*).

62. Without solidarity, there is only a free market and competition, but not equitable prosperity and cooperation.

63. *Trust* governs actions in a society.

It is about trusting ourselves, each other, the future, human ingenuity and its products, and the potential goodness of their applications.

64. Without trust, there is only the management of political power—the market of people as interfaces—but not good politics—where good ideas are marketed and shape public opinion.

65. Politics takes care of the relations, which constitute and connect the nodes of the network, and the nodes themselves (all entities).

    Focusing politics on the primacy of relations rather than the primacy of things means, for example, giving primacy to the concept of "citizenship" rather than that of "citizen".

66. Good politics must move from taking care of the good management of the *res publica* to taking care, above all, of the nature and the healthy growth of the relational network that constitutes a society, its members, and its environment, i.e., the *ratio publica*.

67. The fabric of the ratio publica is the inter-spatiality and inter-temporality of the historical-cultural relations that give society and its members its identity, as well as the natural and artificial environments that host them.

68. Politics malfunctions when the two central relations of *solidarity* and *trust* do not work.

    It follows that politics can be repaired only by repairing these two relations.

69. The *mafia* is a type of *organised crime*, based on a relational and not on a thing-based politics.

70. Any mafia is a form of criminal politics and vice versa. It follows that any dictatorship is a mafia.

    Mafia replaces politics in caring for the relations that constitute and connect things. That is why it is incompatible with the state and survives only by replacing it and becoming a form of governance.

71. Politics, when it does not work, can be repaired only if its relational nature is repaired.

    This should be a reason for some moderate optimism, because it is easier to repair relations than *relata*, i.e., things constituted and connected by relations. For example, it is easier to repair the relation of trust between some stakeholders than to "repair" the stakeholders themselves to make a relation of trust work.

72. Good politics is a meta-project, i.e., it supports the *individual human project*.

Every person can be understood as being on a path of self-fulfilment, in which each one gradually becomes more and more oneself. This individual, open, and autonomous construction (*poiesis*) is a delicate process because nobody exists in isolation. A person is a knot of relations: fragile, influenceable, malleable, and damageable. Politics supports individual *self-construction* (*autopoiesis*) by providing the conditions for its realisation, especially in terms of tolerance, justice, peace, freedom, safety, education, respect and recognition of others, and equal opportunities. Politics malfunctions when at least one of these conditions is not met.

73. Good politics is a cooperative project, i.e., it supports the *social human project*.

Every society strives (even if only implicitly) towards becoming what it would like to be and should be, that is, it can be interpreted as a communal and shared human project, which is also constantly in progress. Good politics is concerned with supporting and implementing the best possible social human project, while also caring for the individual human projects. It must do so in a critical, conscious, and careful manner, in ways that are compatible with the historical circumstances in which it arises, and the opportunities and constraints they contain.

74. Good politics promotes *just tolerance* as a fundamental value.

Since Locke, tolerance has been at the roots of the modern political era, as a demand to keep every individual and communal human life open to choice, change, rethinking, and, thus, improvement. Tolerance must be just, i.e., it must be careful to avoid the adverse effects of its own excessive application. And justice itself must be tolerant of diversity, of mistakes, of the possibility of doing things alternatively or differently, of the possibility of starting again, and counteract the excessive enforcement of automatisms.

75. Justice recognises the logical superiority of tolerance when it (justice) establishes its limit by accepting unpunished injustice rather than unjust punishment.

This is why the foundation of good politics is just tolerance, rather than tolerant justice. Hegel was right in saying *fiat iustitia ne pereat mundus* "let justice be done lest the world perishes", as von Mises would later write. In contrast, Kant was wrong in suggesting *fiat iustitia, pereat mundus*, "let justice be done even if it means the world perishing".

76. Politics does not have a *logout*.

    Socio-political relations can be changed, but not denied. Therefore, the simplistic rhetoric of being in or out (e.g., of Europe) is rendered vacuous by the fact that, in a global relational network (i.e., cosmopolitanism), one cannot disconnect but rather can be connected in a way that is more or less just and consistent with the social human project being pursued.

77. Bad politics does not disconnect (logout), but it misconnects (short-circuits) social relations and the interfaces that should facilitate and coordinate them.

78. Politics is *cybernetic*.

    In Plato, the cybernetic (kybernetes) is the expert pilot of the ship, the one who knows the ship, who has a plan and knows a navigation route, knows how to steer in the right direction even against the tide, winds, and currents, sometimes navigating indirectly and obliquely to reach the destination.

79. Politics is not about managing the speed of change (e.g., technological innovation), but about determining the goodness of its direction.

    Politics can either facilitate or hinder changes, but it does not have its feet on the brake or the accelerator, but rather its hands on the steering wheel of history. The high speed at which a society goes through its transformations can be a wholly positive thing if the direction chosen by politics is good.

80. Democratic politics is *dualist*.

    Democracy is usually defined in terms of shared values (semantics), or common rules (syntax) adopted by a society. In reality, political semantics and syntax presuppose a *structural* separation between two elements: *sovereignty* (i.e., the legitimate and legitimising possession of political power) and *governance* (i.e., the exercise of political power). Without this initial, dualistic, structural condition of possibility, a representative democracy is reduced to a dictatorship (tyranny), in which the majority (which possesses and exercises political power) imposes its will on the minority, whose individual or social human projects are not protected.

81. The space of politics is part of the *infosphere.*

    Today, the space of politics—also understood as a public space (see above) and as a deliberative exercise—is always *onlife*: partly offline and partly online, partly analogue, and partly digital. This also applies to those who are still excluded from the digital revolution (those on the disadvantaged side of the *digital divide*), because their choices are influenced or determined by those who are included. The onlife space influences both the offline and the online spheres.

82. The task of good politics is to make capitalism *sustainable* and *equitable.*

    Capitalism is the best system known to date for producing wealth, but not for producing it *sustainably* nor distributing it *equitably*. In the past, capitalism has been seen as an inseparable counterpart of the world's consumer economy (*consumerism*). However, this link can and must now be severed, in favour of a new coordination between capitalism and the circular and sustainable economy that cares for the world (*fosterism*). By moving from a politics of things to a politics of relations, it is easier to start building a post-materialist and post-consumerist society that favours an economy of services and experiences equitably and sustainably.

83. Good politics promotes and manages *citizenship capital.*

    Every generation enjoys the outcome of the work, efforts, and sacrifices made by the countless generations preceding it, because each generation inherits the past and, in turn, leaves its legacy to the next generation. Politics should adopt strategies to distribute the benefits of the inherited wealth of this kind, ensuring that all members have not only equal opportunities but also the citizenship capital required to support individual human projects.

84. Education is a fundamental part of citizenship capital.

    In order to strengthen the green and blue experience economy (see below), a mature information society must invest in an education that teaches not only how to "read" (i.e., how to use, handle, consult, and exploit the digital), but above all how to "write" (i.e., how to work, transform, design, and improve it). The information society is a neo-manufacturing society, except that the raw material is the digital: digital data, information, processes, products, and services. Therefore, it is necessary to teach not only the languages of human capital, for examples the languages of architecture, art, history, music, law, living and dead languages, and sciences, but also the languages of digital design, including one's mother tongue and English, mathematics, statistics, industrial design, computer science, and so on. Citizens need to be able to read and write digitally to be protagonists in creating and caring for their society and the environments that host it, in a critical, informed, and respectful way.

85. The state is an *interface* that acts as a relational support for society's creative, productive, and cooperative efforts.

The state is a multiagent, meso-social entity. It is not the endpoint of the political-juridical organisation of a polity, which is a political community, i.e., the political order of a society. Instead, it is the relational meeting point, a dynamic interface with various features, between *polities*, i.e., between a society, which organises itself through a state, and other societies organised as other states throughout the rest of the world. The effectiveness and efficiency of the state as an interface can be politically diverse (see, for example, the various models of state organisation: from a federal or presidential republic to a constitutional monarchy).

86. Citizens interact politically with the world through the interface-state, to which they belong, and the various interfaces within the state.

Various dynamic interfaces—e.g., a municipality, a county, a region, a state in a federation, a nation in a union—enable this interaction and communication to take place, which does not require a unique model.

87. The crisis of the modern state is not one of "necessity" but one of "sufficiency".

The state is increasingly necessary and ever less sufficient to take care of the *ratio publica*. The state is only one of the many other equally necessary and individually insufficient agents, such as supranational organisations, international institutions, and multinational companies. It may seem that the state no longer has a crucial function in the digital era of globalisation, and that the alternative is either; (a) a more territorially rooted localisation, with corresponding micro-nationalisms (see the many phenomena of separatism and souverainism in various European states, from Spain to Great Britain, from Germany to Italy), or (b) an international globalisation suited to markets, multinational companies, and intergovernmental institutions. In reality, the state, understood as an interface of communication, interaction, and coordination between local and global realities, becomes simultaneously more necessary and less sufficient, the greater the degree of globalisation.

88. The state is good when it implements good politics.

89. Good politics values the state as an interface.

This is because the state can invest in useful infrastructures and cover the risk of long-term investments; it can free the success of creative and productive strategies from formal (e.g. bureaucratic) or substantial obstacles (e.g. lack of credit, public debt); it can incentivise the development of socially acceptable or preferable strategies, and discourage the development of unacceptable ones, by adjusting or counterbalancing market limitations when necessary or useful; it can delegate the success of strategies, outsourcing and controlling, when possible, any creative and productive activity that does not need public management, to private initiatives; it can coordinate efforts at the national and international level; and finally, it can ensure that doing the right thing is not penalised (i.e. level the playing field). For instance, digitalisation is disrupting the labour market. It is clear that, due to the new forms of automation and information management, many jobs (or at least many functions and, therefore, related tasks) of the past will soon no longer exist or will be significantly transformed, while new ones will emerge that are not yet imaginable. In this context, the precariousness of present situations and the resultant uncertainty about future solutions will increase. A *defensive strategy* that resists digitalisation (e.g., the proposal for a tax on robots) and welfare as the only solution is not a winning one. What is needed is an *proactive strategy*, one that is highly mobile, agile, and flexible, but that also (and precisely for this reason) provides a robust network of social protection. This is because entrepreneurship is promoted and facilitated by reducing the costs and risks of failure. Those who can most easily afford to take risks and fail are not the less well-off. The digital world offers great business and entrepreneurial opportunities, hence the possibility to generate wealth and create jobs. This will be possible if failures in taking advantage of digitalisation are seen as normal and not penalised, and if a robust, supportive socio-economic culture mitigates their adverse effects. A culture of "little but safe" will not take a country to the top of the digital economy but will instead put it in a rear-guard position. Instead, a strategy for an "abundant, even if uncertain" digital economy is needed. This, too, is not an original idea. As written in *Matthew* 13:12: "For whoever has, to him more will be given, and he will have abundance; but whoever does not have, even what he has will be taken away from him".[3]

90. Good politics is *multiagent*.

The state has the force, the *convening power*, and the duty to coordinate (*infraethics*) other agents to take care of the *public ratio*, and its good, effective, efficient, and safe functioning. Above all, the state should call upon all stakeholders (including the business world) to share this responsibility in a visible, transparent, and *accountable* manner, and to make policies together through multiagent agreements guaranteed and managed by the state itself. This is also true at a supranational level where, for example, the EU has the power and the duty to coordinate other states and stakeholders to take care of the European *ratio publica*.

91. Multiagent politics lowers opportunity costs.

This is because the amount of unrealised good increases as social coordination, collaboration and cooperation decrease, a relation that corresponds to the modern state's crisis of "sufficiency". Multiagent politics should be collaborative and cooperative, not merely competitive and coordinated.

92. The state is not entrepreneurial.

It is not the state's purpose or responsibility to transform itself into a company. This is not its vocation, and such a metamorphosis (the entrepreneurial state) would only serve as a straitjacket that generates inefficiency, distortions, and waste. Instead, it is companies that, thanks to the state, must become good citizens, as nodes in the social network, for example, as *benefit corporations*.

93. Good economic policy is an economy of *onlife experience*.

The amount and quality of time at one's disposal is the most valuable, finite, non-transferable, and non-renewable resource that each person possesses. Therefore, the prosperity of individuals, their societies, and their environments is also assessed based on how their individual and social time is managed and valued. The modern era can be broadly

---

[3] New King James Version.

interpreted as the period during which humanity has managed to "heal" more and more time—mainly due to improved living standards, scientific research, and national health systems—as well as to "liberate" more and more time—mainly due to the successive phases of industrialisation and technological development, trade, and socio-political conditions. More and more people live longer, have a better quality of life than any previous generation, and live with much more time and income at their disposal. For this reason, an innovative economy of growth today should focus on the management and valorisation not so much of working time, but of healed or healable time—i.e., time spent without suffering and illness—and of free time or time that can be freed. We can call this time *disposable*—that is, disposable and dispensable, in analogy with *disposable income*—onlife, as it is not bound by work commitments and is usable, because it can be dedicated to activities of one's choice. In a world where healthy and leisure time will increase, the economic activities related to how this time can be managed intelligently and fruitfully will be increasingly crucial. The economy of the future, as an economy of experience, is an *economy of disposable time*.

94. *Design* is at heart of the experience economy.

In a mature information society, increasing emphasis should be placed on design and digital technology to support an economy of individual experience, rather than mass production. Industry, education, health, entertainment, culture, tourism, but also fashion, the advanced tertiary sector, and the agri-food industry, are all sectors that are increasingly moving from the necessity to the insufficiency of the high quality of a product or service. This must be of high quality but cannot be only of high quality, because the added value is provided by the required or at least desired experience, which is often digitally mediated. For instance, if the quality of two pizzas is equally excellent, customers will go to a nice place, with a beautiful view, where they can book both the parking space and the table with an app, read the online ratings, maybe get a discount if they leave a positive comment on the app, etc. The pizzeria must know how to use the data it collects to offer a better experience, optimise costs, and identify opportunities. The pizza must be consistently good, but its quality is now the starting point, not the endpoint of competition. The selfie is the extreme version of this process: it is not the experience of eating the pizza, but the experience of the experience that makes the difference. Every manager should keep a selfie test in mind. The transition from the economy of things to that of experiences is also well documented at the company level. Today, over 80% of the value of the 500 most highly capitalised US companies (S&P 500) is in intangible assets. The shift from the centrality of things to the centrality of experiences represents an excellent opportunity for any country that can combine the green economy of environmental capitalism with the blue economy of digital capitalism. Green and blue are also about the economy of experience. They are not the cherry; they are the cake.

95. *Co-design* is the socialisation of problem-solving.

The digital supports and facilitates group-based project management, where participants contribute creatively and openly to develop new or improved solutions. They do this by identifying problems, constraints, opportunities, and goals, involving end-users, usually through digital platforms, in a networked way, overcoming the barriers of an organisation or a company structure. From education to the design of green and blue solutions, to co-designing as a strategy, intelligence is insufficient: goodwill, a spirit of cooperation, and rules for *governance* are also required. In other words, it also takes a digital ethics and the social commitment of all good forces, because individual efforts alone are insufficient and often fruitless.

96. The solutions of good politics are *green* and *blue*.

Today the solutions found by good politics to pursue the human project must be both green (concerning the economy of natural, social, artificial, cultural, and mental environments) and blue (concerning the digital and information economy). National, social, cultural, and digital environments (i.e., the natural and the artificial) coexist in symbiotic relations that are mutually beneficial. They should not only be protected but also valued as resources for individual and social well-being that should not be wasted. This must be done holistically and systematically. *Fostering capitalism* must replace *consumeristic capitalism*.

97. There are no *externalities*, only delayed *internalities*.

98. The marriage between the environment and digital technology (the green and the blue) is vital for the prosperity of the planet, its inhabitants, and, therefore, every society.

A society should transform its philosophy of mere conservation and care of environmental and cultural assets—the environment and culture as a costly burden for society to look after—into a strategy of promotion and economic valorisation, whereby the environment and culture are valued as capital to be put to good use, to the economic, social, cultural, mental, and even intrinsic benefit of the whole of society that expresses it, involving its members and its environments, also thanks to digital technology.

99. The human project is the kind of individual and social life we would like to enjoy.

100. The human project for the digital age is green and blue.

Postscript – The Information Society in the Time of the Coronavirus

This book was completed during the COVID-19 (coronavirus) pandemic. During this period, the world slowed down abruptly. Living onlife became an even more familiar experience for a growing number of people. As a result of the various health and safety measures imposed by governments worldwide, the time at many people's disposal increased enormously, not only quantitatively, but sometimes even qualitatively. A free, or at least less pressing, agenda makes it easier to think not in fragments but over more extended periods, lengthening the pace of reflection, in the knowledge that there is more time to explore, and that not everything has to be done in a rush. Philosophy can be practised as a hundred-metre sprint, but it is best as a marathon.

The pandemic took the world by surprise, although it is not the first such event, and certainly will not be the last. In this postscript, I intend to highlight three "viral" issues regarding a mature information society: a mistake, an opportunity, and a risk, in order to draw a final conclusion, in line with what I have argued in the rest of the book.

The mistake was made by the mass media, which provoked an "infodemic" about the virus: a vast flow of information of all kinds, correct and incorrect, reliable and unreliable, exaggerated in both a dramatising and trivialising way, created a climate of uncertainty and mistrust. It should be added that, if society had run the Internet less commercially, we could have relied on official sites where we could have obtained trustworthy and fact-checked health information. So-called generic top-level domains (gTLDs) are represented by the final three letters of a website. For example, ".com" is reserved for commercial organisations, in the same way as national top-level domains (nTLDs) are assigned to countries. Around 2000, the World Health Organisation (WHO) and the Internet Corporation for Assigned Names and Numbers (ICANN) discussed the possibility of creating "health", a non-generic, top-level domain exclusively dedicated to health, where accurate and reliable medical information, guaranteed by the WHO, could be found. That would have been an excellent idea. Unfortunately, for various political and commercial reasons, nothing came of it. Competition and coordination won, instead of collaboration and cooperation. The result is that today, domains such as "care", "diet", "doctor", "health", "healthcare", "help", "hospital" and "med" are all private.

The earlier, Italian experience in Europe, tragic in terms of suffering and casualties, did little to impart lessons to other countries, such as the UK and the USA, where the pandemic developed a bit later. In these countries, the same communication mistakes were made, albeit in a different, and perhaps worse, way, given their incapacity to learn from the mistakes of others. Bad politics, bad journalism, a bit of naivety, and media echo chambers that would have confused everyone, prevented good information management, which would have been necessary to alert everyone to the seriousness of the risk and the severity of the consequences, without having to alarm anyone. The cacophony of divergent opinions polarised the public. The terrified treated the virus as if it were the plague, storming supermarkets from Italy to Denmark, from the UK to the USA. The irresponsible underestimated it as if it were a cold or, at worst, a conspiracy, inviting people to have aperitifs in the square, to party in Paris, or to celebrate St. Patrick's Day in Ireland. In the end, all that was left was the increasingly radical application of the precautionary principle and the proliferation of cases. Let us remember, however, that "when in doubt ..." and "you never know ..." are recommendations that end up suggesting that one should never cross any road. This contagious and deadly virus brought many countries to their knees because of its human, health, logistical, social, and economic impact. However, more reasoning and civic sense, and less emotion and rhetoric, would have helped mitigate such effects. Suffice it to say that the term "infodemic" was dusted off by the WHO to talk about the misinformation circulating about the coronavirus, although it was coined in 2003 in connection with misinformation about the viral disease SARS (Severe Acute Respiratory Syndrome). In more than fifteen years, one might have expected there to have been some level of preparation regarding good scientific communication in anticipation of major crises such as this one. Let us hope that the lesson has finally been learned.

The opportunity is obscured in difficulty, but it is our task to find it. It is said that no crisis should be wasted. We have been forced to travel less, to work and interact remotely, to collaborate in virtual spaces, to implement distant learning and so forth—in short, to exploit all those opportunities that have long been available to us thanks to digital technologies but that we have often preferred to ignore. The virus and quarantine have broken old habits and forced us to imagine new ways of interacting and working. While it is disappointing that it took the pandemic to motivate us, we should use this collective tragedy to promote, for example, *e-learning* and *smart working*, in order to increase work autonomy, flexibility, and productivity, to deliver more accountability for results, promote a better quality of life, and make many activities more sustainable. Despite the pain, discomfort, and suffering caused by the virus, and concerns about its long-term consequences, the people and organisations that take advantage of this new digital challenge will emerge stronger from the disaster caused by the pandemic and how it was often mismanaged. They will be prepared to face the next crisis, not *if* but *when* it occurs. Sometimes, the digital sphere has been part of the problem, exacerbating the situation with an infodemic. But now, the digital itself could, and hopefully should, be part of the solution, for societies that live onlife. However, the risk is that the so-called *digital divide* between those who live onlife and those who do not will widen and exacerbate. Therefore, digital policies must also address this problem to ensure everyone can participate fully and equally in today's information societies.

This brings me to the risk implicit in a mature information society. The panic generated by the infodemic should not be followed by the euphoria occasioned by false hopes that the availability of vaccines and other cures would lead to a rapid end to the crisis. I fear that the same pundits who spread apocalyptic misinformation yesterday will spread utopian misinformation tomorrow. When one is suffering, good news can be interpreted as heralding the end of suffering. Unfortunately, this is not the case. The new wave of mass infection in China in 2023 was a terrible reminder. The reality is that it will take a long time, and a great deal of organisation and funding to protect those at risk and fully emerge from the crisis. There is no way to avoid death, but with intelligence and goodwill, it can be postponed, so that one may die, like Abraham, "full of years".

It is precisely the figure of Abraham that enables me to close this book by connecting the pandemic and the human project. As I wrote, our society, unfortunately, rests these days mainly on a political meta-project, one which makes possible and facilitates only individual human projects and does not care about a cooperative project for all of society. It facilitates competition and, at most, coordination, but not collaboration and cooperation. The anti-vax movement epitomises this pure individualism, and the lack of any sense of social responsibilities and solidarity, that has permeated our culture to its core. However, in severe crises, we may realise the fundamental importance of acting together: not as many atoms, but as a relational community of nodes, belonging to the same network. No node can cope alone, but the whole network has the resilience to withstand the impact of a war, a pandemic, a famine, or a natural disaster. If the coronavirus has served to remind us of the importance of having and pursuing *also* a social project for the whole human community, and of emphasising that union is strength, while individualism, left to its own devices, is insufficient and weakens society's opportunities to do so much more, then the virus will have ultimately served a positive role. The lessons learned can be put into practice immediately. Once the pandemic is over, the accumulated experience, the international solidarity that is developing, and the sacrifices that have been made will bear witness to the fact that, with the same determination, the same coordination, collaboration, and cooperation, and the same worldwide effort, we know that we can resolve other major collective challenges as well, such as the ecological crisis and social injustice. Overcoming the pandemic will prove that humanity, when it wants to, can rise to any challenge. It could and should give us confidence in our joint action.

The three monotheistic religions of Judaism, Christianity, and Islam all recognise Abraham as a common patriarch. He is a biblical figure who unites; he is also a symbol of hospitality. It is he who stands outside the tent, in the hottest hour, ready to receive three strangers, and invites them to refresh themselves by saying: "Do not pass over without stopping" (*Genesis* 18:1–8). We should listen to this appeal and not pass by without stopping to reflect upon what humanity can achieve when it acts together.

Acknowledgements

I began working on this book in 2017, following a few meetings with Alessandro Beulcke, with whom I conceived the project, discussed its ideas, and shared enthusiasm for the enormous value that informed, rational, intelligent, and open discussion can have in the pursuit of improving politics. The title and some of the chapter contents have their origin in a pamphlet I published in the Italian magazine *Formiche*. Without Alessandro, I would have had neither the courage nor the confidence to write this book. Therefore, I consider him co-responsible, but only for the good parts. The bad parts are entirely my responsibility.

In addition to Alessandro, several people have contributed to improving the ideas explored in this book. They have greatly helped me with their patience, kindness, intelligence, and with a considerable investment of their time. I really cannot thank them enough. For reasons of privacy, I will not name all of them. But with their permission, I will name a group (which I have sometimes called the *G 18:3*, with reference to *Matthew* 18:3) that has critically been part of the various versions of this book in addition to Alessandro himself: Alessandro Aleotti, Monica Beltrametti, Barbara Carfagna, Luca De Biase, Adrio Maria de Carolis, Massimo Durante, Ugo Pagallo, Sergio Scalpelli, Luciano Violante, and Matteo Zuppi. In addition, I would like to thank Josh Cowls, Fabrizio Floridi, Emmie Hine, Prathm Juneja, Jessica Morley, Kia Nobre, Jakob Mökander, Claudio Novelli, Stefano Quintarelli, Mariarosaria Taddeo, and David Watson who read many versions of this text or its chapters and provided more suggestions on how to improve them than I can remember.

I am most grateful to Thomas Buchheim, Jörg Noller, the editorial team and the publisher of the *Philosophisches Jahrbuch*, and the colleagues who

The Green and The Blue: Naive Ideas to Improve Politics in the Digital Age, First Edition. Luciano Floridi.

took part in the discussion, for the remarkable honour of being invited to contribute to the *Jahrbuch-Kontroverse* series (Buchheim et al. 2021). The scholarly attention paid by colleagues to one's own work is the greatest gift one may receive in academia, even more so these days, when we seem to have increasingly less time to study, think, and dialogue.

My heartfelt thanks also go to Raffaello Cortina, his team and his publishing house for wanting to publish an expanded version of the pamphlet as a book in Italian. This further revised and expanded English version owes much to that original book.

Kia deserves a second mention. As usual, she has been an inspirational muse and a source of joy and serenity, which translate into energy, hope, and a desire to improve the world. She is the source of any optimism the reader may encounter in this book. As if she were not busy enough with her research, she kindly offered (she really insisted, I assure you) to listen to my reading of the final draft and, as always, made many excellent suggestions. It is a rare privilege to interact with such a brilliant mind.

To all these people, named and unnamed, goes my deepest gratitude. If the things I have written in this book are not entirely wrong, it is thanks to our discussions and the feedback I received from them. None of the nominees is responsible for the remaining mistakes, which are mine alone, and I mean that. Above all, none of the people who helped me underwrote the ideas presented in this book, for which I take full responsibility.

References

Alterman, Hyman. 1969. *Counting People: The Census in History*. New York: Harcourt.

Arendt, Hannah. 1998. *The Human Condition*. 2nd ed. Chicago; London: University of Chicago Press.

Aristotle. 1996. *The Politics and the Constitution of Athens*. 2nd ed. Cambridge: Cambridge University Press.

Bacon, Francis. 2000. *The New Organon*. Cambridge: Cambridge University Press.

Bergson, Henri. 2014. *Time and Free Will: An Essay on the Immediate Data of Consciousness*. London: Routledge.

Bobbio, Norberto. 2005. *Liberalism and Democracy*. London: Verso.

Brandeis, Louis, and Samuel Warren. 1890. "The right to privacy." *Harvard Law Review* 4 (5):193–220.

Brynjolfsson, Erik, and Andrew McAfee. 2014. *The Second Machine Age: Work, Progress, and Prosperity in a Time of Brilliant Technologies*. New York: W.W. Norton & Company.

Buchheim, Thomas, Verlag Karl Alber, Volker Gerhardt, Matthias Lutz-Bachmann, Isabelle Mandrella, Pirmin Stekeler-Weithofer, and Wilhelm Vossenkuhl, eds. 2021. *Philosophisches Jahrbuch*. Rombach Wissenschaft.

Burgess, Matt. 19 June 2020. "Why the NHS Covid-19 contact tracing app failed." *Wired* https://www.wired.co.uk/article/nhs-tracing-app-scrapped-apple-google-uk.

Cassirer, Ernst. 2003. *Substance and Function, and Einstein's Theory of Relativity*. Mineola, N.Y: Dover Publications.

Cellan-Jones, Rory. 2021. *Always on: Hope and Fear in the Social Smartphone Era*. London: Bloomsbury Continuum.

Cheng, Edwin, and Susan Podolsky. 1996. *Just-in-Time Manufacturing: An Introduction*. 2nd ed. London: Chapman & Hall.

Clayton, James. 7 July 2020. "TikTok: Chinese app may be banned in US, says Pompeo." *BBC* https://www.bbc.com/news/technology-53319955.

Copeland, B. Jack. 2006. *Colossus: The Secrets of Bletchley Park's Codebreaking Computers*. New York; Oxford: Oxford University Press.

Council of the European Union. 2016. "Position of the Council at first reading with a view to the adoption of a REGULATION OF THE EUROPEAN PARLIAMENT AND OF THE COUNCIL on the protection of natural persons with regard to the processing of personal data and on the free movement of such data, and repealing Directive 95/46/EC (General Data Protection Regulation) ST 5419 2016 INIT - 2012/011 (OLP)."

Cicero, Marcus Tullius. 2000. *De re publica ; De legibus, Loeb classical library*. Cambridge, Mass ; London: Harvard University Press.

Ding, Alexander. 2003. "Youth are more sensitive to price changes in cigarettes than adults." *The Yale Journal of Biology and Medicine* 76 (3):115.

European Data Protection Supervisor. 2015. "Opinion 4/2015 towards a new digital ethics data, dignity and technology."

Floridi, Luciano. 1999. *Philosophy and Computing: An Introduction*. London; New York: Routledge.

Floridi, Luciano. 2013. *The Ethics of Information*. Oxford: Oxford University Press.

Floridi, Luciano. 2014. *The Fourth Revolution - How the Infosphere Is Reshaping Human Reality*. Oxford: Oxford University Press.

Floridi, Luciano. 2015. "'The right to be forgotten': a philosophical view." *Jahrbuch für Recht und Ethik - Annual Review of Law and Ethics* 23 (1):30–45.

Floridi, Luciano. 2018. "Soft ethics, the governance of the digital and the general data protection regulation." *Philosophical Transactions of the Royal Society A: Mathematical, Physical and Engineering Sciences* 376 (2133):20180081.

Floridi, Luciano. 2019. *The Logic of Information - A Theory of Philosophy as Conceptual Design*. Oxford: Oxford University Press.

Floridi, Luciano. 2023. *The Ethics of AI - Principles, Challenges, and Opportunities*. Oxford: Oxford University Press.

Flusser, Vilém. 2005. "The city as wave-trough in the image-flood." *Critical Inquiry* 31 (2):320–328.

Forgács, Éva. 1995. *The Bauhaus Idea and Bauhaus Politics*. Budapest; New York: Central European University Press.

Hammond, David. 2011. "Health warning messages on tobacco products: a review." *Tobacco Control* 20 (5):327–337.

Hegel, Georg Wilhelm Friedrich. 2019. *Lectures on the Philosophy of World History. Volume 1, Manuscripts of the Introduction and the Lectures of 1822-1823*. Oxford: Oxford University Press.

Hobbes, Thomas. 1983. *De Cive: The English Version Entitled, In the First Edition, Philosophicall Rudiments Concerning Government and Society*. Oxford: Clarendon Press.

Hobbes, Thomas. 1996. *Leviathan*. Cambridge: Cambridge University Press.

Holford-Strevens, Leofranc. 2005. *The History of Time: A Very Short Introduction*. Oxford; New York: Oxford University Press.

Huxley, Aldous. 1994. *Grey Eminence : A Study in Religion and Politics*. London: Flamingo.

Kant, Immanuel. 1991. *Political Writings*. 2nd ed. Cambridge: Cambridge University Press.

Keynes, John Maynard. 1930. *Economic Possibilities for Our Grandchildren*: Published in Keynes' (1972), also freely available online.

Keynes, John Maynard. 1972. *Collected Writings Vol. 9: Essays in Persuasion*. 2nd ed. London: Macmillan.

Koyré, Alexandre. 1957. *From the Closed World to the Infinite Universe*. Baltimore: Johns Hopkins Press.

Lardinois, Frederic. 26 October 2019. "In a victory over Amazon, Microsoft wins $10B Pentagon JEDI cloud contract." *Tech Crunch* https://techcrunch.com/2019/10/25/in-a-victory-over-amazon-microsoft-wins-10b-pentagon-jedi-cloud-contract/?guccounter=1&guce_referrer=aHR0cHM6Ly93d3cuZ29vZ2xlLmNvbS88&guce_referrer_sig=AQAAAD0t1DHxCM6fwLaUQcWgzybxg-ICOHj-16l865mpamf4HalyDCfDL-SSPc9GbAfe4GiaLyy5dFF3fQyuODzE71s27lftyQqIhJjD3kd3AoNTr5UHOO0iUr0NClaqGuPyofVGEC4j6z5ADzFG8aiYL0lL7YPK-x0I0OmEW60aRkQz.

Latour, Bruno. 1984. "The powers of association." *The Sociological Review* 32 (1_suppl):264–280.

Latour, Bruno. 1987. *Science in Action: How to Follow Scientists and Engineers Through Society*. Cambridge, Mass.: Harvard University Press.

Law, John. 1992. "Notes on the theory of the actor-network: ordering, strategy, and heterogeneity." *Systems Practice* 5 (4):379–393.

Law, John. 1994. *Organizing Modernity*. Oxford: Blackwell.

Lee, Richard B., and Richard Daly. 1999. *The Cambridge Encyclopedia of Hunters and Gatherers*. Cambridge: Cambridge University Press.

Locke, John. 2010. *On Toleration*. Cambridge: Cambridge University Press.

Machiavelli, Niccolò. 2003. *Discourses on Livy*. Oxford: Oxford University Press.

Machiavelli, Niccolò. 2019. *The Prince*. 2nd ed. Cambridge: Cambridge University Press.

McCarthy, John. 1997. "Review of Kasparov vs. Deep Blue by Monty Newborn." *Science* 6 June.

McCarthy, John, Marvin L. Minsky, Nathaniel Rochester, and Claude E. Shannon. 2006. "A proposal for the Dartmouth summer research project on artificial intelligence, August 31, 1955." *AI Magazine* 27 (4):12–12.

McLuhan, Marshall, and Barrington Nevitt. 1972. *Take Today; the Executive as Dropout*. New York: Harcourt Brace Jovanovich.

Mill, John Stuart. 2015. *On Liberty, Utilitarianism, and Other Essays*. New ed. Oxford: Oxford University Press.

Moreno, Carlos, Zaheer Allam, Didier Chabaud, Catherine Gall, and Florent Pratlong. 2021. "Introducing the "15-Minute City": sustainability, resilience and place identity in future post-pandemic cities." *Smart Cities* 4 (1):93–111.

Mukherjee, Supantha. 20 July 2020. "China may retaliate against Nokia, Ericsson if EU bans Huawei: WSJ." *Reuters* https://www.reuters.com/article/us-china-huawei-europe/china-may-retaliate-against-nokia-ericsson-if-eu-bans-huawei-wsj-idUSKCN24L1NW.

Orwell, George. 1949. *Nineteen Eighty-Four. A Novel*. London: Secker & Warburg.

Peirce, C.S. 1994. Peirce on Signs: Writings on Semiotic. James Hoopes, ed., Chapel Hill, North Carolina: University of North Carolina Press.

Pirolli, Peter. 2007. *Information Foraging Theory: Adaptive Interaction with Information*. Oxford: Oxford University Press.

Posner, Michael. 29 May 2020. "What's behind the Trump-twitter clash?" *Forbes* https://www.forbes.com/sites/michaelposner/2020/05/29/whats-behind-the-trump-twitter-clash/?sh=46ba9bbc54f5.

Rawls, John. 1999. *A Theory of Justice*. Revised ed. Oxford: Oxford University Press.

Rousseau, Jean-Jacques. 2019. *The Social Contract and Other Later Political Writings*. 2nd ed. Cambridge: Cambridge University Press.

Sayes, Edwin. 2014. "Actor–network theory and methodology: just what does it mean to say that nonhumans have agency?" *Social Studies of Science* 44 (1):134–149.

Schmitter, Philippe C. 2001. "What is there to legitimize in the European Union… and how might this be accomplished?" *Working Paper, Wien, Institut für Höhere Studien, 2001, Political science series, 75IHS Working Papers, 2001* accessed 7 August 2023 https://jeanmonnetprogram.org/archive/papers/01/011401-01.html.

Singh, Manish. 29 June, 2020. "India bans TikTok, dozens of other Chinese apps." *Tech Crunch* https://techcrunch.com/2020/06/29/india-bans-tiktok-dozens-of-other-chinese-apps.

Stiglitz, Joseph. 2011. "Of the 1%, by the 1%, for the 1%." *Vanity Fair* 11. Available Online https://www.vanityfair.com/news/2011/05/top-one-percent-201105.

Taylor, John, and Tahu Kukutai. 2016. "Indigenous data sovereignty: toward an agenda." Acton, ACT, Australia: Australian National University Press. https://library.oapen.org/handle/20.500.12657/31875.

Tocqueville, Alexis de. 1955. *Democracy in America.* Cambridge: Cambridge University Press.

The Economist. 11 April 2011. "Inequality and politics - Stiglitz and the progressive Ouroboros."

The Economist. 15 April 2011. "Inequality - the 1% solution."

Toffler, Alvin. 1980. *The Third Wave.* London: Collins.

Torpey, John. 2018. *The Invention of the Passport: Surveillance, Citizenship, and the State.* 2nd ed. Cambridge: Cambridge University Press.

Tsidulko, Joseph. 30 July 2020. "Pentagon CIO: JEDI cloud 're-announcement' should come by end of August." *CRN* https://www.crn.com/news/cloud/pentagon-cio-jedi-cloud-re-announcement-should-come-by-end-of-august.

Turing, A. M. 1950. "Computing machinery and intelligence." *Mind* 59 (236):433–460.

Verhofstadt, Guy. 2006. *The United States of Europe: Manifesto for a New Europe.* London: Federal Trust for Education and Research.

Verne, Jules. 1995. *Around the World in Eighty Days.* Oxford: Oxford University Press.

Vítečková, Karolína. 22 June 2020. "The story behind Google Plus shutting down." *Wiredelta* https://wiredelta.com/behind-google-plus-shutting-down.

Von Mises, Ludwig. 2005. *Liberalism: The Classical Tradition.* Indianapolis: Liberty Fund.

Wiener, Norbert. 1954. *The Human Use of Human Beings: Cybernetics and Society.* Revised ed. London.

Wittgenstein, Ludwig. 2001. *Tractatus Logico-Philosophicus.* London: Routledge.

Index

Page numbers in *italic* indicate figures; page numbers followed by 'n' indicate footnotes.

World Health Organisation
(WHO), 234
writing, invention of, 60